The Long Death of Brit

The Long Death of British Labourism:

Interpreting a Political Culture

Willie Thompson

Pluto Press

LONDON • BOULDER, COLORADO

First published 1993 by Pluto Press
345 Archway Road, London N6 5AA
and 5500 Central Avenue
Boulder, Colorado 80301, USA

British Library Cataloguing in Publication Data
A catalogue record for this book is available from the British Library

ISBN 0 7453 0580 6 hb
ISBN 0 7453 0581 4 pb

Library of Congress Cataloging in Publication Data
Thompson, Willie
  The long death of British labourism : interpreting a political
culture / Willie Thompson.
    190pp. 23cm.
    Includes bibliographical references and index.
    ISBN 0-7453-0580-6. – ISBN 0-7453-0581-4 (pbk.)
    1. Labour Party (Great Britain)–History–20th century. 2. Great
Britain–Politics and government–1945– I. Title.
JN1129.L3T48 1993
324.24107'09'04–dc20   92-47378
                                                                CIP

Designed and Produced for Pluto Press by
Chase Production Services, Chipping Norton
Typeset from author's disks by
Stanford DTP Services, Milton Keynes
Printed in Finland by WSOY

Contents

Preface

This book makes no claims to originality in research or the unearthing of new factual material. (Even the title has been used previously, albeit in an obscure context.) In respect of the evidence used to sustain the argument I have drawn on the published studies of individuals who are, I hope, adequately acknowledged in the text and notes.

What I am attempting to do is instead to highlight certain characteristic aspects of the British labour movement which flourished and declined in the second half of the 20th century in relation to particular attributes of the centralised and deferential political culture and monarchical state in which it operates.

Moreover, the argument presented here constitutes the merest preliminary sketch. Every dimension of these relationships requires a much more far-reaching study than I have given it; in particular the question of the changing composition of the workforce over these 45 years and the impact of that upon prevalent social and political attitudes.

Willie Thompson
June 1993

Introduction

In a country which once possessed the biggest concentration of industrial workers of any in the world, with a single unified trade union centre and a winner-take-all electoral system, the Labour Party has nevertheless held a very shaky grip on office. In the present century, six of its eight electoral victories (out of 24 general elections) have produced minority governments or negligible majorities, a fate never suffered by its Conservative rival.

The political right would attribute such a paradoxical state of affairs to the balance and good sense of the electorate. Certainly Britain, England especially, is blessed or afflicted, depending on one's viewpoint, with a profoundly conservative political culture; but the question is why, given the country's social composition, it should have evolved in that direction. The left, nearly always on the defensive, would claim repeated betrayal by the leaders of the movement[1] but, accepting that premise for the moment, any such thesis has to explain why the labour movement continues to elect traitorous leaderships.

It makes more sense instead to see the labour movement and the party which it sustains as having emerged from a rigidly hierarchical society, which has remained intimately connected to a centralised, authoritarian and traditionalist conception of the state and political system, within which the party's reforming purposes had to be achieved. That relationship embodied a fierce contradiction, all too evident even in the party's one episode of triumph, the 1945 election and subsequent five years of government, and still more apparent afterwards as Labour struggled to reconcile its reforming traditions with its deep veneration for the ancient authoritarian ones of the British state and culture.

The incompatibility has prevented the labour movement from achieving the social hegemony to which it might reasonably aspire. British labourism drew its authoritarian temper from an intensely elitist culture embedded in the country's past, but more dynamic movements of the left have encountered the same sphinx coming from other directions. The political notion of 'the left' had its origins two centuries ago in revolutionary France, where St Just the Jacobin declared that

1

'Happiness is a new idea in Europe'. At the same time he was dispatching his colleagues to the guillotine. The contradiction here between aspiration and execution was central not only to the events of St Just's own time but has since resonated through all subsequent endeavours to shape social reality in a manner conducive to extended happiness.

The character and significance of the French Revolution remain the subject of bitter debate, but what is incontestable is that it marked the first attempt in Europe, probably anywhere,[2] to remould socio-political institutions in a systematic fashion, designed to be more in accordance than those of the past with secular notions of human welfare, and to regard all (male) inhabitants of the nation, at least in principle, as citizens of equal social worth. In this respect it initiated a process which has never ceased and which has proceeded in parallel with and linked to the transformations of technology, production and material lifestyle which have likewise continued through to our own time. The materially affluent society of civil liberties and democratic institutions has become the planetary norm of achievement and the accepted purpose of government – enjoying verbal deference from nearly every state power on earth, even and especially from those ones which violate them most systematically in practice.

The process however has been accompanied all over the globe with the most desperate human and social traumas and suffering, and not all of that can be put down to the perverse resistance of outdated social groups and forces.[3] It would scarcely be an exaggeration to say that it has been carried along upon a river of blood. Perhaps the contradiction arose right at the beginning, because the first regime in modern times which could make any pretence to democracy in its formal constitution has gone down in history as the 'Jacobin dictatorship', which as soon as it came to power indefinitely suspended its own constitution and imposed a much more authoritarian style of government than the one it had lately overthrown. In doing so it set a grim precedent which has been followed on countless occasions by subsequent revolutionary administrations.

Even in the political sphere therefore, the French Revolution, conducted under the slogan of liberty and representing, so to speak, the 'big bang' from which the modern political universe was formed, reshuffled the pack of authoritarianism rather than changing the rules of the game. The facility with which authoritarian practices came to be accepted as a suitable vehicle for the advancement of liberty is suggestive of certain deep-seated assumptions at the very roots of social consciousness, independent of radical or conservative political ideology. This is all the more evident when we recall that, outside the political arena, at the level of civil society, structures of authority were scarcely changed at all. The ascendancy of men over women, of parents over children, of employers over workforces, of masters over servants, of charity-givers over recipients, was maintained and even consolidated. Citizenship did not affect relations of that sort and the dominant Jacobins actively prevented such attempts as did occur to transgress these traditional limits, denouncing them as the instrument of faction and counter-revolution.[4]

By behaving in this way the revolutionary leaders were giving unquestioned acceptance to traditions far more ancient than the images of classical Greece and Rome to which their rhetoric habitually appealed. The very first written evidence reveals all the agricultural societies that first made written records had already become authoritarian – and patriarchal – in the highest degree and at every level. The voice that has echoed down the centuries has been the voice of command.

Precisely why this should have been so initially is not our immediate concern, although in functional terms it is readily explained. Unquestioned obedience is, in the short run, the easiest and most economical way of achieving collective objectives and of organising collaborative labour; the more so in conditions of scarcity or danger where individual wills and desires are made to submit to a collective will embodied in authority. The age-old principle of the authoritarian collective reached its perfection and paradigm of expression in the modern military organisation, which reveals, in its purely functional command structure and principle of absolute obedience, the ideal type towards which its historic predecessors have tended. To this must be added the fact that the exercise of authority and the status and the symbols which accompany it are (or quickly become) very enjoyable and gratifying experiences for most people who have the opportunity to experience them, irrespective of culture or gender.

Whatever their exact origins, it is safe to assert that authoritarian relationships propagated themselves in settled agricultural communities by a process of natural selection, as a social mechanism which ensured more effective control over the natural environment. The bearers of authority fulfilled a functional role. In due course, by the usual processes of fetishistic alienation to which all historic cultures appear to have been subject, the principle that the subordinated producers existed only as secondary beings *for the benefit* of the bearers of authority and consumers of the social surplus – a principle which received its perfect expression in the institution of chattel slavery, where humans were regarded as articulate domestic beasts – was entrenched in all the classical civilisations from Egypt and Sumer to China and Rome.[5]

Absolute and unaccountable power was implied by such a perception, an implication that the governing powers in the ancient civilisations strove to turn into reality whenever the opportunity offered. Two conflicting traditions did exist, that of classical Greek democracy and that of the Hebrew prophets, both of which insisted that authority was rightfully circumscribed, whether by human or by divine limitations. The latter, which castigated iniquitous kings and their oppression of the poor, by being incorporated into the Christian tradition, was passed on to medieval Europe and, in combination with the dispersed and diluted sovereignty that was the essence of feudal government, stipulated that rulers had responsibilities as well as privileges. All that, however, had little bearing on the authoritarianism endemic in civil society.[6]

Leadership comes in many guises and there is more than one way of enforcing authority. Among the most rapid and easily deployed methods, however, are fear and the cultivation of fear. In all ages and literate cultures fear has represented the sovereign device for social control and been regarded as the salutary and proper cement of interpersonal and institutional relations. In the explicitly political form of the Terror it was employed to save the Jacobin republic, another sinister portent for the future. Subordinates related to superiors above all through fear, whatever other sentiments might be supposed to accompany it. More than one Roman emperor is reported to have said: 'Let them hate me so long as they fear me.' It is only in the present century, and by no means everywhere, that the instillation of fear has ceased to be the recommended central principle of child-rearing, or of matrimonial relations, for that matter. In the cultures formed by the monotheistic religions the terrors of divine wrath were added to more concrete methods of inspiring fear: the whip, the dungeon, the rope, the axe and the stake.[7] 'The fear of the Lord' – and of punishment in the hereafter – 'is the beginning of wisdom.'

Background

The society and culture in which the British labour movement had its beginnings was thought by contemporary observers to be somewhat less socially authoritarian – at least in England – than its continental counterparts, but it was very much a relative difference and a matter of degree. From the 1790s to the 1840s indeed, authoritarian practices were being intensified, politically and socially. The establishment of factory production in certain areas of textile manufacture introduced an unprecedented level of authoritarian control into work processes which took place in establishments whose resemblance to prisons was scarcely accidental and staffed wherever possible by women and children precisely because that sort of workforce was easiest to intimidate and terrorise. Nor was it accidental that the legal category into which all waged employees were placed was that of 'servants' and the statutes regulating their relations with their employers termed the Master and Servant Acts. The legal, administrative and ideological offensive against political dissent during and after the French Wars mightily raised the repressive profile of authority in state, local government, religion and workplace. Independent association and activity on the part of labourers were made criminal acts. In the 1830s and 1840s the new Poor Laws, with their deterrent workhouses in England and equivalent institutions in Scotland, marked a fierce enhancement of the terroristic discipline imposed upon the indigent; and police forces, instituted as much to combat political subversion as crime, became a country-wide phenomenon. Among the early 19th century British middle class every authoritarian and socially conformist tendency was enormously strengthened and validated by religion and custom. 'Victorianism' was well established before Victoria ascended the throne. Even cleaning out corruption and implanting the service ethic in collectives such as the public schools or civil service meant their adoption of a much more authoritarian character. The trend continued into the second half of the century, when in the 1860s, with the Contagious Diseases Acts came the attempt to police publicly as well as privately the sexual activities of British women, and the creation of a public education system with a hidden curriculum of submission equal in importance to the overt one of learning. Even today in England, male teachers are still frequently referred to as 'school*masters*'.

Although the early British labour movement, from the Corresponding Societies to the Chartists, was formed as much as anything in resistance and opposition to such developments, experience taught it that it could not even survive, let alone flourish, without taking on much of their coloration, in terms of discipline, good order, submission to the rhythms of industrial life and the sober requirements of organisational bureaucracy and bookkeeping. A very different sort of outlook may have survived as an underground tradition from the antinomians, the moral anarchists of the 1650s, and found final expression in the mystic poetry of William Blake: Robert Owen, although himself an authoritarian personality of the first order, may have founded in the 1830s a quasi-religion of exactly the opposite character, nonetheless the principles of the industrial society were irresistible – and although they were no less revolutionary than those of the Jacobins they were also no less authoritarian.[8] Moreover, they were erected on top of the unthinking, ingrained authoritarianism of gender and age relations, the patriarchy, status differentiations and snobberies endemic within the manual workforce, exemplified in the brutal and terrifying initiation rites which accompanied admission into the skilled trades.

The cultural matrix of the late 18th and 19th century politically conscious British labour movement may have been a compound of traditional and modern authoritarianisms, but in all its phases until 1850 it could be said to have had an essential revolutionary purpose (albeit much weaker after 1820) in its denial of the legitimacy of the prevailing state power and the series of confrontations in which it challenged the ruling class grip upon the apparatus of government. From the middle of the century that attitude was to change decisively and it is in the developments of that period that labourism has its origins.[9]

Naturally, we have to propose a definition of 'Labourism'. Certainly it resembles in many respects European social democracy, an interesting case of convergent evolution, with similar environmental forces producing parallel outcomes from very different starting points. But there are also critical differences. British labourism represents a very particular, almost unique, social and political formation. Its divergence from the standard European pattern has constituted both a strength and a weakness.

First, I will advance the following definition and understand by Labourism the organising principles, ethos, perceptions and socio-political project of what is conventionally referred to as the British labour movement. By this I mean bodies established to represent the collective interests of the workforce in its relations with employers and with wider authority – above all the trade union structures of a predominantly manual workforce, most importantly the individual unions but also the trade union centres, the TUC and STUC and trades councils. Secondly, I mean the Labour Party, in its manifestations of branches, constituency committees, the NEC and the parliamentary party along with associated institutions and bodies like the retail co-op movement, bodies like the Fabian Society or other collections of particular or minority interests. Labourism is therefore an orientation towards a certain social and political reality and not necessarily articulated in any coherent or theoretical fashion. It would not be inaccurate to define it as an ideology and praxis. Certainly there have been and are bodies and tendencies

[handwritten note] ? CO-OP PARTY = POLITICAL WING WHICH COMPRISED IN ITS PARLIAMENTARY MEMBERS "THE GANG OF THREE/FOUR" DAVID OWEN, SHIRLEY WILLIAMS ROY JENKINS?

within the labour movement consciously and explicitly antagonistic to
the labourist ideology as I am defining it. Part of the argument of what
follows is that these have themselves been deeply penetrated and strictly
moulded by a labourist consciousness.   ??? NT   ☀

Labourism has taken its colour from the conditions to which the
mainland British industrial workforce was exposed in the second half
of the 19th century and the opportunities available to those who
composed it. Whatever the exact character of the change which set in
from around 1850, it is incontestable that the dynamic mass movement
associated with Chartism, one highly aware of irreconcilable conflict with
the powers-that-be over the nature of the state, was utterly eclipsed. It
was replaced with a more loosely articulated, much less politically
ambitious network of organisations and agencies, willing to pursue
their objectives within the framework of established political and social
institutions under the mixed aristocratic/bourgeois hegemony which
commanded the British state and social order.

Tom Nairn has argued that E P Thompson's classic *The Making of the
English Working Class* should in reality have a title like 'The Unmaking
of the British Working Class Revolutionary Tradition'. Nairn identifies
the definitive turn as occurring prior to 1820 – well before even the
working class was fully formed as a distinct entity – with the crushing
of all insurrectionary projects within the industrial districts and the
extirpation of the Jacobin tradition deriving from the French Revolution.
Thereafter, it is true, the surviving traditions of political radicalism
during the following 20 years took for granted the perpetuation of the
existing political structures centred upon Parliament, and directed their
energies towards cleaning it up or capturing its commanding heights.
The legitimacy, indeed the mystique, of Parliament as an embodiment
of the general will became an article of faith and, as is well known, the
formal Chartist programme had no concerns beyond its democratisation.

Labour historians have long understood in a sketchy manner and John
Saville's book on 1848 has at last documented *in extenso*, that Chartism
did not simply vanish of its own accord in April that year. But it
cannot be denied that its hold on the popular imagination must have
been weakening severely for the final collapse to have been so rapid,
for the hoary and antiquated governmental system to sustain no significant crisis for another 60 years but instead to add a further enormous
world empire to the one it already had. These things give a measure of
the effectiveness with which public consciousness – even that of the dis-
enfranchised masses – was bent and manipulated into conformity with
that of the ruling elite.

THE LABOUR MOVEMENT AS DEFINED P. 6, IS RIDDLED ☀
WITH SABOTEURS AND SELF-SEEKERS

The hold was all the firmer in that, 14 years before the Chartists went down, the last mass movement to reject parliamentary constitutionalism altogether had suffered an even more crushing debacle. The primitive syndicalism of the Owenites did indeed reject, root and branch, the whole apparatus of the established constitution and wanted to translate the economic weight of productive labour directly into political hegemony through assemblies based upon producer co-operatives and linked to the all-embracing Grand National Consolidated Trades Union. For several months in 1834, evidence suggests that major sections of the wage-earning population adhered to it with a nearly messianic fervour. Uncompromising repression (of which the Tolpuddle episode has entered folk memory) destroyed this enterprise completely before the close of the year, discredited and ended for ever any serious notion of replacing the recognised parliamentary functions in Britain with a rival authority.

Certainly it is most unlikely that the British political system would have found permanent stability but for the extremely advantageous economic circumstances of the following half century. The 'Great Victorian Boom' of c. 1850–73 rested on the foundation that the British economy was the only one in the world to have achieved something approaching a fully industrialised condition and consequently was, by and large, a monopoly supplier of industrial goods to the world and a monopoly purchaser of industrial raw materials. The consequential benefits, it would appear, reached only a minority of actual producers in terms of growing incomes, but catastrophic trade swings with prodigious unemployment, on the style of 1842, appeared to have become a thing of the past, and rising profits made possible a degree of 'social' investment in the industrial connurbations in the shape of public health projects and building controls.[10]

The 'Great Victorian Depression' which followed between 1873 and 1896 did not retard the trend of relative mass improvement; if anything it extended and deepened it. Depression or not, the industrial economy continued to grow, though its profit margins were squeezed. Unemployment rose, but not dramatically, and employed workers registered real income gains from an overall price deflation of 40 per cent (greater in the case of basic consumption). In short, between 1850 and 1900 the balance in the labour market remained, on the whole, favourable to the workforce: not until the beginning of the 20th century did inflation and a dynamic employer counter-offensive begin to erode working class real incomes.[11]

The ruling class, a complex and structured amalgam of landed, mercantile and industrial capital, had also reformed its lifestyle and its internal institutions, principally as a measure of survival in response to the threat from the potentially insurgent masses earlier in the century. The more spectacular sorts of elite corruption, racketeering and patronage, were cleaned up in a lengthy process stretching over the years between the 1830s and the 1870s, from local government through public schools and the universities to parliament and the military. Legitimacy was withdrawn from the customary practice of using public office for private gain and in its place industry, rectitude and probity (functionally speaking, the attributes needed to flourish in an economy of non-monopolistic capitalist production) were acclaimed as necessary qualifications for a career in public service of any sort. Such commendable developments were part of a package deal, the 'reformation of manners' aspired to by the evangelical zealots of the early 19th century who, in their anxiety to employ morality and religion as an instrument of social control of the masses, never ceased to warn their betters of the dreadful revolutionary consequences liable to follow from their own irreligion and dissolute morals. Thus the ideological drive behind the purification of institutional mores in the later 19th century infused the public discourse at the same time with an atmosphere of stifling moralism and sententious religiosity. The extension and rationalisation of the school, workhouse and prison systems fortified the perceived necessity to enforce moral discipline and correction upon their inmates, adding a yet further dimension to traditional or functional forms of authority exercised by the ruling class as well as those prevailing in family relations or other informal networks. The degree to which this public discourse reflected the realities of late Victorian Britain is, for our purposes, a secondary question; what matters is that it was propagated in innumerable classrooms and pulpits and through all the printed media from newspapers to adolescent magazines. There is little reason to doubt that, by and large, the Victorian elite took the moral dispensation seriously rather than cynically if the agonised self-scrutiny of its most articulate members is anything to judge by.[12]

The origins of labourism as a definable outlook are to be found in the trade union organisations, comprised of mostly skilled male workers in certain trades (a definite minority, it has to be stressed) that emerged in the 1850s and 1860s as the most significant of working class collectives. They were able, through collective bargaining, to use the favourable conditions prevailing in that labour market to the advantage of their members as well as acting the role of benefit societies in a state without any public provision apart from the Poor Law. To do these things effectively they had to turn themselves into hierarchical, disciplined, authoritarian organisations with strong-minded and strong-willed leaderships, emphasising prudent management and stringent bureaucratic procedures. Without these qualities they could not have survived or functioned: the less disciplined workers' associations established in the same period tended continually towards fissure, bankruptcy and collapse. Whether these unions were also compelled to embrace the bourgeois ethos both in public affairs and lifestyle is perhaps more questionable: at any rate they did so. In the perceptions and statements of their leaders (there is no evidence of being out of touch with their rank and file in this regard) the socio-political universe was perceived as eternal and unchallengable, as were its existing systems of property ownership, market relations and the intrinsic subordination of labour to capital.[13]

The strategy adopted by the 'amalgamated' unions (christened 'New Model' by the Webbs) was to exploit the labour market by restricting the supply of labour as far as they could. This was explicitly and unashamedly acknowledged. Hence they devised elaborate and deterrent rules, both formal and informal, around the admission and training of apprentices and even provided encouragement and financial backing for union members to emigrate. Manipulation, not overthrow, of the existing structures became the central principle and with this came declarations of ideological adherence to the market economy and the cultivation of amicable relations with employers so far as possible. None of this precluded a rhetoric stressing the dignity of labour (or at least the sober and industrious part of it), claims for expanded political rights, or strike action when it was felt to be the last and only resort. Labour developed strongly what has been termed a 'corporate consciousness', acutely aware of its separateness, the rights it had won and its aspirations to a better share of national resources, but it remained incapable of challenging the dominant hegemony either politically or ideologically. Instead, the organised working class (or rather, the organisations of the working class) absorbed the Victorian values outlined above and was deeply coloured by them. In part this can be understood as a defensive reaction. The only way in which organised labour could get a hearing and be taken seriously where it mattered was by parading its respectability and ethical tone; but again there can be no doubt that its members, and most particularly its leaders, at all levels absorbed and were genuinely motivated by an ethic that was ultimately rooted in dominance, submission and coercive moral invigilation, and this even at a time when more intellectually adventurous groups among the bour-

EMPLOYERS IN THE MAIN, CHARGED A FEE TO ENROL APPRENTICES AND FOLLOWING SERVICE OF SAME DISMISSED THEM

geoisie were starting to call it into question. It is encapsulated in the notorious assertion that the British labour movement owed more to Methodism than to Marx; this remark is of very dubious accuracy, but it is the fact that it became current which is significant. The fact too that in middle class discourse 'respectable labour' was contrasted emphatically and continuously with the 'dangerous classes' (the 'residium') cannot have been lost on the consciousness of those who fell into the approved category.[14]

Labour was one interest group among many others and, although not unimportant, it was far from being the most influential. Like the industrial bourgeoisie before it (and unlike their continental counterparts) it did not form a separate political party even after 1867, when the electoral system was sufficiently expanded to make that practicable, but attached its political interest to one of the pre-existent great parties with experience of Westminster and governmental affairs, the Liberal Party. The fact that this party also represented industrial capital (and even sections of the landed interest) constituted a further intangible bond between British trade unionists and their employers. It enhanced the general social and ideological pressures which impelled them towards identification with established social, constitutional and cultural structures and, in due course, to the imperialist ecstacies of the 1880s and 1890s, along with the presumption that the traditional governors had in the last resort the best right to run the state, or at least to fix its essential direction.

The skilled and relatively secure element of the working class was not in the end to be the only component of the emergent labour movement, nor was liberalism to become the latter's ultimate political destiny, but their experience and orientation was stamped indelibly upon the regrouped and realigned forces of British labour which arose from the influx of fresh occupational or social groups and events on either side of the turn of the century. Those who came to remould the reorganised labour movement found themselves working with habits, traditions and outlooks formed in the earlier period and from which they could not escape.

The emergence in the 1890s of unions of unskilled workers holding, for a variety of reasons, to a more radical disposition than the older cohort, seemed for a time to promise a marked change of direction, the more so in the light of their initial connexions with the socialist individuals and organisations appearing on the scene in the 1880s, especially when combined with the reconstitution in 1889 of a Socialist International under the inspiration of the 'revolutionary' German Social Democrats.

THE INFLUX OF FOREIGNERS, PARTICULARLY FROM SCOTLAND AND THE CONTINENT, INTRODUCED A HIGHER AWARENESS AND INTELLIGENCE

Simultaneously, and partly deriving from the work and activity of these same socialists, the extent and depth of poverty and deprivation among the working class became a public issue in a fashion not seen since the time of the Chartists, and middle class opinion began to perceive the spectre of a revolutionary threat – and perceived a more concrete one too – as the dialectic of imperialism entangled the state in military alliances and the prospect of a continental war in which a stunted and sickly male population would make a poor source of cannon fodder. In the advanced circles of bourgeois thinking *laissez-faire* was discredited and the reputation of Herbert Spencer began its journey to oblivion. Humanitarian sentiment, action to forestall the spread of revolutionary notions, imperialist motivations – all pointed in the same direction: towards governmental initiative to ameliorate the social disasters which market mechanisms had created and were incapable of remedying. Out of this amalgam was forged the New Liberalism of the early 20th century, drawing its inspiration in part from Bismarck's social insurance experiments and in part with a project designed to accommodate social reform within the existing social and political structures.

In the meantime however, labour's political consciousness had also evolved. A need for distinctive political representation was seen both by the leaders of the unskilled workers' unions and by the socialist organisations as indispensable to a mature class identity. Adverse tendencies in the labour market after the mid 1890s and the more evident political debility of traditional liberalism brought eventual success in 1900, after a severe struggle within the TUC, with the formation of the Labour Representation Committee and the subsequent adherence of most trade union organisations to it.

The Rise of the Labour Movement

The labour movement now had a political party (it adopted the Labour Party title in 1906) and soon found itself represented at Westminster, where it had to adjust to the rituals and etiquette of the British parliamentary system. The peculiar circumstances of its birth have marked all of the Labour Party's subsequent career and determined the nature of the ambiguous and uncertain relationship it has since maintained with the labour organisations which gave rise to it.

The original name itself is significant: the Representation Committee's remit was to secure independent representation for working men in parliament – and nothing further; indeed any more far-reaching aim was specifically excluded. Policies have changed, but not the fundamental initial purpose, the decisively *parliamentary* character of the party has never varied. Parliament and electoral activity – with their parallels in local government – has not been an important or even the most important aspect of this political party – it has been its essential being.

Not only that, but the Labour Party has been able to appear dynamic and efficient only when in government – and even then only on occasions when the social and economic tides were running in its favour, when the administrative and bureaucratic energies of its leaders were channelled towards implementing reforms which had popular support – in short, when not called upon to resist and combat the powers-that-be. Its record as a party of parliamentary opposition has been one of almost unrelieved wretchedness and in extra-parliamentary terms more feeble still. Conceived initially as an adjunct to the trade union struggle, it could not fail to develop subsequently a life and identity of its own, but it scarcely appears in the records of the period 1911–22, when massive confrontations between capital and labour amounted to sustained class warfare. Almost overnight, in the four general elections between 1918 and 1924 it displaced the Liberals as the main opposition party and even briefly formed a minority government. Not even its most sympathetic historian would attribute this startling rise to a brisk and strenuous political education of the masses on the part of the Labour Party leadership. Rather it was the beneficiary of shifts in social consciousness which it had done nothing to initiate and little to direct, and thereby established a sorry tradition which has carried on down to the present. Ralph Miliband's classic *Parliamentary Socialism* analyses its characteristic weaknesses but misperceives their implications. The following examples may especially be noted.

The pursuit of governmental office, local and central, as an overriding priority and the consequent focus of the party's energies on the electoral process, together with the dominant role at all levels of its elected representatives, is most characteristic. There is no reason why *in itself* this practice should necessarily disable a political organisation from mobilising and rallying support by other means as well. For a party with mass support, vigorous electoral campaigning should be perfectly compatible with other forms – indeed they could well reinforce each other. In practice this has not occurred.

It is a wholly respectable argument that, to achieve anything in the British political system, office is a necessary condition and that the nature of British political culture would deny office to a party which embraced certain objectives or policies, even those which might be desirable in principle – abolition of the monarchy for example. It is therefore at the very least myopic to berate the Labour Party as Miliband tends to do for betrayal of socialist principle in order to win parliamentary majorities. There is a case for accepting long-term minority status until sufficient of the electorate has been persuaded to vote for the full programme. There is also a case for adapting that programme to what the electorate is known to find tolerable so as to exercise such powers as the system makes available. Either option can be presented as an instrumental choice, but to do so *only* on that level is to ignore not only the question of conflicting ideas about fundamental objectives within the labour movement itself, but also the manner in which 'parliamentary socialism' actually came to be the political consummation of labourist objectives.

Parliament has been taken by the dominant Labour Party tradition not pragmatically, as a political institution possessing certain possibilities and limitations, an instrument of greater or lesser usefulness for building the co-operative commonwealth, but treated instead with the reverence and sanctity due to a sacred object, replete with dignity and wrapped in ceremonial. The early Labour Party leaders unquestioningly adopted (often with the utmost alacrity) the posture of the traditional rulers. On these grounds the Parliamentary Labour Party has claimed, and generally obtained, exemption from any control or supervision by the wider party. (The ostensible justification, that MPs can be responsible only to their constituents, is easily recognised as a thin and hoary pretext for submitting to a mystical taboo. It is of course reinforced by the practical benefits to MPs of such autonomy.) The problem has been less the mainstream Labour Party's timidity in challenging the bourgeois state, important though that undoubtedly is, than its insidious absorption of that state's sacramental values, which has rendered it incapable of distinguishing between pragmatic or contingent reasons for adopting or rejecting a standpoint, and unquestioned devotion to the procedures and institutions of the venerable British constitution. There is substance in the gibe that Labour is the really conservative party.

From this follows the explanation for Miliband's bitterest grievance and focus of attack, the strict separation of 'industrial' (and, we might add, other forms of mass mobilisation) from 'parliamentary' struggle, and the total illegitimacy used to stigmatise any action seen as 'coercing parliament', or even the calculated defiance of legislation endorsed by parliament in due form. It springs not, as Miliband implies, from ill-will and malice intended to weaken and divide the force of the labour movement, but from the deeply conditioned horror evoked by sacrilegious violation of sanctified parliamentary space.

The veneration which in British political culture surrounds the abstractions of government and state, together with their ceremonial aspects, contrasts strikingly with the slightly disreputable air which attaches to 'party politics', despite the latter's integral place in the state structure. To announce a measure as being 'non-political' or 'above party' used to be a gambit intended to confer legitimacy on controversial or dubious proposals; indeed one of the most serious of charges against Margaret Thatcher from the political centre was that she had 'politicised everything'. Tom Nairn's analysis of the 'dignified' parts of the constitution,[15] the parts that are formally powerless (with the monarchy of course at the pinnacle), demonstrates that, far from being redundant or irrelevant, they in fact provide the glue which holds the entire rickety structure together. In this sense the Head of State is supremely 'non-political' (a blatant contradiction in terms) and every endeavour is made, in the approved public discourse surrounding the British monarchy, to assimilate its role to that of private family life, to forget that it is a political institution. 'The Crown can do no wrong' – so if wrong has been done it must have been done by the fallible ministers, not the infallible state itself. Politics is the arena where public wrong can be done, hence the field of conflict and suffering. It is also the arena where authority is legitimately challenged; consequently it has to be surrounded with implicit denials and ritual defusings. The very term 'parliamentary language' is symptomatic. In the British case this takes the form of the pretence that its parliamentarians, like juries, proceed in their deliberations insulated from all contaminating outside influences and that if we must have parties only their parliamentary fractions are to have any real authority. Government can be compared to sex: it is a central reality in public life as sexual relations are in private, and because of its potent and fearful character it is required to be surrounded with all sorts of concealments and ritual pretences which everybody knows to be false while simultaneously having to affirm them. To exert political force outside the accepted channels, to try for example to influence legislation by industrial action, is a bit like removing your trousers in public. It may also help to explain why the regimes of the former socialist bloc, where the identification of the state with a specific form of politics was not merely the reality but publicly insisted upon, found it so difficult to have their legitimacy taken wholly seriously by the western powers. It was not only the content of their politics which gave offence: in an indefinable fashion they appeared in this light to be not real states but usurpations – rather as nudists are incapable of achieving an acceptable social identity.

British labourism has been a (predominantly) worker's movement which has unreservedly committed itself to this conception of the state and its relationship to political life. Therefore, of necessity, it has embraced the principle which so excites Miliband's indignation: the rigid compartmentalisation of the industrial and overtly 'political' aspects of the movement – which join effectively only at the level of funding. Certainly the trade unions have had the constitutional power to make, or at least share in the making of, Labour Party policy through the mechanism of the annual conference and other formal mechanisms, but the really significant facet of this relationship is that it has always evoked unease within the labour movement itself, been the object of frenzied media scorn and been exercised with shamefaced embarrassment. The argument that it violates constitutional proprieties has never been forcefully met and challenged, is implicitly conceded and, in reality, the trade union leaders have always, except on specifically trade union matters or when strongly pushed by their own rank and file, deferred to the parliamentary ones.[16]

The 'British Constitution' illusion also prevents the Labour Party's deploying its great membership and resources in effective campaigning strategies outside the boundaries of electoral contests. The Labour Party as such has only once mounted an impressive, successful, extra-parliamentary campaign. It has been structurally incapable of organising such activities on a country-wide scale, of combining a parliamentary assault with co-ordinated manifestations of public anger organised in its own name – far less of linking that with a strategy of *industrial* action.

In practice such campaigning, from the conflicts over trade union law in the first decade of the century to their equivalents in the 1980s, by way of campaigns over unemployment, social welfare, fascism at home and abroad, colonialism, war and peace – have been left to the trade unions or single issue movements with individual Labour Party organisations joining in on an haphazard and *ad hoc* basis. Consequently, and paradoxically, trade union consciousness has often appeared to be more advanced and radical than that of the workers' supposed political leadership, especially when, as often in the 1960s, the campaigns were directed *against* the policies of Labour governments.

The Labour Party

There are numerous components to labourism. One cannot omit, for example, the heritage of the 19th century nonconformist conscience or the passion for authoritarian if beneficent social control embodied in the

Fabian Society. The central element, however, has been the symbiosis between a movement of organised male workers seeking space for collective bargaining and social improvement on their own terms, and a state which has remained, beneath its outer layers of parliamentary democracy, profoundly authoritarian and traditionalist (even if the traditions were 19th century manufactures more often than not). This relationship exists on the foundations of a society and culture in which the ethic and values of a pre-industrial elite remained astonishingly resilient.

This account of the decline and fall of British labourism begins with the apotheosis of that form of politics. With its overwhelming parliamentary majority in 1945 came formal control of the state and constitutional power to legislate. Running with a tide of popular acclaim, Attlee's administration did indeed legislate in a manner which embodied the basic objectives of labourism's social programme. More importantly, these objectives were almost universally regarded not as controversial impositions liable to future reversal but as embedded in granite consensus and fixed for all time. At the same time this government did not escape the heritage of the British state and its own traditions – authoritarianism and subordination. While it wasted incalculable resources on what was, from any point of view other than that of the British elite, a demented ambition to remain a Great Power, it put on its model of socialism a stamp of authoritarian bleakness and unfeeling bureaucracy. Even worse, it deliberately and consciously promoted the resumption of capital export and the reestablishment of the City of London as an international banker, while it remained incapable of initiating any strategic project to modernise and re-equip the economy's productive base. The possibility of a different strategy, one which prioritised industrial renewal at the expense of the City, did not go unrecognised, indeed it was, as we shall see, mooted – and rejected.[17]

Nonetheless, the Labour settlement was destined to survive and be incorporated into the accepted wisdom of the following decade as a world boom lifted even the leaky British economy to unheard-of heights of consumer affluence. The same process weakened and undermined the traditional, inherited social and cultural disciplines upon which labourism depended for its internal cohesion and transmission to subsequent generations – for the left no less than the mainstream of the movement.

The recovery of government office between 1964 and 1970 served only to expose the incapacity of the labourist tradition to master the problems of what was, by then, agreed upon all sides to be an obsolescent and stagnant economy or, correspondingly, to mobilise the reserves of popular solidarity and attachment on which its predecessor of 1945–50 had been able to rely when in trouble. Instead, through its shortcomings, it promoted the emergence of a much more broadly based left current than had been previously seen – partly inside, partly outside the traditional organisations of the labour movement. The argument of this book however is that the left trend was in its various manifestations, from the communists to the Trotskyist sects, itself deeply afflicted and disabled by the characteristic labourist ailments.

The Labour Party, I have argued, whether in office or opposition cannot be understood except in its symbiotic relationship with the British state. Indeed, the eventual bankruptcy of the Wilson government's course arrived when it attempted to apply, through the exercise of state authority, the establishment panacea for an ailing economy by curtailment of trade union powers. That the ministers who attempted it had neglected the central dialectic of labourism was evidenced by their failure and humiliating climb-down in the face of union strength. The relationship with the state could only be viable if certain limits in relationships with the movement were not overstepped.

The deficiencies of the labourist tradition are no doubt the most evident characteristic of its history, but its assets of strength and loyalty could never be discounted, as the Conservative prime minister Edward Heath discovered in 1974 when the trade unions in effect overthrew his government after it had tried to continue the aborted Wilson policies. I shall argue that, following this episode, a brief interval of opportunity existed for labourism to transcend its past and to initiate developments which could have marked a turn in the structures of the British state and economy. Moreover, I shall argue that in failing to capitalise on these possibilities the left was more or less as culpable as the right. Instead, all sections and tendencies remained helplessly stuck in postures which historical reality had rendered obsolete and which allowed each of them to be outmanoeuvred and crushed by a force which appealed over their heads to a combination of the consumerist greed, which labourism has never understood how to handle, and the authoritarian populism intrinsic to the labourist tradition itself throughout its existence.

Once in office that same force, labelled Thatcherism, implacably changed the rules of the constitutional game which had been played for 130 years, exploiting the legal but hitherto quiescent absolutism which resides within the Crown-in-Parliament. The main artery which connected labourism to government was severed, spilling its lifeblood of consensus and negotiation.

The argument of this book is that there is no possibility of labourism's being reconstituted in the sense which the name implied up to the 1980s, because the conditions which permitted it to exist and sometimes flourish have passed away forever. The electoral revival of the Labour Party since 1987 has depended upon its abandoning some of its most distinctively labourist features and the continuation of that recovery is made possible only by persistence in the same course. Thatcherism has permanently altered the political map and the terminal crisis of labourism was seen only too clearly in the inability of any of its constituents to make any headway whatever on either the political or ideological plane against a government which tore apart the social consensus and enforced miseries and deprivations which would have been regarded as unimaginable in any previous decade since 1945. The demoralisation was thoroughgoing and mirrored most publicly in Labour's abject performance within the parliamentary arena, the abiding focus of all its political hopes. Only the belated recognition that the movement was trapped in a political dead end, accompanied by the entanglement of its enemies in the consequences of their own economic and social nostrums, at length began to alter the balance of forces.

If any new and viable construct is to be consolidated out of the death of labourism, however, it will have to be one in which the lessons of history have been understood and absorbed. It will reject centralisation and authoritarianism, both in its own structures and in the form of society which it envisages. It will have to abandon labourism's sacramental attachment to the forms of the state and the archaic constitution. Only the barest beginnings of such a development are visible so far. Finally, that successor movement will aspire to transformations of state structures and of personal relations no less than transformations of the economy or of the welfare services.

1 Labour in Office 1945–51

The Labour Party's astonishing electoral victory in July 1945 represented a concentration not merely of the hopes inspired by the war and the memories of the 1930s, but of those which sprang from half a century of social struggle which had employed the strategy of using central and local state power to redress and allieviate the material and cultural inequities produced by the operation of market forces.

Still, it must be kept in mind that, even in 1945, the Labour Party received well under 50 per cent of the popular vote. The overwhelming size of its majority was determined by a crucial shift in electoral geography occasioned by the fact that large numbers of previously Liberal and potential Liberal voters transferred their votes. It represented a successful appeal, based on the discredit of prewar conservatism and the credibility of Labour's wartime performance and promise, to the more socially conscious and politically progressive sections of the middle classes, sufficient under a first-past-the-post electoral procedure to give Labour the edge in many marginal constituencies.

The events of 1945 in Britain invite comparison with the establishment of the Popular Front governments throughout liberated Europe, or at least the western ones. Although the latter were explicitly alliances of divergent anti-Fascist parties identified with particular class interests, the British instance could not unfairly be regarded, in the coalition of interests which the Labour Party manifesto had assembled, as the native form of broad class alliance expressed through the peculiarities of the British electoral system. The other common feature was the character of the programme on which the Labour as well as the Popular Front governments assumed office: of economic reconstruction and a perspective of far-reaching social reform which would alter but stop short of overturning the essential class relationships of capital and labour.

The differences in the respective situations were no less significant. Not the least of these was that, while in Europe the prewar order and ruling elites had been discredited by defeat and collaboration, British social, political and cultural traditions were, on the contrary, reinforced and even consecrated by their association with the heroic saga of World

War II and ultimate victory: they would serve as the scaffolding for the new Jerusalem. Secondly, as a victorious power which counted as one of the Big Three, the assumption prevailed, both among governing elites and at a popular level, that the British state would continue to perform as a major world power in line with its imperial traditions both on a European and a global stage; this presupposition was to do much to structure the character and policy of the incoming Labour government. It was a megalomania to which no other European power – with the partial exception of France – was subject.

The Leadership

The personalities and backgrounds of the Labour leaders corresponded very closely to the cultural norms which the movement had evolved in the course of its adaptation to and symbiosis with the traditional practices of national politics. Four individuals together exercised an unchallengable domination over the Labour Party and, as far as structural limits permitted, the state. They summed up in their personalities the virtues and vices of British labourism at its apogee.

Clement Attlee's insignificant appearance – which was that of a browbeaten bank clerk – belied his skill at using the movement's traditions and rhetoric to establish a consensus behind the objectives which his party leadership in government wanted to pursue and to confirm his own indispensibility. Of middle class extraction and Oxbridge education, he had been a lawyer before he entered Labour politics. As a stopgap, compromise, leadership candidate in 1935, his direction of the Party's fortunes between then and 1940 was undistinguished at best. The formation of the Coalition in May 1940, which connected the Labour Party firmly and solidly for the first time to state power, gave scope to his fruitful emergence as Churchill's deputy, due to his talent for conscientious and untiring administrative labour. His persona was one which reflected the self-sacrificing collective dedication, utter probity and middle class moralism in which the labour movement had been schooled throughout its tribulations.[1] Personally reticent, modest, inarticulate, with all the emotional hangups of his class and generation, at the same time there was no suspicion of anything effete about him. He had served as an officer during World War I and, possessed of a 'simple, almost military attitude to authority and responsibility', subsequently cultivated an air of schoolmasterly authority.[2] Thus he was perfectly attuned to the labourist culture of the 1940s.

Ernest Bevin represented a different sort of labour leader; a childhood victim of multiple deprivation, coarse in his address and interpersonal relations, he even looked the part of the stereotype working class bully-boy. Like Attlee an extremely able organiser, he was also very nearly a caricature of the authoritarian trade union leader, adept at shouting down and intimidating opponents within the movement, ruthless in the manipulation of trade union office to enhance his own authority. These qualities had made him invaluable within the Coalition cabinet in organising the allocation and discipline of the workforce during wartime. When he unexpectedly became Attlee's Foreign Secretary in 1945, they also made him soft as putty in the hands of his Foreign Office permanent officials. 'He's a big bumble bee caught in a web and he thinks he's the spider,' sneered Aneurin Bevan [3]

Herbert Morrison lacked both Attlee's negative charisma and Bevin's brutal presence but, as with the other two, administrative expertise proved to be his strong suit. His imagination was narrow and his personality authoritarian. His attachment to public ownership was genuine but instrumental, he valued it as a source of economic efficiency and counter-cyclical intervention and for him its potential benefits to consumers, let alone the workforce, were very much secondary considerations. As the supremo for the Labour government's nationalisation programme, he was at pains to ensure that the new publicly-owned enterprises remained as similar as possible in their internal organisation to their commercial predecessors and that they would operate according to commercial criteria.

The fourth member of the Labour Government quadumvirate, Hugh Dalton, was in many respects the most interesting and atypical. His background was as about as unlikely for a labour leader as it is possible to imagine. His father, an obscure clergyman, so successfully ingratiated himself into Queen Victoria's favour that he was made tutor to her two grandsons (one of them the future George V) and a canon in the Windsor chapel, in which surroundings Hugh passed his childhood. The royal connexion was one reason, and not the least, for the particularly virulent hatred in which Dalton was held by the Establishment. They regarded him as a class traitor.

Dalton was neither an agreeable figure nor a particularly admirable one. From the beginning to the end of his political career he was notorious among his colleagues as an ingratiator, buttonholer, bully and intriguer. Yet this graduate of the royal household, Eton and Cambridge, had more imaginative grasp of the possibilities available to a social democratic regime that took its mission seriously than did his Cabinet colleagues of less exalted background. Dalton's commitment to a significant and far-reaching scale of income redistribution within British society was far more serious than that of the other leaders, whose horizons were limited to stable employment, social welfare and rising income levels; the elimination of poverty and enhancement of opportunity rather than any sort of class restructuring. Moreover, Dalton, a professional economist, had given considerable thought to how it might be done and, as Attlee's Chancellor of the Exchequer, he assumed office with both the opportunity and the motivation to try. A further irony here was that his appointment was a direct consequence of his relatively radical reputation: he had wanted and expected to be made Foreign Secretary and was denied that more august responsibility by Establishment antagonism and pressure applied upon Attlee through King George VI. Dalton's own strengths and limitations, as well as those of the party he represented, are illustrated in his relations with his Bishop Auckland constituents. No MP or minister could have done more to look after them, to bring employment and services into the area, yet all the while he strove to keep the local party as small and moribund as possible; a large and active one, he was convinced, would restrict his scope and cramp his style. The relationship was exclusively one of paternalism, and so in essence was Dalton's posture towards the masses on a national scale.

Equally influential in the counsels of this government to any Cabinet minister was that temporary civil servant, the economist J M Keynes who, although mortally ill, was dispatched to the USA to try to secure the resources, in the form of a loan on easy terms, which would permit the Labour programme to be implemented. The severity of the constraints, both natural and human, which that programme was to face, had not yet disclosed itself and the perspectives through which Attlee's administration viewed the economic future combined, on the one hand, the traditional Labour formulas of public ownership and macroeconomic planning through physical allocation and controls with, on the other, Keynesian notions of demand management in an open market.[4]

Under the best imaginable circumstances the new administration had a formidable undertaking ahead of it, and those circumstances did not long remain very favourable. Measured against the obstacles they faced, the achievement of Attlee and his colleagues was most impressive, perhaps the more so in that they did not hesitate to load themselves with additional massive burdens. In some part these extra impositions were inescapable, but not always: in important cases they were avoidable but deliberately chosen.

The Inherited Structure

Even supposing that Labour had lost in 1945, it is most unlikely that there would have been any repeat of the industrial confrontations and climatic class battles that followed World War I. The reason is not simply the wartime experiences in social welfare and industrial co-operation, which a Conservative government led by Churchill would have found very difficult to dismantle: it is even more fundamental.

Since the General Strike (in fact the trend had begun even sooner, for all the bitter antagonisms of the earlier 20th century) a growing element of mutual interest and collaboration was evident between government, employers' organisations and the trade union leadership. From the 1930s, the terms of the implicit bargain were, on the government side, the maintenance of low interest rates, tariff protection and policies favourable to industrial concentration which enhanced the role of the major unions and, on the employers' and trade union side, a climate of industrial peace and repudiation of extremist politics such as those represented by the NUWM. By 1937 trade union representatives were sitting on numerous committees appointed by the Ministry of Labour, and Ernest Bevin was able to state in that year that, 'The trade union movement has become an integral part of the state.'[5] Keith Middlemas, in his fascinating *Politics in an Industrial Society* which details the course of this hitherto little understood development, refers explicitly to 'corporatism' and uses the term 'Corporate state'.[6] Middlemas describes Bevin as a more enthusiastic corporatist than any previous politician because he fully appreciated the power of government to affect economic decisions. The rather cosy relationships which had been established can be judged by Arthur Deakin's reaction, in 1942, to the proposal to introduce family allowances: he opposed the idea on the grounds that it might be used to curb wage increases.

In circumstances where the Labour Party was politically enfeebled, with little foreseeable hope of forming a government, all this little publicised but critically important relationship could be convincingly seen as the most effective way in which labour's interest was being represented, and it served as the foundation for the absolutely central role that a trade union leader was to take in the wartime Coalition. It is said that if the Germans had invaded in 1940 Churchill intended to put the defence under a Committee of Public Safety consisting of himself, Beaverbrook and Bevin, and Eden contemplated for the postwar era a centrist coalition headed by himself and Bevin. 'The trade unions now became political and industrial insiders as never before.'[7]

The trade unions emerged from the war loaded with honour and authority. Following the ravages of the 1970s and 1980s it is hard to recollect how enormous their prestige was then. The leaders of the major unions, especially the biggest, the T&GWU, were men of overwhelming authority who regarded themselves as the only legitimate spokesmen for organised labour. Although Bevin was now permanently transferred to government, his successor, Arthur Deakin was scarcely less monumental. Their achievement rested, certainly, on their organisational and personal hold over their memberships, but in equal measure on their semi-integration, collaboratively with employers, into the government apparatus.

With the establishment of Labour in government, the Party had become the senior rather than the junior partner in the labour alliance, but the success of its programme, indeed the survival of the government, would depend on the continuation of the close working relationship both with the trade union leaders and those of private industry. In the abstract, the advent of Labour to office could have led to greater strains and tensions with the union movement had the latter expected greater advances from 'their' government and been disappointed. In the event, nothing like that occurred and this harmony must be attributed to the common values and perceptions of national interest shared by both and in tune with popular feeling.

The lynchpin of the postwar corporate consensus was not a particular piece of legislation but the White Paper on Full Employment issued by the Coalition Government in 1944. After the experience of the interwar years this was absolutely crucial, and so long as the Labour administration could deliver it, the movement was likely to put up with any impositions and sacrifices that seemed necessary for the purpose. Most likely a Conservative government, if it had been capable of doing likewise, would have got a similar response, though perhaps with greater difficulty.

It has to be said that, battling against the odds, the Labour government fulfilled its electoral mandate as well as any and probably better than most. Simultaneously it was implementing, if not exactly a hidden agenda (although some of it certainly was), a programme that had no warrant in the 1945 manifesto and was grounded in the traditional and longstanding imperatives of the British state. Both were expressions of labourist ideology: the first aimed to bring the corporate and political power of labour to bear in the interests of social improvement, in the most material sense, while the second advanced no alternative definition of national interest to that maintained by the established authorities and their ideologists, above all the City, Treasury and Foreign Office, but rather aspired to promote that interest with zeal and dedication.

Although certainly an oversimplification it would not be essentially a mistake to conclude that the notion of social progress which characterised this government was 'economistic' – not, that is, a recognition that any worthwhile social or political programme required a secure economic foundation, but an assumption that getting the economy and welfare system right was all that really mattered so far as the public at large were concerned. All other aspects of policy and state concerns could be and ought to be conducted according to traditional norms. Needless to say, the traditions in *those* areas remained intensely authoritarian, but the same applied to the mode in which the new economic and social initiatives were conceived. The elementary structures of social organisation and civil society were unquestioned, and indeed it would become a source of pride for Labour that they should be strengthened and consolidated by the great measures of reform. Welfare and housing would be managed on the assumption that, typically and overwhelmingly, the users of these services would be nuclear families with non-working mothers. In the nationalised industries and services employer/employee relations were to proceed on exactly the same principles that characterised those in the private sector, namely authority and subordination. Education was to operate a tripartate system, with pupils graded according to traditional norms of ability and operating under unchanged disciplinary codes. In medicine and health, for all the profound changes that were to follow regarding availability, medical authority and hierarchy would be perpetuated in an unaltered fashion. In this, as in the range of welfare cash benefits the relationship was *experienced* as one of donor and client, despite their enhanced levels – above all in the bottom-line, means-tested benefits which fell outside the scope of the National Insurance system (now retitled National Assistance in place of the discredited name of Public Assistance; although in reality unchanged). In spite of all endeavours to the contrary, the aftertaste of the Poor Law remained. The reform programme, extensive and ambitious though it was by the standards of the British past, failed to embody a philosophy either of individual or collective self-determination: it assumed that social identities would remain unchanged under the new economic dispensation.

In this respect, official attitudes towards the public role assigned to women in the early postwar years is both revealing and instructive. With the end of the war, the heavy emphasis on women as an essential component of the industrial labour force came to an end, as might be expected. It would be an oversimplification, however, to imagine that an immediate drive followed to return women promptly to the domestic sphere. Labour shortages were expected, and Attlee, broadcasting in September 1945, stressed that: 'We are desperately short of manpower... we require an increase of about five million workers.' Women were therefore subject to contradictory propaganda messages: on the one hand they were being offered work, on the other the worthy task of adjusting the national birth-rate.

In 1947, as acute labour shortages emerged, an actual publicity drive was undertaken, using the slogan 'Women must Work' to recruit more women into paid employment. However, the emphasis was different from that of the war years. Heavy industry and management were no longer regarded as suitable. Women were encouraged instead to take up traditional female employment in manufacturing industries, such as textiles, or to go into the caring professions.

The officially-sponsored demand for female labour was reconciled with the increasing natalist ideology of the time by an attempt to exclude mothers of young children from the workforce. So far as possible these were not wanted. In 1945 and 1946 financial provision for day nurseries was slashed: '... motherhood and paid employment were seen as (virtually) irreconcilable options. One economist concluded that unequal pay ensured that "motherhood as a vocation is not too unattractive compared with work in the professions, industry or trade",' and the TUC made its contribution by demonstrating the distinctive and unequal character of male and female employment: 'It was also a powerful influence urging women to reconstruct the family as their foremost duty.'[8]

It is suggested that the failure of the 1947 recruitment drive was an important motivation in the adoption of the policy to recruit unskilled labour from the Commonwealth nations: 'Propaganda (or education) prepared the xenophobic British workforce to accept this "temporary" solution even less than it had encouraged men to accept women into industry during the war.'[9]

Labourism repesented a refusal or inability to envisage (far less act upon such a vision) any profound transformation in social structures or relationships beyond the limits of what had come, over a century, to be tacitly accepted and defined as lying within the legitimate boundaries of political action, signalising the character of ideological hegemony in mid 20th century Britain.

The sorts of unquestioned presuppositions which the leaders of the Labour Party and trade unions carried into the postwar era reveal the extent to which they remained prisoners of a tradition and understanding of British culture, a perception of what it meant to *be* British that was defined with the approval of the traditional powers-that-be, that took for granted the rightful privileges and superiority of an elite which saw itself as God's gift to humanity, providentially placed to hold the barbarous Russians in check while giving lessons in statecraft to the unlettered and naive Americans.[10]

The first set of presuppositions to be noted in this connexion are the ones regarding state and empire. To say that the monarchical constitution was accepted unquestioningly would be a gross understatement; it was deeply revered. The baroque farrago of precedent, convention, fancy dress and mummery was imagined to represent the ultimate in political wisdom. 'If I am fit to represent the working class of Merthyr I am fit to attend a garden party at Windsor,' asserted Keir Hardie, expressing his deference along with his class pride.[11] Symbolically, Attlee's government gave way to Churchill's insistence that the bomb-gutted parliament building be rebuilt along its ancient lines rather than as a modern debating chamber equipped with appropriate facilities. Here for sure the heritage of dead generations weighed like a nightmare on the brains of the living. In short, for the government leaders the state was a sacred mystery with which they had no inclination to tamper. Rather they intended to worship at its shrine and to invoke its powers to achieve their social goals.

Adoration of the symbolic and traditional nonsense was one thing – though very indicative – but this state had more concrete attributes. It featured a highly centralised sovereignty embodied in the omnicompetent Crown-in-Parliament, itself further centralised by the absence of a written constitution, the accepted norm of one-party government and cabinet management. Further, the British state (while it was many other things as well) was the political expression of a ruling class whose sources of profit were world-wide in extent and guarded by a military apparatus of corresponding awesomeness and power, traditionally in the shape of a hypertrophied navy and global pattern of bases. 'Spheres of interest' and major leverage in international relations were regarded as natural accompaniments. On the domestic front the state upheld a social order that was, in principle at least, among the world's more coercive polities and incorporated severe standards of hierarchic patri-archical authoritarianism in gender and sexual relations as well as in its provision for the public maintenance of the destitute – even if these had been somewhat modified by wartime community spirit. Except in that last dimension the project of the incoming administration conflicted with none of these realities, rather they were looked upon as part of the natural world.

If Labour's attitude to the economy was more radical in principle, there too unquestioned presuppositions marked out the boundaries. Public ownership and planning formed the centrepiece of the strategy, but these were conceived as operating within market-dominated structures and having no fundamentally different objectives from those of private capital. More specifically, the character of the financial apparatus and its overseas alignments were not called into question. Evidently Britain, as an island economy dependent upon foreign trade, had in the nature of things to be very conscious of its sources of supply and the means of obtaining them, but making the demands of the City of London and its international monetary transactions the first priority of economic management was another matter altogether.

The Attlee government was, by the standards of British development, a great reforming administration, undoubtedly the most far-reaching of the century. The well-known limitations in the content of these reforms can be related to the sets of presuppositions mentioned above, in holding to which the Party leadership accurately reflected the sentiments of its constituency and the popular culture of the times. The limitations in the *manner* and *form* of its achievements can be considered in relation to a third set of presuppositions even more deeply embedded in the culture. These involved the way that people relate to each other and these assumptions were implicitly – and often enough explicitly – authoritarian ones. The Victorian Poor Law threw its shadow over the newborn welfare state, the managerial system was maintained quite unchanged in the newly socialised enterprises.

The consequences of each set of presuppositions should now be considered in turn.

Attlee's first act following the electoral landslide was to break the rule instituted in the aftermath of Macdonald's debacle that the Party leader should consult the Party and movement before accepting any Royal invitation to form a government; instead he departed for Buckingham Palace forthwith. In the general euphoria little notice was taken of this incident, but it was significant. More significant still was the new Prime Minister's agreement, under Royal inducement, to alter his intention of appointing Hugh Dalton to the Foreign Office and replace him with Ernest Bevin. It is certain that Dalton was regarded as too left wing and it may be that his betrayal of his class origins was held against him, but a more significant explanation is that Dalton was notorious in his wartime ministerial career as a politician with a mind of his own who had given his civil servants an extremely rough ride and he would have certainly refused to have been manipulated or intimidated by the Foreign Office mandarins. In acting thus, Attlee not only revealed himself to be pliable to establishment pressure even where he had no need to be, but also underlined his acceptance of the constitutional convention which made a prime minister solely responsible for the selection of his cabinet without reference to his party or anybody else apart from the monarch.

Thus the new government showed clearly that it planned no fundamental innovations in the manner in which Britain was governed and that, in that respect, even crying abuses would remain unmolested if they had acquired traditional respectability. Consequently the Orange police statelet in Northern Ireland was not interfered with in any fashion and its rulers permitted to continue to mistreat the Catholic population without any whisper of criticism from official circles, far less any concrete sanction from the battery of powers which on paper Westminster had available to it. On the mainland by contrast, but within the same tradition of rule, the centralism inherent in the British polity was intensified. The longstanding Labour Party commitment to Scottish devolution, reaffirmed informally as late as 1945, simply disappeared; it was regarded not merely as being no longer necessary but as a positive impediment to reform and planning now that Labour had the power of the central state altogether at its disposal. A similar pretext – that it would complicate and confuse the administration – was used by Herbert Morrison to shoot down even the modest proposal to appoint a secretary of state for Wales. Military, civil service and judicial hierarchies and modes of operation, needless to say, stayed totally intact. It must not be imagined, however, that cowardice, class treason or perversity determined the attitudes and behaviour of the Attlee government in these respects. Quite apart from the deep labourist tradition which had wholly absorbed the sacremental character of British institutions, from monarchy to judicial fancy dress, these same institutions had taken on a democratic, even heroic, patina as the foundation of the British state which had fought and won the conflict with the dictatorships.

Foreign Policy

During the war years, foreign and strategic affairs had been very much the preserve of the tory leaders of the Coalition. Churchill's war aims had been directed as much to the preservation and enhancement of the formal and informal British empire as to the defeat of the Axis and, from the point early in 1943 when it became evident that victory was assured, had devoted much thought and attention to limiting the postwar influence of the Soviet Union in European and international contexts, whether by striking deals with Stalin over southern and eastern Europe or, much more significantly, drawing the USA, with its military and economic resources, into a coalition directed against the former wartime ally. The strategy further implied the maintenance by the British of a very large overseas military establishment of their own, with a string of bases in Europe, Africa and Asia, both to prove their worth as a partner to the Americans and to be capable of exercising coercive military force on their own account, establishing in the groundwork of postwar military policy an obsession with 'commitments'.

All this was inherited and adopted virtually without alteration by the incoming administration. The one significant point of difference was the Labour Party's publicly affirmed intention of conceding independence to India.[12] Even so, it is perhaps doubtful how fast this would have proceeded had it not become clear on the one hand that India would soon be ungovernable unless the commitment was upheld and on the other that withdrawal presented no immediate threat to British or western economic interests. For the rest, the Churchill line was continued zealously down to the last stop and comma.

It would be a serious mistake to suppose, however, that all that was involved was a calculation founded upon material interests, important though these undoubtedly were. The record shows beyond doubt that of nearly equal importance in the eyes of the British elite was their self-image as the leaders of a 'Great Power' and that it was worth making very considerable sacrifices to maintain that image. A recurrent theme in the top-level discussions of the postwar years is the fear of being reduced to second-class status in the international domain, quite separately from considerations of what such an outcome might imply in material terms. To sit at the top table, to be at the very centre of world affairs, to be star players in the great game of diplomacy was in a sense the life project of the high-ranking generals and diplomatic functionaries.[13] Orme Sargent, a leading Foreign Office official, was fearful that the Labour election victory would result in communist hegemony in Europe, social revolution in Britain and 'the reduction of England (sic) to a second-class power'. He was soon to be made head of the FO. The ruling class at large certainly shared his view, and similar values had become acceptable by the populace. The Labour leaders needed little or no persuasion to take them over undiluted, even if the Labour Party as a whole was less enthusiastic.

The first fruits of this continuity were gathered when Bevin continued Churchill's use of military force to uphold the monarcho-fascist regime which had been installed by British power in liberated Greece to counter a communist-led popular insurgency. The conflict had started in 1944 in furtherance of Churchill's concept of safeguarding British interests in the eastern Mediterranean and Middle East from the presence nearby of any potentially hostile power – such as a communist-dominated Greece was presumed to be. For Stalin, anxious at all costs as the end of the war approached to maintain good relations with the west, ideology was irrelevant and he deemed the Greek communists and popular movement expendable. With the Churchill-Stalin agreements of late 1944, confirmed at the Yalta conference in February 1945, Greece had been allocated to the British sphere of interest.

Some elements of the repressive actions taken by British forces round the world during Bevin's period of office could be – and were – publicly justified, however tendentiously, on the contention that resources vital to public wellbeing were at stake. Malaya, which supplied most of the world's rubber and much of its tin, was a case in point. No such argument could apply to the Greek events. They can be understood only on the basis that the megalomaniac and paranoid obsessions of the Foreign Office establishment impregnated the consciousness of a government which had come into office with quite different conceptions, and which genuinely believed itself to be the guardian of a national interest that went beyond that of the traditional rulers. They were persuaded, and their labourist ideology enabled this, to identify that sectional interest with the national one.

It was, of course, a formidably expensive posture and implied a prodigious waste of the resources of a very straightened economy carrying other ambitious projects – those on which the election had been won. Indeed, resources were so stretched that Attlee was moved at one stage to question whether it was really necessary to continue such a massive military presence east of Suez, but he quickly allowed himself to be overruled by Bevin and the chiefs of staff.[14] It must be stressed that these decisions were made well before the US government began to press for large-scale rearmament by its allies – they were a British choice.

Nor was the USA involved in another crucial and breathtakingly expensive decision by the Attlee government, to manufacture a British atomic bomb. On the contrary, for the US, which resolutely refused to pool any atomic information with the British, it was irrelevant and a distraction grudgingly accepted by Washington in order to gratify the sensitivities of a foreign government which was so accommodating as to turn its national territory into an unsinkable aircraft carrier for the US bomber command.

The sort of pragmatic justifications noted above might be quoted – or invented *post facto* – for many or most of the objectionable foreign policy decisions adopted by the government, but the atomic bomb project – initiated long before there was any reason to suspect that the USSR might soon possess an atomic weapon[15] – is understandable *only* on the basis of the elite obsession that if Britain ceased to be, if not Top Nation, then at least one of the Big Three, history would come to an end.

A crucial meeting ... took place on 25 October 1946, with Dalton and Cripps protesting fiercely, on financial grounds, against developing a British nuclear weapons programme. To the alarm of Portal, the Chief of Staff, the British bomb seemed about to disappear from history. Then Bevin ... returned from a lengthy lunch engagement to sweep away the economists' reservations and bully them into submission. He argued that it was important for the Union Jack to fly over a British bomb.[16]

This vignette encapsulates vividly the combination of motivations and relationships which determined this aspect of Labour's military policy, which was kept a close secret from both parliament and public during the entire stretch of the government's existence. '... Ministers as senior as Morrison or Bevin often had views ... which hardly took account of the political, military or financial realities after 1945.'[17] The factors at work are further underlined by the circumstance that, among the government's key advisors on the policy, was a Conservative front-bencher, Sir John Anderson.

The government's foreign policy was made incontinently more arduous, as Dalton and Cripps had foreseen, by its imperial and nuclear obsessions; the balance of payments deficit in 1947 was £600 million, of which one-third represented overseas military expenditure. The Labour government became so dependent upon US resources for its programme and indeed its bare survival that it was no doubt unavoidable that it should become integrated into the US global military system, which is not to say that the terms on which that happened need have been as exacting and demeaning as they in fact were. Other states which joined NATO managed to avoid a similar degree of entanglement and subordination, and there seems little reason to imagine that the British state could not have got as much or more for less infringement on its sovereignty. Attlee's administration, however, wanted other things from the Americans than simply the material resources to sustain an ailing economy: nothing less than the underwriting by American power and wealth of British international and imperial pretensions – including its atomic weapons programme. For this they were prepared to mortgage the country's future, endanger their own social programme and risk disabling rifts within the the trade union movement, the Labour Party and even the Cabinet itself. No price was too great: the arms budget in early 1951 stood at £4.7 billion, 14 per cent of the national income. Rational considerations, even malign ones, cannot in themselves explain this posture, which followed the norms of the state inherited from the prewar, even pre 1914, era, and which can be interpreted only in terms of the labour leaders' complete absorption into their own consciousnesses of that state's principles and ambitions, which they had infused with a quasi-sacramental legitimacy. The scientific advisor, Lord Tizard, observed that even proposals which accepted the basis of western atomic policy, but which proposed to concentrate the weapons in the possession of the USA were greeted 'with the kind of horror one would expect if one made a disrespectful remark about the King'.[18]

Arthur Balfour's notorious remark, made in 1906, that the great Conservative Party, whether in or out of office, was entitled to guide the destinies of the great British empire, could never have been more apposite than as applied to the international policy pursued between 1945 and 1951. It is less a proof though, that Attlee and Bevin set out deliberately to do what the Conservatives, or for that matter the traditional rulers, wanted, and more a tribute to the degree to which patriotic and national values had become identified in popular consciousness with conservative ones and a more specifically left wing or critical understanding marginalised. Reaction and conservatism had habitually wrapped themselves in the flag since the French revolutionary wars and Churchill's role between 1940 and 1945 had restored a credit that was in danger of becoming exhausted. National requirements, defined from the right, were seen as properly transcending sectional interests. It is by no means necessarily to the discredit of Attlee and his ministers that they should have followed a vision of national considerations which reached beyond the corporate class claims of the movement that they directly represented – if only that interest had been interpreted in less conservative terms.[19]

Economic Reform

In the sphere of economic affairs, less mystically regarded, the Conservative presumption, to embody the national interest, was certainly contested and vigorously rebutted, although even here a legitimate sectional claim was recognised.[20] Public ownership and planning certainly proclaimed a repudiation of traditional conservative standards although it has to be said that, after the experience of the 1930s and the growing acceptance of Keynesian perspectives, opposition tended to be perfunctory rather than real – at least until proposals for the national-isation of productive industries was placed seriously on the agenda in the late 1940s. Not coincidentally these, particularly that relating to the steel industry, were the economic proposals for which the Labour leadership showed the least enthusiasm and the greatest reluctance. It is understandable that they should have done so, for the industrial portion of their programme, in both its ownership and planning aspects, was embarked upon in part to advance the material situation of the workforce at the point of production and above all to eradicate mass unemployment forever. But it was also intended to furnish the services and infrastructure for a thriving productive economy, the greater part of which was assumed to continue indefinitely in private ownership. Meantime, planning of that industrial economy, which turned out to be principally planning for shortages, was conducted by planners who were drawn directly from the ranks of private industry. 'The Government's first priority was economic survival, which meant survival of existing economic arrangements.'[21] That, in the event, was how nationalisation worked, to the distress of its more wholehearted proponents, but the point is that it was *intended* right from the beginning to work in that fashion. As the dissolution of the wartime Coalition approached, there was no worked-out scheme of public ownership available to Labour's leaders and they proceeded in an *ad hoc* fashion under grass-roots pressure from the Labour Party Conference, which had forced extensive nationalisation proposals onto the programme as late as December 1944. So it was that most of the publicly owned sector, 20 per cent of the economy eventually, was made up of those bankrupt and decrepit though vital enterprises that private capital could not sustain, like the mines and railways, or else ones like electricity, gas and road transport where private control might have raised the costs to man-ufacturing industry to an unacceptable level. For the first three years after Labour took office, wartime government controls on private industry were continued; however, ministers did not view them as the framework for an alternative economic system but only as necessary instruments to be used in conditions of shortage.[22] From 1948 onwards they were increasingly relinquished. According to Keith Middlemas, any hope of a unified transport system or coherent energy policy 'died in the lifetime of the Attlee government',[23] although the TUC, generally in complete harmony with government economic thinking, remained 'wedded to the idea of a planned economy' in terms of industrial boards, directed investment and wealth redistribution.[24]

There was, however, another field of economic strategy influenced by presuppositions connected with those prevailing in international relations, which had both a material and a national–ideological dimension. Very early on in the life of the government a decision was reached in principle to treat as a central priority the resumption and restoration of capital export from Britain (overseas holdings having been liquidated on a considerable scale to meet the wartime emergency) and, in spite of the country's much weakened economic position, to retain sterling as a reserve currency at all costs. Although an argument can be made that a long-term contribution was thus made to the viability of the nation's overseas trading position, on which her material economy depended, the immediate effect was to increase the burden on a balance of payments which was already under heavy strain. The beneficiaries were, more than any other element, the banking and financial interests of the City of London.[25] Again, it would be facile to conclude that the Labour administration subordinated the interests of the masses to those of finance capital in full consciousness of what it was doing.[26] Rather,the aura of the country's greatness cast its lustre on this aspect too of governmental responsibility, for which the pound sterling functioned as a symbol both of power and of illustrious prestige.

It is hardly necessary to emphasise that by the adoption of this approach the basic line of development imparted to the postwar economy involved the resumption of a traditional orientation and once more prioritised the needs of finance and international commerce over those of industrial growth, or even of reconstruction. The character of the decision was indeed recognised at the time, for proposals had been advanced for government to adopt a much more forcefully directional approach to the private sector. That approach would have involved retention and even strengthening of wartime controls, the physical allocation and direction of raw materials, capital and labour, all capped by the reorganisation of the Board of Trade into a Ministry of Industrial Planning.

The conception was advanced in different forms on several occasions during the lifetime of the government, but it was always rejected, it would seem, without very much deliberation, and traditional norms were reasserted. The 1944 package had envisaged the establishment of

government-supervised Industry Boards to oversee development and
technological renewal, but the FBI easily avoided their implementation
as 'Labour leaders were increasingly persuaded that the objectives of
private industry harmonised rather than conflicted with the aims of a
Labour government.' At the end of 1944 decisions were made which
implied that the Treasury, with its financial priorities, would be the centre
for economic planning and management at the expense of the Board
of Trade and the Ministry of Labour, and the Treasury won the point
that the main aim of planning was to get investment timing right, not
to regulate the competitiveness of private firms, as the Board of Trade
wanted. It is true that, in the summer of 1947, Stafford Cripps had got
through an Industrial Organisation and Development Act and been made
head of a new planning ministry which was to oversee all the other
departments with production concerns, but its remit was limited and,
in any case, Cripps and his new ministry were reintegrated into the traditional nexus when he was appointed Chancellor only a few months
later. Treasury dominance was thereby consolidated. Finally, in 1950,
Harold Wilson, then President of the Board of Trade, tabled a paper
entitled *The State and Private Industry*, which incorporated the kind of
dirigiste perspective he would resuscitate as Labour Party leader 13
years later. It was rapidly sunk by combined opposition from Whitehall,
the FBI and the TUC, indicating in the case of the trade union leaders
a considerable weakening in their attachment to economic planning
compared with their outlook during the first Attlee government.[27]

Thus we discover, in this sphere too, labourism identifying itself with
the traditional purposes of the state and accepting a role as the custodian
of unquestioned values.[28]

Why should it appear self-evident that the manipulation of money
should take precedence over the promotion of industrial growth,
indeed that resources should be diverted and the public urged on to make
sacrifices in their energies and consumption in order to provide it with
a secure foundation?

It is in this connexion that Perry Anderson's thesis is worth consideration.[29] Its argument, roughly speaking, is that, even before
industrialisation got underway in the 18th century, Britain was a highly
developed agrarian and commercial capitalist economy, the world
leader in fact, and that the shape and character of its ruling class and state
institutions was determined particularly by this circumstance. Developing
British industry, for all its scope, strength and even world leadership was,
so to speak, overlaid on this earlier capitalist structure, which continued
to shape the essential directions of the economy and to subordinate

industrial growth to its own purposes. While 19th century industry grew prodigiously, financial power, with the City of London as the nerve centre of a world trading economy, enjoyed a still more breathtaking expansion. Industrial capital, isolated in its northern strongholds, the argument continues, was never capable of seizing the commanding heights of society, either by a political challenge or by inducing the traditional ruling class to recognise its own future in industry and applied science. It wasn't only that cabinets were dominated by landowners up to the 20th century, but that classical bourgeois values never prevailed where it really mattered.

Consequently, once Britain began, from the late 19th century onward, to encounter commercial and political challenges from emergent rival capitalist powers, the resulting conflicts between sections of the British ruling class were always resolved by the sacrifice of the politically weaker element, industrial capital. Prior to 1914 capital flooded overseas, technology in Britain lagged in comparison with that of Germany, the USA or even France, and plans for introducing a strong emphasis on technical education were deliberately frustrated by the devotees of classics established in high places. During the 1920s the desperate situation of the export industry was made even worse in order to maintain the gold standard and the parity of sterling, while in the postwar era industry and technology were once again left to its own devices, so far as any central strategy was concerned, while the Bank–Treasury–City nexus ensured that government concentrated its efforts on easing the path for sterling's international role.

Anderson's model has evoked very considerable criticism, and from a wide political spectrum.[30] The principal ground for offence is that it advances a very different characterisation of British capitalism than that which Marxists have long accepted. Also, its emphasis on the long-term subordination of industrial capital, even in the climactic 'age of capital', appears perversely to contradict the self-evident nature of the 19th century economy. Certainly the model is vulnerable to criticism in detail: Anderson has rather too great a tendency to seek its legitimisation in the exegisis of Marxist texts, too marked an inclination to read off the political consciousness of different fractions of capital from their grading in the socio-economic hierarchy and too little attention to comparable cases – Germany and Japan spring to mind – where the industrial bourgeoisie started off with an even less promising social and political heritage.

Nonetheless, with all reservations noted, in its general scope the Anderson model remains a convincing framework for analysis and suggests a line of explanation for otherwise mysterious features of British economic and social evolution. It would, after all, be hard to imagine that there is *no* connexion between the emphasis on capital export, the centrality of financial considerations in the economic policies of all governments, the wretchedness of British industrial performance and the archaic nature of its political system, exemplified particularly by the besotted royalism that saturates it.

The symbiotic relationship of labourism with a state erected for purposes quite alien to the prime objectives which Labour ostensibly pursued but, nevertheless, the vehicle through which they had to be achieved, is borne out in the administrative style and forms of human relationship embodied in the great reforming programme of the government.

Nationalisation was in due course to assume an almost totemic significance and probably to figure more significantly in retrospect than it ever did before the 1945 election, when the eyes of the electorate were fixed on social justice above all, and public ownership counted only as one means among others of reaching that goal. Certainly the original labourist conception of nationalisation was wholly pragmatic, a specific remedy for paticular enterprises where private capital had failed the producer or consumer (the mines above all) or else was reluctant to take the risk. Perhaps it was this which distinguished labourism's ideology most sharply in the pre-1914 period from that of all the socialist groups, whether parliamentary or revolutionary, from the ILP to the SLP. Clause 4 of the Labour Party constitution, instituted in 1918 in response, like the nationalisation programme adopted in 1944, to a groundswell of grass roots feeling, was an elastic formulation capable of multiple interpretations, but the one that prevailed had its sources in the experience of 19th century municipal enterprise and government management of key industries during the world wars. So far as the economic purpose of the nationalised sector was concerned, it was to serve and not to dominate the privately controlled one.

It is not surprising, therefore, that the initial programme of nationalisation legislated in the government's first years evoked only perfunctory opposition, but that the intended second tranche, including industrial life assurance, sugar, cement and – above all – steel, was a very different matter. Business interests mobilised to combat the programme with energy and determination. Nor is it remarkable that the question of nationalisation of the steel industry, the only major profitable manufacturing industry scheduled for public ownership, marked the divide between right and left in the labour movement along basically differing conceptions of how a welfare orientated economy should be run.[31] The symbolic importance was equal to the material and focussed antagonistic claims of moral legitimacy as between public and private ownership – which was the inherently worthy form and which was to operate on sufferance?

It is very much to be doubted whether the attitude adopted by the Labour leaders towards nationalisation was based on any conviction such as that developed in the 1950s by the circle which centred around Gaitskell and Crosland that the greater portion of the economy was best left under private ownership; on the contrary, they were probably convinced, in the light of the political tradition in which they had been formed, that public ownership *was* the better option *in principle*. Their reluctance to exceed or even approach the bounds of the 1945 manifesto should be recognised rather as reflecting the conditioned deference of their relations to established forces and traditions, and their inherent respect for the basic structures both of existing civil society and of the state which protected that society.[32] The fiercely anti-Labour *Economist* nevertheless thought that what Labour had done was the very least that a socialist government, equipped with such a mandate, could have aimed at, and regarded oil as a surprising oversight.

The same caution and impoverishment of vision is apparent in the character of the public ownership which was instituted at that point. Howell refers to the 'Party's lack of concern with the distribution of power within industry'. To call the industries state-owned is something of a misnomer. Although government retained ultimate control over the direction of their operations, formal ownership was vested in each case in an independent corporation (modelled ultimately upon the BBC). It is notorious that the boards of these corporations were dominated by the same individuals who had run the enterprises in the days of private ownership.[33] It is notorious that grossly excessive compensation was paid to the shareholders of bankrupt industries likes the mines and railways (which compensation they proceeded to invest in the still profitable private sector), while the run-down sectors were obliged to borrow enormous sums at commercial rates to restore and re-equip their physical capital. It is notorious that residuary government control was used to enforce pricing policies which seriously underpriced the nationalised goods and services supplied to the private sector. These policies prevented the publicly owned industries accumulating reserves, stigmatised them as inherently inefficient and unprofitable, and banned them from expanding into other manufacturing areas as they were legally entitled to by their charters and in which they were equipped to operate.[34]

Perhaps of greater consequence in the long term than any of these shortcomings was the deliberate and complete lack of accountability of the nationalised sector both to its workforce and to those of its consumers among the ordinary public. As a matter of principle the workforce were excluded from any share in managerial decisions; traditional managerial principles were considered to be sacrosanct. 'Workers' control' was considered anathema in labour politics and, of course, readily caricatured as syndicalist fantasy. Herbert Morrison even refused the Union of Bank Employees any voice in choosing the Governor of the newly nationalised Bank of England. The Party leaders did not have to appeal to the loyalty of the trade union chiefs to win endorsement for this approach, on the contrary, none were more fervent opponents of meaningful worker participation in management. No doubt they were conscious of possible implications for their own authority. Nor was any institutional mechanism considered necessary for the expression of any grievances the general public might possess. They were, after all, electors and the government was democratic and ultimately responsible to the electorate: that should be sufficient. In their day-to-day relations with nationalised industries and services they would have to accept what was provided by people better qualified to judge the public interest. Nationalisation, which was for all its ambiguities undoubtedly a major departure in the economic sphere, did not have its potential extended into the wider area of public relationships and thus a real opportunity to enhance and deepen the application of democratic and participatory norms was missed. Democracy remained confined to the narrowly understood field of a highly imperfect British political tradition.

Welfare Reforms

Similar principles applied to provision of the new welfare benefits. Once again, it is clear that the system initiated by the National Insurance Act was less revolutionary than the contemporary euphoria took it to be.[35] Lord Beveridge, whose Report of 1942 is generally regarded as its founding charter, was very much a minimalist in his calculations of a basic living standard. He believed strongly that welfare provision should be organised on a contractual basis and that individual defaulters from the contract should be punished. His Report, and the subsequent legislation after 1945, were of course based on the insurance principle. Although the early 20th century socialists (including Fabians) had contested this in favour of universal funding out of taxation, it was now accepted unquestioningly, and represented a development upon, rather than a break with, the forms of provision instituted by Conservative and Liberal governments prior to 1939. Moreover, the same authoritarian principle which operated at all social levels prevailed here as well, embodied in the client/provider relationship which the recipients automatically took on in relation to the government or, in fact, to the offices through which the benefits were administered. Even in the National Health Service, which was funded on a more universal principle than the cash benefits and available at need, the consumers – the patients – were in effect wholly passive receivers of 'good things' from an immense bureaucratic apparatus rather than citizens exercising their social dignity in being healed. The BMA tendentiously exploited this point in its anti-NHS propaganda by warning the public that the new system would destroy the intimate relationship they had hitherto enjoyed with their family doctor.[36]

The full degree of authoritarian rigour implicit in the welfare structure was reserved for and became open in the case of those in the residual category these not covered or inadequately covered by insured benefits, who were dependent therefore upon means-tested National Assistance. Humiliation and bureaucratic arbitrariness were built-in features of its operation. The insured benefits were initially intended to be sufficient for a bare but adequate standard of living. With inflation, however, they quickly ceased to be so and the majority of individuals who were dependent long-term upon benefit found themselves compelled to supplement these incomes with National Assistance and everything that involved. They constituted a minority group, so were no great political embarrassment, but the group included most pensioners.

The standards of authoritarian conduct prevailing between public employers and their workforces and between welfare providers and their clients were replicated, and sometimes intensified, at the level of local authority which, under the auspices of central government, actually supplied a great many of the services. In the postwar era housing was probably the most significant of these. The provision of municipal housing on an extended scale was something which had certainly gripped the imagination of the electorate, to the extent that the Conservatives found it worth promising in 1951 to build even faster than Attlee's government had done. And yet it was probably here that consumer dissatisfaction was the most marked of all. The dissatisfaction arose not only over the understandable delays caused by the speed of erection and the way in which allocations necessarily caused lengthy queues (though these things certainly caused major and bitter resentments) but also because of the petty and arbitrary restrictions which were often imposed upon the new occupiers; these extended to matters of exterior and sometimes even interior decor. Moreover, it was the councils in the areas of longstanding Labour municipal control which acquired the worst reputations; their leaders were often intoxicated by the security of unchallengable power, which made them indifferent to the feelings of an electorate upon which they were confident they could always rely. In areas like north-east England, Liverpool, south Wales, or west Fife, moreover, serious degeneration had set in and Tammany-type control and connexions been established so that these municipalities came to be run by political cliques which resembled local mafias, and were subject to irresistible temptations to indulge in actual corruption.[37]

Achievement or Failure?

Depending upon how you look at it, Attlee's first administration can be seen either as a remarkable achievement or as a depressing failure. Both perceptions are valid. The economic reconstruction was accomplished and the welfare system instituted against phenomenal material difficulties and unrelenting pressure to make the minimum concessions to public feeling and the maximum to private wealth and privilege. To satisfy both these constituencies, and the US government besides, was no mean undertaking for a cabinet which comprised vain, backstabbing prima donnas led by a singularly undynamic traditionalist. Seen in the long term, on the other hand, the achievement was fundamentally flawed. They missed the opportunities, which were perceived but not grasped, for a more far-reaching reorganisation and re-equipment of the industrial base, and so a fatal heritage of economic weakness was handed down; and by constructing the framework of social welfare in such a way as to minimise public involvement and participation, they made it above all the achievement of central and local *government*. This alienated its character so that it became possible for a later government to dismantle it because the majority were indifferent or even opposed to it.

The strains imposed by these simultaneous lines of policy soon came to the surface. The country's financial structure cracked under the joint burdens of upholding a commodities export drive, a capital export drive, a reserve currency and a world imperial role underpinned by massive rearmament commitments undertaken just as the pressures were reaching their most intense. The indications of strain were repeated balance of payments crises and critical shortages of dollars. The response was not to reduce the scale of commitments – except at the margin, for example the withdrawal of British forces from Palestine in 1947 – but to exhort the working population to miracles of productive effort designed to bridge the export gap, and the consuming public to curtail their claims upon national resources for the sake of the balance of payments. The principles of austerity and collective self-sacrifice continued from wartime into peace, and in some instances rationing was even tightened. From 1945 to 1947 the pressures were unremitting and things grew worse, but at any rate the country enjoyed low inflation, a balanced budget (for all Dalton's expansionist sentiments), an improving balance of payments, industrial recovery, and a high degree of political harmony.[38] Undoubtedly the cushion of the US loan was crucial to this success. When that was punctured by the convertibility crisis of the summer of 1947, cuts and austerity received still greater emphasis, resulting in longer hours, lower investment and less purchasing power.[39] The nation could scarcely have been said to be enjoying a sybaritic extravaganza in the first two years of the administration, yet that was the public impression that the media contrived to put about regarding Hugh Dalton's mildly expansionary financial policies.

By contrast, when the term 'austerity' came into public currency under the regime of Dalton's successor at the Treasury from November 1947, Stafford Cripps, a deliberately puritanical rhetoric was adopted. The nation made to feel it was being administered a purgative for its past excesses. Public opinion polls of the period would seem to suggest that such dubious claims and relationships did carry conviction with the public to which they were addressed and give a foretaste of the effect of similar governmental postures in the years of Thatcher's first term. The notion that nasty medicine, however unwelcome, is necessarily good for you, appears to be one which is deeply embedded in the British psyche.[40]

If exhortations were liberally supplied so, in a more restrained manner, was coercion. Rationing can perhaps be viewed in this light, a coercive control upon consumption (which is not to impugn its necessity in the circumstances). More unmistakably coercive was the continuation of wartime restrictions on strike activity; the combination of appeals to loyalty and self-sacrifice, on the one hand, with compulsion, or the threat of it as the alternative, can be seen in the acceptance by the TUC in 1948 of a government-sponsored wage freeze aimed at reducing inflation.[41] Needless to say, this departure was possible only with the co-operation of the leaders of the major unions, whose authority and authoritarian style was used to dragoon the rank and file into line. Equally, even the likes of Deakin would have found such an endeavour beyond their strength if the trade unionists and their delegates had not been fundamentally willing to be so dragooned.

> In the first place workers who are accustomed to industrial discipline expect it in other fields, and when it is provided in a trade union they do not question its presence ... There is a tendency to admire aggressiveness.[42]

In 1946 the miners and the ETU had been ready to approve wage planning as a component part of a socialist programme. By April 1946 a proposal for a national wages policy was supported by officials in the Board of Trade, the Treasury and the Cabinet Office. It was to be operated through a National Incomes Commision on which government, industry and the TUC would negotiate wage rates. The idea at that juncture found no favour with Attlee, Bevin or the TUC chiefs but, after the experience of the TUC endorsed wage freezes, Deakin had become a vehement advocate of wages policy and regretted its abandonment in 1950.[43] In November of that same year Gaitskell proposed a National Wages Board as a 'neutral arbiter between management and unions' [44] in the context of the economic crisis resulting from the Korean War. 'In the end, predictably, the argument came back to wages.'[45]

With the inflow of Marshall Aid and the upturn in European and world commercial activity which followed, conditions began, in general though not always in particular,[46] to ease after the sterling devaluation crisis of 1949. The worst was over, but it had become clear beyond dispute that to combine what the establishment saw as the world role of the British state with the welfare advances of the years following 1940 required access to US resources and goodwill, for which the price was military and financial subordination. British airfields were prepared to receive a USAF atomic bomber fleet. The original idea of NATO was attributed to Ernest Bevin, or more likely his officials, but Britain accepted a level of dependence upon the superpower far beyond what was required of any other of the major NATO powers, in order to sustain the labourist project. In 1948, the Board of Trade estimated that without Marshall Aid the country would be suffering hunger and deprivation while unemployment would be at 1.5 million and rising.

Commentators at the time and historians subsequently have been unanimous in their verdict that this government encountered no serious problems or challenge from the political left either inside or outside the ranks of the Labour Party. In that sense at least it was truly, in Ralph

Miliband's phrase, 'the climax of labourism'.[47] 'The government dominated all such relationships with its backbenchers, with the National Executive and with the Party Conference.'[48] Intransigent critics in the parliamentary party, of whom there were never many in any case, were picked off piecemeal, censured or expelled. Those in the constituencies were routinely abused and ignored. '[Many Labour MPs] were essentially nationalists, just as prepared to accept a bi-partisan foreign policy to withstand Stalin as their predecessors had accepted coalition to resist the Kaiser'.[49]

Only the Communist Party, with around 50,000 members, two MPs, a smattering of local councillors, and a strong presence in certain trade unions, presented any coherent or significant alternative on the left. In the areas of its greatest strength, such as the 'little Moscows' or parts of London, it was able to sustain a political counter-culture of the sort lovingly chronicled by Raph Samuel. In circumstances of disillusion or disappointed expectation with the government's performance, the CP might have been expected to thrive and attract growing support. In fact precisely the opposite happened. In great part this was certainly attributable to the impact of the Cold War, and the campaign of unremitting guilt by association directed against the CP on account of Stalinist atrocities both real and imagined elsewhere in the world. The CP, of course, zealously confirmed the association by endorsing every one of the atrocities and absurdities. However, the question is why the Cold War withered the CPGB in a way which did not apply to the French or Italian parties. It must be concluded that, while the CP was temporarily able to gain credit from very positive wartime attitudes towards the USSR and was drastically revising the content of its political perspectives, preparing to replace *For Soviet Britain* with *The British Road to Socialism*, a revolutionary orientation of any sort was profoundly inimical to the British political culture, in a way which is not the case in continental Europe.[50]

The CP's situation was not helped by the fact that, as revealed in sensational exposees by former members such as Bob Darke or Douglas Hyde, whatever *policy* changes might have occurred, the Party's internal regime had not altered much from its prewar Comintern style. It retained quasi-military organisational forms with rigid disciplinary procedures and made authoritarianism a point of honour. Communist trade union leaders when they were in commanding positions needed no lessons in authoritarian crudity or bureaucratic manoeuvre from their Labour counterparts. Among the west Fife miners Abe Moffat ran the NUM with an autocratic style that Deakin or Bevin might well have envied. Although there is no reason to suppose that the ballot rigging engaged in by the communist electrician leaders in 1961 was instigated or approved by the CP leadership, equally without doubt it was a logical product of the contempt for meaningful democratic processes which afflicted the CP to a greater degree than it did the Labour Party or trade union machines. The ETU culprits were unique only in getting caught.

As subsequent decades were to show, the government of 1945–50 certainly did not conduct the social revolution that the more incautious of its protagonists and propagandists claimed for it. Neither can it be viewed as a betrayal of the best hopes of 1945 for a socialist future, a sellout to capital and imperialism – whether because of incorrigible depravity on the part of its leaders as the CP of the time believed and Miliband is inclined to do today, or because of intrinsic weaknesses in the nature of the Labour Party itself, as David Coates argues. Nor, finally, can it be regarded simply as a mixture, some positive achievements, certain negative shortcomings. Its triumphs and disasters were all of a piece, part of a coherent project, a vision of what a humane Britain ought to be like, as its leaders strove, according to their lights, to make the best of impossibly difficult circumstances in giving to their constituency what had been promised in the election programme. That their lights were dimmer than they might have been should occasion no surprise, their backgrounds made them part of the culture of a decaying imperial power where deference was endemic and whose decay was yet unrecognised. Such was labourism.

The 1950 Election

Certainly the labour and trade union constituency itself, whose members bore all the impositions inflicted upon the community by the government's contradictions, saw it in a most positive light. Individual Labour party membership grew steadily throughout these years and, most remarkably, the government's by-election record was staggering: it did not lose a single one. The wartime Coalition, by contrast, could hardly contrive to win any. Labour's vote and share of the poll rose in the general elections of both 1950 and 1951. Communists and independent left-wingers were wiped out. Overwhelmingly, the Attlee brand of labourism was endorsed by the mainstream of the British working class.

In spite of that, there is a considerable difference between an endorsement for a political party which is seen both as the best guarantor of social

achievements so far won and as the most likely prospect of their
extension, and positive enthusiasm in the expectation that Jerusalem is
about to be built. The mood in which the 1950 election was fought
could not have contrasted more with that of 1945. Churchill described
it as 'demure'. Even in the mainstream, enthusiasm had weakened and
ideological commitment softened. Given that the only political initiative
asked of the masses during the lifetime of the government was to
respond without argument to appeals for harder work and restricted consumption, doubtless it could not have been otherwise. The left was
thoroughly soured, albeit more because of foreign policy than the
inadequacies of the domestic programme. In view of their virtual helplessness at that point, their dissatisfaction was no immediate problem,
but in changed circumstances it was capable of becoming one.

On a broader front, the relationship of the government to public
feeling was complex and ambiguous. That its basic line of policy was
popular is undeniable; we need look for no more convincing proof than
the fact that its opponents took its essentials into their own programme.
During the 1945 election campaign Attlee had accused the Conservatives of being in thrall to the notions of Frederich von Hayek. Whether
or not he himself took this seriously, he could not have been more
mistaken.

But did expectations among Labour voters run ahead of or behind
what the government was doing? Here the evidence is contradictory.
Did the more radical programme which delegates to the 1944
Conference pushed upon a less than enthusiastic leadership represent only
the attitudes of Labour Party activists, or wider levels of political
expectancy? How would the public mood have responded to the more
robustly socialist approach which the left then and since would have
wished to see?[51]

Certainly in its public pronouncements the government was fastid-
iously concerned to make constitutional distinctions, to avoid any
party emphasis and to address its audience in the mode of a government
speaking to its citizens rather than as the leaders of the Labour Party.
'[Attlee] never attempted to communicate the government's strategy to
the electorate.'[52] No compensation for this omission was provided by
the Labour Party as such working energetically to mobilise the masses
behind its government.

Woodrow Wyatt, then on the left of the party, declared in 1945: 'At
present the country is far to the left of Labour Ministers.' Public
opinion surveys later on did not bear this out, the majority of respon-
dents expressing the view that the government was 'too socialist'.

The British people, in particular the working class, were conscious of entering a new era in 1945, with hopes and expectations of a kind never experienced on earlier occasions and, so far as such a phrase can represent a complex reality, determined to construct a new world. 'They are looking forward to a postwar levelling of class distinction and a redistribution of wealth,' warned the Postal Censor in 1941 on the evidence of the private correspondence his officials were employed to read. The war years had brought about something resembling a transformation of consciousness, but of course such transformations are never complete, the spirit is not wiped clean and reborn. Their consciousness also brought with it into the postwar years countless assumptions, habits, traditional ways of thinking, limitations of perspective, unexamined prejudices. These derived from the old world of imperial arrogance, elite power, mass unemployment, rigid and finely multiplied class barriers, gender and age relations more rigid still – all of which would continue their malign tradition and grow more attractive in retrospect as the new age revealed its contradictions. 'What gives her that *prewar* look?' an advertisement caption could enquire in the age of austerity beside a smiling and sexually provocative image of a young woman. Following 1945 there was a rash of knighthoods for trade union leaders, and in most cases 'the reaction of the ordinary members has been eulogistic rather than critical'.[53]

Traditional consciousness also reasserted itself in Labour's loss of the middle-class electoral constituency which it had briefly gained in 1945. Its share of that vote dropped from 21 per cent to 16 per cent in 1950. Under a first-past-the-post procedure this was crucial to the party's future electoral prospects. The loss can be attributed in part to the experience of austerity, with which the middle class was less well acquainted in their traditional daily life than the proletariat, and with the dawn of the future consumer society which was likely to strengthen their dissatisfaction with the Crippsian regime. (Orwell's *Nineteen Eighty-Four* was written primarily as a satire on 1948.) The loss can also be attributed to the real imperfections of the nationalised services, as well as the assiduous propaganda in most newspapers which assigned an inefficient and bureaucratic image to those industries. The press also highlighted anecdotes of parasitism in the welfare services. The British Housewives League denounced the welfare state as an anti-middle class conspiracy and the speeches of its leader, Mrs Irene Lovelock, read eerily like those of Margaret Thatcher three decades later.[54]

It would have been better for the Labour Party if it had lost the 1950 election outright instead of winning it with a wafer-thin majority.

Forced to govern for a further 18 months, its exhaustion and ideological bankruptcy emerged all too clearly as it became enmeshed in further balance of payments crises, the consequences of the Korean war,[55] colonial humiliation in Iran and public leadership splits.[56] The aftermath of that period in office was to be felt long afterwards in labour politics. It was all the more ironic in that the economic position in 1951, which looked exceptionally bleak and contributed much to the party's loss of nerve, was on the verge of unparalleled advance as a result of the world boom initiated by Korean War demand.

But, in reality, labourism had achieved all that it was capable of and the questions it left behind were unanswerable in its own terms. It had given Britain a system of elementary social justice and led it to the gateway of the consumer society, and thus it had fulfilled its historic mission. The Party's main election plank in 1950 was the tory threat to full employment and the welfare state: this was repeated in 1951 with additional stress on the Conservatives' warmongering record. The Labour Party's working class supporters were sufficiently convinced to vote for it in unprecedented numbers, but in other sections of society the removal of burdensome social and economic controls was a more enticing prospect. Labour's political leaders may well have believed that the return of a Conservative government posed a real threat to the corporate consensus embodied in the legislation passed between 1944 and 1948 and to the practice of tripartate co-operation between government, industry and unions. The trade union chiefs knew better, and hastened to assert their willingness to put aside political considerations and co-operate with the new administration, provided that it was on the same terms as they had enjoyed with the old.

'It was specifically stated that our relationship with the Government must continue regardless of the colour of the Government ... We shall not be guilty of fractious opposition to the Government merely for the sake of playing politics. That would be suicidal. It would be contrary to the best interests of the masses of people in this country,' declared the TUC. 'Moreover,' Allen adds, 'no sensible trade unionist, least of all Arthur Deakin, wanted to sever the relationship which the General Council had established with the Government since 1940.'[57]

2   Labourism in the Affluent Society 1951–64

In the general election of October 1951 the Labour Party recorded its largest ever poll and percentage of the popular vote. Thanks to the vagaries of British electoral arithmetic it also lost its parliamentary majority – the distribution of the vote transformed it into a small but workable Conservative one. The middle class vote which had given Labour so many of the marginal constituencies in 1945 had underlined the trend of the 1950 election, switching to the party of economic and consumer freedom; which also inherited most of the shrinking Liberal vote.[1]

Paradoxically, the 13 years of Conservative government which followed have a strong claim to figure as Labourism's high point of achievement and culmination of its long-term project.

In the most obvious sense that appears to be an absurd proposition. Between 1951 and 1963 the Labour Party lost three general elections with a widening gap on each occasion; the party was torn by internal conflict over policy, organisation, the personality of its leader; friction manifested itself between its trade union and political wings, a pervasive feeling of malaise and demoralisation afflicted its rank and file membership.

Yet it was during these same years that the measures pursued by the 1945–51 governments really came to fruition and functioned less problematically than would ever be the case again. The postwar integration of the country into a world economic system dominated by the USA was rewarded by general boom conditions, near full capacity working, overall rise in incomes and expanding consumer satisfaction. The apparatus of economic management and welfare provision inherited from the 1940s kept local breakdowns and irregularities under control and diffused the resulting prosperity more equitably than would have been feasible in the absence of the welfare state. The legal immunities and bargaining rights of the trade union organisations, if not exactly unquestioned, were never seriously threatened or even challenged in the course of more than a decade.

Above all, political and social affairs at every level proceeded under an accepted wisdom that the advances of the 1940s were permanent and irreversible and that the substance of political debate was about further advance within that framework. It would not be fanciful to claim that labourism at that point had attained hegemony within British public life. If its principles were being implemented by a Conservative administration, a parallel could be drawn with the late 19th century, when the heyday of the industrial bourgeoisie was overseen by governments most of whose personnel derived in the main from the landed classes.

An expanding capitalist economy with an orientation to overseas investment, full employment and a minority but extensive public sector: a level of welfare not less than that existing in 1951: a state retaining its Great Power pretensions but subordinate to the imperatives of its US partner: such was the common ground between the Labour and Conservative front benches and such was the origin of the term Butskellism, derived from the names of the parliamentary leaders who it was felt most vividly embodied the consensus. Ben Pimlott, in challenging the existence of such a consensus, has pointed out that the term originated as one of disdain, but the very fact that it came from the labour left, seeking a discreditable phraseology to stigmatise a consensus they could not overturn, and the speed with which the word became embedded in political discourse, are all indicative of how potent a reality Butskellism actually was.[2]

In the long view it can be seen to have been the dominant reality of the years between Labour's loss of office and Gaitskell's own death. Butskellism did not exactly embody the vision of the Labour Party's pioneers; in particular its consumerism and meritocratic emphasis contradicted their attachment to community values, and its 'defence' postures were opposed to their anti-militarism. Still in terms of the advancement of labour to a strong bargaining position, in the unprecedented diminution of primary poverty, and in what passed for equality of opportunity, it could plausibly be claimed to mark a fair approximation to their essential objectives. Hugh Gaitskell, with his Oxbridge and civil service background, expressed precisely in the parliamentary context the political assumptions and social desires of the then leaders of British Labour. He was the man of the hour, the fitting successor to Attlee to adjust Labour to the social world it had done so much to create yet whose consequences had surprised it and outdated the values and traditions of its heroic phase.

To an extent, Gaitskell and the circle around him, particularly Anthony Crosland, were capable of appreciating that a policy of simple consolidation was inadequate. If the Labour Party was to have any hope of assuming governmental office again a more far-reaching vision was required than the mere completion of minor unfinished business inherited from the great reforming administration. The Labour leaders claimed confidently to have carried through a social revolution: what further purpose could they have? Hence arose the necessity to redefine the nature and perspectives of labourism, to embrace more unreservedly the ethos of consumer capitalism and to discard many of the traditional values and practices associated with the movement. Electoral considerations featured as well. The Labour Party leaders supposed, accurately enough, that the popular mood since 1945 had shifted away from collectivism as a principle and was continuing to do so to a growing extent. Within the institutional movement, however, traditional labourist outlooks remained strongly embedded and had largely informed the movement's greatest triumph. Friction and tension between the parliamentary and trade union leaderships was therefore the outcome, a process overlaid and cross cut by the perennial right-left dispute.

Labourism in the Trade Unions

For Britain the 1950s marked the Indian summer of the traditional industrial economy. Restored to capacity working by the wartime emergency and the reconstruction phase, coalmining, steel, engineering, shipbuilding and textiles experienced sustained growth in output and employment. Though the output of some, such as coal and textiles, began to falter from the early 1950s, others continued to thrive in the conditions of global boom and all remained major elements in the industrial structure. Indeed, 1955 saw the largest percentage of the workforce engaged in manufacturing in Britain ever attained.[3] Simultaneously, capital export thrived, the accumulated balance growing by three times in the decade 1946–56 and the investment income by six times.[4] The cardinal priorities of government policy were to preserve the social peace underpinned by full employment, to maintain the profitability of overseas investment and uphold the aspirations to Great Power status signified by enormous overseas military commitments and sovereign possession of nuclear bombs.

The pursuit of the three objectives interacted to generate other recurrent sources of economic and social instability. This dominated British politics from the 1940s to the 1970s and proved to be a major factor in the ruin of both the Attlee and Wilson governments.

As far back as 1946, in *Studies in the Development of Capitalism*, Maurice Dobb discussed the likely economic and social consequences

of a full employment British capitalist economy. He predicted accurately
that the improved bargaining position for labour implied by such a state
of affairs would favour wages against industrial profits in a way that would
be unacceptable to capital in the long run.[5] The relationship manifested
itself in an inflationary tendency and, in tandem with the tendency of
a full capacity, high income economy to suck in imports, generated an
adverse balance of payments which frequently turned into crisis when
the scale of capital export and government military spending abroad
pushed that balance deep into deficit.

Economic management therefore pursued self-contradictory
objectives, principally by the use of fiscal policies rather than administrative control. Full employment and rising levels of consumption
demanded the encouragement of growth with a variety of devices
such as regional policy to steer that growth towards areas of the country
less attractive on specifically market criteria. The protection of the
exchange rate and the City's place in the international financial network
required precisely the opposite, the dampening down of economic
activity by means of borrowing restrictions, taxation policy and the
manipulation of investment in the public sector. The alternating phases
of the process were designated the stop-go cycle. Underlying the cycle,
however, a progressive deterioration was going on in the competitive
strength of British manufacturing relative to that of other capitalist
powers. This erosion sprang from a reluctance to re-equip and update
in the traditional sectors, tardiness in developing new ones, the diversion
of research and development towards military objectives and, above all,
the hegemony of the financial sector and emphasis on foreign
investment.[6]

By and large it was a state of affairs very favourable to labour corporatism. Finding a modus vivendi in the labour market which would
not interfere with the opportunity to make profits in boom conditions
was very much the disposition both of government and management;
for their part the trade union leaders did not seek to exploit to the full
the favourable bargaining position in which organised labour found itself.
Instead, with the formative experience of the 1940s behind them and
their attachment to the Keynesian consensus, they were only too
willing to practice a pragmatic restraint in return for a recognition of
the movement's importance and their own consequent standing.[7]

Instead, the opportunity which was afforded to workers by the
condition of the labour market then existing was seized on the shop floor
rather than in the union headquarters and the typical industrial action
of the time was the unofficial strike led by shop stewards in shipbuild-

ing, motors or mining: but even these only represented an iceberg tip of constant shopfloor pressure to produce innumerable local variants which improved on national agreements.[8]

The character of this bargaining and the settlements which resulted from it are significant. Overwhelmingly they were about earnings – even those disputes which were ostensibly over working hours usually concealed forms of pay bargaining, their object being to extend the proportion of the working day which counted as overtime rather than to shorten the day overall.

This of course gave rise to striking disparities in earnings according to skill, situation and the degree of organisation that it was possible for different sections to achieve, between, for example, electricians or engineers on the one hand and farm labourers, shop assistants or nurses on the other. That particular side of the problem could not be said to be one which greatly exercised the minds of the labour movement of the time at any level. The presumption was that there would be a trickle-down effect whereby the successes of the best organised would be emulated by the less well placed.

The male industrial workforce, through industrial action or by threatening it, sought to secure the key to the consumer paradise that managed capitalism appeared to promise. In accordance with the traditions of the movement and British industrial culture, they sought it through a labour market wholly exempt from any centralised organising, policing, or legally binding agreements. The movement did not concern itself with the historical character of the British economy, its structural weaknesses or how, overall, it might relate to the resourcing of the welfare system. No doubt the TUC chiefs would have preferred a Labour administration, yet the relationship of the official trade union movement with government between 1951 and 1962 was not discernibly different from what it would have been had the Labour Party been in office.[9]

The implications of the consumerist framework within which industrial relations proceeded were multi-faceted. It is not necesssary to accept the once fashionable thesis of the 'affluent worker' rapidly absorbing bourgeois values to appreciate that a consumerist climate and the privatisation of leisure time, represented especially by television, was bound to erode the bonds of social and political solidarity and to dull any consciousness of long-term perspectives for the labour movement, no matter how clearly it might be recognised in principle that strong shop floor organisation was the goose producing the golden eggs of improved earnings. In any event, the Labour Party was never able to repeat, let alone improve upon, the votes and percentage of the poll it received in 1951.

In these halcyon years organised labour was itself inserting the thin end of a wedge which, in a very different economic climate, would split its solidarity apart. The attitudes formed in the 1950s formented after 1979 a *sauve qui peut* reaction when unemployment threatened loss of access to the fruits of consumerism or large redundancy payments offered the only manner of prolonging it temporarily. Both cases rendered impossible an effective united response to government economic depradations and incursions into immemorable legal rights.

The Failure of the CPGB

Within the frame of British labour culture, the only significant alternative to labourism was the Communist Party, and that only until 1956; the forerunners of the far-left groups and parties of later decades numbered no more than a few dozen individuals and were wholly inconsequential.

The CP was certainly of consequence, but represented no threat of any sort to the labourist hegemony. In 1951 it adopted a programme with national perspectives that definitely rejected the soviet (if not the Soviet) model to which it had adhered since its foundation,[10] but this did not make it any more acceptable to the working class or the electorate. So far as it identified itself with shop floor militancy it was favoured by the trend in that direction, and was able to continue or construct well established organisation in certain industries, most notably mining and motor vehicles, but it had virtually nothing else going for it. Its revolutionary and internationalist rhetoric struck no sparks in the midst of a profoundly anti-revolutionary and nationalist political culture. The loss of both communist parliamentary seats by large majorities in 1950 was indicative, and all sympathetic tendencies inside the political labour movement were crushed or had evaporated. Thereafter, only the trade union leaders had to face any significant communist challenge and they had no difficulty in portraying the party as the domestic mouthpiece of a foreign power and a sinister and barbarous one at that. The bleak collective material impoverishment which supplied the dominant image of existing socialist society was, of course, the very antithesis of developing consumer promise. In terms of the influence it did exercise the CP was effectively marginalised and ghettoised within its trade union strongholds (even these were not immune from attack and overthrow) and a few local communities with lengthy communist traditions.

'Not antipodes but twins,' was the way in which the cynical and mendacious Stalin had once characterised the relationship of social democrats to Fascists. British communism and British labourism in the 1950s may not have been twins exactly, but they were certainly far from being antipodes; they were marked far more by the cultural presumptions they shared than by the politics which divided them. Both had a high esteem for authority, subordination, deference to appointed leaderships and conformity to received social norms. The internal regime of the CPGB may have been centralised and dictatorial: it was scarcely more so than that of the apparatus of the major trade unions under such supremos as Deakin, Williamson or Carron.

The dominant ethos within the labour movement, reformist or revolutionary, remained the tradition of discipline and self-sacrifice necessary to organise in difficult conditions and to fight industrial struggles, coupled with the self-help philosophy of late 19th century skilled labour with all its stress on hard work, useful education, deferred gratification and suspicion of frivolity and enjoyment.[11]

It was this structure of attitudes which consumer culture tended to dissolve, especially among generations unacquainted with the discipline and control needed to cope with deep poverty and a merciless social environment.[12] In material terms, full employment made the discipline of the workplace, whether imposed by bosses or by informal social networks, easier to defy or escape, at any rate diluting its awesomeness: possession of secure and independent incomes reduced deference to boss, trade union bureaucrat, traditional social authorities and political spokespersons alike. These same incomes not only allowed people to accumulate personal possessions in hitherto unimaginable quantity but permitted an unheard-of degree of subcultural and lifestyle experimentation. Television, which spread rapidly and grew less anodyne after the institution of commercial broadcasting in 1955, provided a constant reminder of untraditional role models now within the reach of young people in the working class. A distinctive youth culture and style made its appearance, crystallised especially by the advent of rock music, which was itself assisted by technical developments in recording and the first portable radio sets. The teddy boy cult at the same time epitomised the expanded scale of lifestyle opportunity, its class dimension and the social disapproval it evoked.

After 1945, the numbers who went on to higher education was also significant. The principal beneficiaries were the lower middle classes, but now, unprecedentedly, a significant, if still tiny, proportion of working class youth found its way into the university system and some of them began to articulate the contradictions of a consumer culture structured by class differences, suffocating traditionalism, philistinism and the 'poverty of desire'.[13]

The years 1952–55 marked the high tide of expansionist consensus, in the economy a phase of largely unproblematic growth, with British industry supplying traditional manufactures to a reviving world economy in a climate exempt from serious inflation or further balance of payments crises. Limitless horizons of personal consumption in a stable economy, underpinned by an adequate if not munificent welfare system, now crowned labourism's ten heroic years of sacrifice and achievement. It was against such a background that Anthony Crosland published *The Future of Socialism*, in 1956. It was intended both to celebrate the alleged social revolution and to endeavour to define the future of labourism in a consumer culture.

From around the middle of the decade however, signs of tarnish began to appear upon the gloss. The relative inferiority of Britain's economic performance compared to that of her resurgent competitors became apparent and was a source of deepening concern to manufacturers and government. It imposed a growing strain upon the harmonious relationships of the previous half-decade and nurtured rank and file dissidence with the established direction of union leadership.

In these same years, hitherto unquestioned aspects of the state's imperial and military roles blew into storm centres of government crisis and were publicly and dramatically called into question by mass demonstrations and movements overwhelmingly composed of young people. The labour movement was thrown into agitation, partly by reaction to conflicts within and around the state, partly through the maturing of its own inner contradictions.

After securing his re-election in 1955 on the basis of an appeal, as he noted, to skilled workers, Anthony Eden's government found itself beset in the following year with balance of payments difficulties which stemmed from an obsolescent, militarised, finance-orientated economy running on full throttle. The options were deflation, welfare cuts, and state intervention in the labour market. But all of them implied a deterioration in the relationship with organised labour and intensified potential conflict.

Before that potential had significantly matured however, Eden's administration was overtaken and overwhelmed by a spectre from the imperial past when Franco-British atavisms and Israeli expansionist drives clashed with the realities of international relations in the 1950s and the higher interests of US policy.

The invasion of the Suez Canal area in November 1956 by a Franco-British expeditionary force under cover of excuses to which the government hardly even tried to give a convincing gloss, violently ruptured the nearly complete bipartisan consensus on foreign affairs which had prevailed up to that point. It is, indeed, the only really significant instance of Labour/Conservative disagreement in that area during all the postwar years. A further unprecedented aspect of the Suez crisis was that it represented the only occasion in its entire existence since 1900 when the Labour Party acted as an effective and energetic extra-parliamentary (or for that matter, parliamentary) opposition, the one instance on which it mounted a serious and country-wide *campaign* for other than electoral purposes.

This dramatic, if short-lived, political earthquake was made possible only by a rather unlikely combination of circumstances: the indignation of Commonwealth governments and above all the expressed hostility of the White House gave the Labour leadership, passionate atlanticists, the establishment buttressing necessary to fire their resolve against their own government. Even so Gaitskell hesitated, while at the grassroots indignation at such exhibition of primaeval toryism was stirred beyond anything since the war. Consequently, mass demonstrations erupted across Britain and gigantic crowds applauded Bevan's denunciations in Trafalgar Square. Indeed, Labour leaders for once performed so effectively that Eden thought of censoring them from the broadcast media. The episode illuminated for a brief space the potential mass active support which the Labour Party has never known how to mobilise or develop.

But most significantly perhaps, the aggression and the debacle which followed – leaving aside the temporary material inconveniences which flowed from increased petrol prices – struck a blow at the traditional mystique of government and authority in Britain whose effects were felt over the long rather than the short run. I recollect vividly a heated argument in the classroom at the time, at the end of which the teacher asked plaintively, 'But don't you realise that Sir Anthony must know better than anybody else?' It is hard to imagine such a sentiment being seriously voiced at any later period – at least before the Thatcher regime became well established.

Traditional certainty and authority in another direction likewise suffered acts of spectacular demolition in the same year. The content of Khrushchev's secret speech at the CPSU Twentieth Congress in February began to leak out in the spring, to be followed in June by the appearance, without any Soviet repudiation, of an English text. The

Manchester Guardian's title of its pamphlet version, 'The Dethronement of Stalin' was all too apt. For all communists (and sympathisers), however they might in practice react, the conceptual universe which has justified undeviating loyalty to a Soviet leadership which embodied uncompromising revolutionary virtue, was irreparably damaged. The destruction in November by the Soviet army of a Hungarian government trying to withdraw into neutralism would have been traumatic enough in itself for British communists: combined with the previous events of the year it produced the most searing crisis in the organisation's history up to that point and both the CP and Young Communist League lost some of their most distinguished industrial and cultural talent. A year later, at a special congress, the badly reduced Party reaffirmed its traditional positions, but the old self-confidence was gone for ever.

The New Left

From the resulting political ferment emerged the first significant challenge since 1940 to the labourist ethos. The original New Left came into being, composed of former communists, some adherents of the traditional labour left and a more diffuse stream of freshly politicised young people.

One of these sources, the ex-communists, began to publish the journal *New Reasoner,* which centred its attention on a critique of Stalinism and the communist tradition, but also gave a lot of space to cultural analysis, both in the sense of high culture and of what was in time to be termed 'popular' culture. The latter was the forte of another journal, which became the second major source of inspiration for the New Left, *Universities and Left Review.* It included items such as Stuart Hall's 'A Sense of Classlessness', or Richard Hoggart comparison of the television channels, which appeared in issue five, but it did not neglect economic and political discussion. These publications amalgamated in 1960 as the *New Left Review.* Associated with the journal there appeared a network of Left Clubs, around 40 in number, stretching from Aberdeen to Southampton. One even insisted on referring to itself as a political party, Lawrence Daly's Fife Socialist League, which was able to win council seats and make a respectable challenge in the 1959 election.

Other than this, the New Left comprised only a series of discussion circles composed in the main of educated young people grouped around a journal, and attempts to turn it into a more coherent organisation came to nothing and it had no successor organisation. In the course of 1962–63 it vanished as a collective, although the journal survived in a very different form from what its founders had intended. In spite of its ephemeral character and lack of immediate political impact however, the New Left was important in two respects.

First it raised the question of cultural politics for the first time within the labour movement as a serious issue. Secondly, the very meaning of 'left' was redefined, to incorporate a range of approaches and practices foreign to traditional notions. The beginnings of an alternative to labourism were sketched out, a reflection in the politics of the left of the same erosion of ancient authority structures that expanded consumer choice was promoting among the young population at large. The degree of long range influence which it may have exercised upon the development of the Communist Party in the 1970s and 1980s is also an interesting question.

In the immediate term, however, its failure was nearly complete and this, although probably not unavoidable, was certainly on the cards given the character of the movement and the nature of its aspirations.

The New Left, arising in protest against the grubby underside of British consumer society, found it difficult to continue to gain public attention in that mode of denunciation once the novelty had passed and the machinery of consumer society – even if viewed with greater unease than before by its members – went on delivering for most of them the goods which they had come to expect. New Leftism accelerated its own decline by repudiating on principle any sort of internal organisation and discipline which might have compensated in some degree for the ebb of popular interest.

In the post-Suez and Hungary backwash, Gerry Healy's Socialist Labour League was also expanding and, blurring for the meantime its specifically Trotskyist principles, attracted a number of CP refugees and made headway inside the newly-established Labour Party youth movement, the Young Socialists. Its overtures to the New Left, however, were unsympathetically received and summarily rejected.[14]

A more specific consideration in the early demise of the New Left lies in the vehicle it sought to realise its political aspirations – the Labour Party. To have set itself up as an electoral rival would have been far beyond its capacities and ambitions (in spite of Laurence Daly's attempt in 1959). By encouraging its supporters into the constituency Labour parties, the New Left caused them to become bogged down in the Byzantine internal manoeuvres they encountered there and so diffused their energies. More critically still, it made the anti-labourist values of the New Left hostage to the evolution of the Labour Party itself.

Hugh Gaitskell and the Macmillan Government

Clement Attlee, like Churchill, retired in 1955 full of years and prestige, outlasted all his leadership rivals and rendered his last service to the party he had led for 20 years by staying in office long enough to prevent the election of the decrepit Herbert Morrison. Hugh Gaitskell, his succesor and, like Crosland, a protege of Hugh Dalton was, apart from being a convinced atlanticist and cold-war partisan[15] perceptive enough to understand the widening divide between the mass endorsement of labourist values ten years earlier and their public perception in an increasingly consumerist society (the assessment of which he altogether shared with Crosland). His strategic answer was to initiate a process intended to replace labourism with social democracy on the contemporary German model. This made an unashamed and avowed commitment to capitalism and grounded the Labour Party's credibility in claims to be its most effective and humane political supervisor.

The time appeared to be opportune, the more so as Bevan had made his peace with the Labour Party establishment in return for the position of shadow Foreign Secretary, abandoning and demoralising the supporters for whom his personality above all had been the symbol of the traditional left. More, with the Conservative Party confused and demoralised in the aftermath of the Suez debacle, the prospects of electoral victory had very considerably brightened and, once attained, would have enormously reinforced Gaitskell's own standing and capacity to push the Party in the direction he wanted it to go.

But the entrenched foundations of traditional labourism were not to be so readily overturned. It is doubtful if Gaitskell could have succeeded even with the dominant trade union barons of the early 1950s still in office and with the cachet of electoral success. In the event he had neither and instead the left inside the labour movement acquired a foothold which it managed to retain and develop in spite of subsequent political defeats.

At around the same time age overtook several TUC stalwarts of the Bevin regime and circumstances prevented them from handing on their offices to men of a similar disposition as themselves, or at any rate with the capacity to enforce the same lines of policy. Their successors tended to be individuals more temperate in their reactions to the Cold War and to the British left and who, as lower-ranking officials, had experienced rather than collaborated in the perceived betrayal of the brightest hopes of 1945 during the dreary passage between 1947 and 1951.

They were also on the whole a less autocratic group of men than their predecessors – perhaps it was a generational tendency – and were likely to reflect a temperamental difference socially conditioned by some weakening of authoritarian traditions, especially during the years of wartime radicalism when they were at a more impressionable age and situation than their seniors. Certainly they were a great deal more accessible to rank and file sentiment within their organisations.

The evolutionary change within union structures marked by this shift was accompanied by two further pressures which tended to disrupt the stable relationships of authority which had existed both within the labour movement and between it and government from the return of the Conservatives to office until the Suez episode. One of these was the re-emergence of balance of payments crises which brought to government awareness the steady erosion of British competitive strength in export markets and caused it to seek around for a long term remedy. A faction within the administration, for which Peter Thorneycroft was the spokesman, began openly to advocate abandonment of the state's commitment to full employment, the cornerstone of all domestic policy since 1944, and to recommend a programme of severe deflation and curbs on trade union bargaining power. They lost the battle against the tory leadership's positions of consensus and Thorneycroft was sacked,[16] but the sunny landscapes portrayed by Crosland were immediately over-shadowed and the secure continuation of the social revolution which he had proclaimed was put into question. In any case, although the new advocates of unregenerate toryism were beaten for the time being, a degree of deflation was still imposed. This raised in public conscious-ness the concept of the stop-go cycle and in its wake brought sharper industrial conflict and gave more legitimacy within official labour structures – if not in the press or public consciousness – to shopfloor militancy. In terms of conventional expression British labour, both politically and industrially had, since the first half of the decade edged leftwards. This was an unfavourable climate for the success of Gaitskell's project.

The second development, which was to mount the first (temporar-ily) successful challenge since the 1930s to the authority of a Labour leadership, grew out of the radical questioning by many thousands of young people of the Cold War pieties and continued British preten-sions to great power status which had previously been taken for granted. Opposition to the presence of nuclear weapons in Britain, although led by longstanding radical figures, was overwhelmingly a youth movement and one whose logic brought in question the central premises upon which NATO was established. Impatience with the frozen postures of anti-Sovietism manifested itself in this movement, and would doubtless have become more far-reaching but for the damage to Khrushchev's credibility caused by the Hungarian invasion. A cardinal contrast between CND's activities and the earlier campaign against German rearmament (apart from the scope of the issues involved) was that CND, with its mass support, placed the main focus of its activity upon public campaigning and demonstration: the earlier conflict had been an almost exclusively internal affair. The CP hesitated before committing itself to support CND. It would complain that the movement, apart from being tactically inopportune when bilateral superpower negotiations were in prospect, was simplistic in failing to distinguish between peaceloving Soviet intentions and aggressive western ones. Indeed, the bedrock presumption behind the movement was that no government on principle could be trusted with the destructive powers which science had made available. It represented a novel outlook which was itself as profoundly shocking to establishment mentality as the actual content of CND's objectives. The New Left was intimately linked with CND, and its influence began to spread among rank and file trade union activists, as evidenced by resolutions and votes in union conferences.

The anti-nuclear campaign was received with greater hostility by the Labour leaders than their Conservative counterparts – doubtless because the former were its more immediate targets, but as its influence expanded among Labour's politically conscious supporters it represented an additional major problem for Gaitskell and his colleagues. It was an immediate threat which had to be dealt with, which made it impossible for them to concentrate their energies and propaganda upon securing the objective of changes to the Labour Party constitution, forcing them, in working for the immediate aim, to rely upon and bargain with trade union leaders suspicious of the social democratic revisionism with which Gaitskell was identified.

Nor did Gaitskell have the advantage of electoral good fortune. Tory demoralisation over Suez, the government's electorally embarassing deflation of 1955–57 and the restoration of parliamentary Labour unity appeared to augur well for Labour's chances in the next election; on the precedent of the Attlee government things should have only got worse for the tories. Unhappily for Gaitskell, the tories in their crisis found a leader with a masterly grasp of the public mood who could play like a virtuoso upon the strings of consumer sentiment.

Harold Macmillan not only declared the Conservative's continued commitment to full employment and rising levels of consumption but sacked his Cabinet neanderthals to prove it.[17] 'Life's better with the Conservatives!' proclaimed the central tory slogan of the 1959 election; claiming credit, not surprisingly, for the undoubted fact embodied in the first two words. 'Don't let Labour ruin it!' was the slogan designed to evoke the memory of austerity and postwar tribulations. Macmillan's most renowned saying – slightly misquoted – 'You've never had it so good!' captured the mood to perfection; the speed at which it became a byword indicates how well it resonated with public feeling.

More, in a political arena increasingly dominated by television and the need to fulfil the requirements of media presentation, the contrasting political styles of the two leaders told badly against Labour. Macmillan projected himself as a very likeable personality (whatever the reality may have been is another matter). His pose was one of upper-class insouciance, while contriving simultaneously to convey the impression that he didn't take the role with complete seriousness, that he was guying it or camping it up. When he appeared on television, for which he had a natural gift, he contrived to make his listeners feel that he was taking them into his genially irreverent confidence. The point was emphasised by the fate of Vicky's cartoon character: 'Supermac' was conceived for the purpose of savagely mocking the prime minister, but the public transformed it almost at once into a figure of cuddly endearment. Against such a maestro Gaitskell had no chance at all. Attlee's utter lack of charisma had been no great disadvantage, compensated as it had been by his aura of austere probity. Gaitskell's style, allowing for differences in age and background, was in essence somewhat similar, but he came across as an ill-tempered and humourless stuffed shirt, in Bevan's brutal but accurate characterisation, 'a dessicated calculating machine'.

The leaders of the big unions distrusted Gaitskell's ambitions to reformulate the Labour Party's purposes, not only or even principally on grounds of ideological difference, but because they feared that it tended – as it did – to reduce their own political influence while still requiring them to continue as the Party's financial mainstay. While waiting on the 1959 election the differences were held in check, but the defeat that October convinced Gaitskell that the only way to stem the deepening erosion of Labour's electoral base which the poll showed was to pursue strenuously the changes which he advocated and thereby, most importantly, to transform the image of the Labour Party in the electorate's perception.

Gaitskell's campaign let loose a far-ranging debate within the labour movement in which he confronted the traditional left, the New Left and the weight of trade union sentiment, while simultaneously antagonising by his intransigent pro-nuclear stance any parts of the movement not necessarily identified with the left but influenced by the arguments of CND. The latter made rapid progress; it mobilised a respectable vote at the 1959 Labour Party Conference and actually had its resolution carried in 1960. Gaitskell viewed reversing that vote the following autumn as his most urgent priority. But in order to muster sufficient union leadership support he was obliged to give way on the proposal to abolish Clause 4 in the Party constitution, the issue which had become symbolic of the entire debate.

Gaitskell, like many another labourist Labour leader, though perhaps to a greater extent than any before or since, was accused of wanting to manage capitalism better than the capitalists.[18] Perhaps it would be more accurate to suggest that under Macmillan, between 1957 and 1961, the Conservatives, whatever tensions there may have been under the surface, followed a labourist policy more easily and effectively than a Labour administration could have done in relation to British affairs, and in the foreign sphere there is no reason to imagine that Gaitskell, supposing he had won the 1959 election, would have been any less subservient to Washington than was his rival, or any more adept at handling the decolonisation process.

Postwar labourism got its second wind from developments which, with an important exception, were contingent, unpredictable and outside the historical dialectic of the times. The exception, which followed from Macmillan's option of 1957 not to deflate, was the recurrence of severe balance of payments crises in 1961, a deflationary response from the Treasury and a consequent increase in unemployment worse than in any previous year since 1947, which went some way towards discrediting Conservative pretensions to infallability in economic management. Such a hiatus or little local difficulty was far from being necessarily fatal,[19] but after eleven years in office the Conservative leadership was becoming frayed at the edges and Macmillan was losing his touch. He sacked a third of his cabinet in 1962, thereby furthering the impression of wanting to evade responsibility. This image was reinforced in the following year when sexual scandal erupted in the Cabinet especially, but not exclusively, around the person of the War Minister John Profumo; the Prime Minister's explanations for his lack of supervision sounded increasingly lame and plaintive. In a short space of time what had been the attractive image of insouciant competence and largesse started to look like sleaze and irresponsibility.

The 1964 Election

The other adventitious factor was the premature and unexpected death of Hugh Gaitskell in 1963, making possible the reassertion of traditional relationships within the labour movement, under the guise of modernity. With Harold Wilson trade unions, constituency organisations and parliamentary party eased their tensions and resumed their accustomed places in the framework. Wilson achieved this feat by picking up the growing public unease with the underlying strength of the British economy and structuring his rhetoric around a cure-all solution which effectively avoided addressing of the foundations of the problem. Equally, he reunited the Labour Party by diverting attention away from the fundamentals of what had divided it during the previous five years.

The rejuvenating elixir which he served up was modernisation and, more than that, virtually cost-free. 'The white heat of the technological revolution' became a catch-phrase almost as renowned as 'never had it so good'. The formula was modernisation in the technology of British industry (of course), modernisation in management practices (and possibly trade union ones as well, although not much was said about that) and modernisation in government and state structures.

There can be no doubt that Wilson's programme was an ideological construction in the worst sense of the term, a false consciousness designed to motivate action by masking reality but, like every such construction, with a basis in truth. The truth in this instance was that there was indeed a widening gap between the technical sophistication of most of British industrial plant and products and those of its major capitalist competitors. The essential premise was that Britain's economic problems sprang from an insufficient application of scientific method. The question begged by Wilson's rhetoric was why this should be the case. The only explanations he provided were traditional attitudes and deficiencies in education. The character, functioning and history of the British economy were left wholly out of the picture, as indeed was class structure. Without explicitly saying so it was based upon the premises Crosland had developed, assumed the reality of a 'social revolution' and saw government in terms of a technocratic commanding force giving the necessary impetus and stimulus to an economy made moribund by contingent rather than structural causes. However, the formula proved to be ideal for reuniting the Labour Party behind its leaders, for it permitted all sections and trends to believe what they liked about the implications of the programme: the 'revisionists' saw it as operating wholly within the terms of the postwar consensus; the left saw it as incorporating an attack on wealth and privilege and even, potentially, the ruling class ascendancy. Oppositional tendencies dissolved. Both the New Left and CND faded from the political map in the course of 1963. Frank Cousins was reconciled with Harold Wilson, as indeed were nearly all the grassroots dissidents for whom the T&GWU leader had been a symbol.

During the 1964 election campaign, the Labour Party made considerable play of the slogan 'thirteen wasted years', unaware of the irony that time was to prove them to have been wasted for the labour movement most of all. The combination during that period of a favourable economic climate, full employment and the absence of government responsibilities had provided a unique opportunity for Labour to think about the future of industrial society without the pressure of emergency policy making or emergency action. But all that emerged from leadership circles was the insubstantial and factually misconceived Croslandite thesis, which took for granted the indefinite continuance of a precariously balanced economic growth which even the Treasury mandarins were aware could not survive in its existing form.[20] Towards the end of the 1950s discussions of the 'Swedish model' were much in vogue as a possible exit from the deadlock imposed by the trinity of uncontrolled wage demands, inflation and retarded innovation, but the discussion omitted any mention of the fact that the Swedish economy was neither carrying a crushing military burden nor supporting an international speculative currency: as always in the social democratic universe it assumed the possibility of an organisational solution to a problem arising out of structural conditions which went unexamined and unquestioned. The response of the left in its various guises was in general no more appropriate. For the traditional Labour and parliamentary left, the problem was identified as one of mistaken policies – mostly involving weak commitment to public ownership and compounded by lack of rank and file control of parliamentary and trade union leaders. These positions can be recognised as upholding the original labour socialist tradition, best exemplified by Bevan, which was directed towards using the powers of the British state (once the right people had got hold of it) to establish a state-owned, centrally planned economy. That irreconcilable contradictions might exist in the essential nature of that state was not part of their vision. Nor did they appreciate that the existing industrial economy, however impossible it was to foresee its future transformations, could not escape being a historically transient phenomenon.

The CP was, of course, aware of the deficiencies of the Labour left's assumptions about the state – so far as domestic policies were concerned this constituted virtually the only area of profound disagreement between them. Since 1951 the CP had abandoned, along with the programme *For Soviet Britain*, the last remnants of its Comintern inheritance and had declared its commitment to the essential values of the British liberal political culture as it had evolved over the previous century. Yet they were no more capable than their Labour Party counterparts of questioning the perspectives of indefinitely rising consumption within the framework of authoritarian and hierarchical social and personal relations. They might take seriously the overthrow of bourgeois rule and eventually, in a distant future even the withering away of the state but (unlike Engels) certainly not of the family nor of gender divisions.

It would of course be hopelessly unhistorical to imagine that any element of the labour movement, from the Croslandites to the communists, could have been capable in the circumstances of imaginatively transcending the productive, social and organisational forms which, from their different angles, appeared to have served working people so well by winning the war and subsequently attaining for them the historic breakthrough into a socially equitable society of mass consumption – for the labourists the British 'mixed economy', for the communists the 'soviet achievement'.

Nonetheless, deep questions about the very character of industrial society and its meaning for social and individual identities *were* beginning to be asked,[21] both by the New Left in a tentative and groping manner and, by implication if not directly, by the rise of anti-nuclear sentiment. The tensions which these produced were potentially creative ones, and it is not wholly fanciful to imagine that they could have been worked out in such a manner as to have given the labour movement the intellectual equipment needed to cope with the developments of subsequent years, though it has to be admitted that the odds were very heavily stacked against any such happy resolution. By dissolving the tensions and instead committing itself to Wilson's emollient programme of technological revolution – which was founded on a whole stack of unanswered questions and unstated presuppositions – British labourism embarked upon its endeavour to restore the consensus of the 1940s on top of the material gains of the 1950s – and in the process opened the door to the hard-faced men (and women) who had never believed in that consensus in the first place.

3   Breach of Promise 1964–73

The Government Programme

An irony worthy of fictional melodrama is visible in the circumstance
that the Labour Party's political defeat in 1951 was followed by a perpetuation and strengthening of the labourist consensus under a Tory
administration: the return of Labour to office in 1964 ushered in a phase
during which the presuppositions upon which labourism was founded
started to crumble and the labourist bloc began to fall apart.

In revisiting the scenes of Harold Wilson's administrations between
1964 and 1970 it is difficult not to be overwhelmed with contempt.[1]
Indeed the performance was contemptible, but it has to be recognised
that the multiple failures and political scandals of this government in
virtually every sphere of its responsibility were not the simple products
of cowardice, incompetence and ill-will (although there was plenty of
all of these). Rather they were symptoms of a malaise rooted in the contradiction between the then capacity of the British economy and the
demands which it was called on to support, a contradiction which steadily
eroded the foundations of the postwar consensus. The long-term crisis
of an antiquated industrial structure was starting to manifest itself.

'They entered office equipped to run a high-growth economy,
anticipating that the barriers to growth would be technological and
scientific. They in fact inherited a low-growth economy, where the
barrier to growth was primarily a financial and competitive one.'[2]

The minor tremor of 1957–58 and the somewhat more significant
shock of 1961–63 presaged a developing trend towards a state of
extended crisis as, in an open world market, uncompetitive British manufactures succumbed to the restored postwar economies of industrial
rivals. In 1953 the British share of world trade had been 19.3 per cent,
by 1960 it had dropped to 16.3 per cent and by 1965 was down to 13.7
per cent. Between 1958 and 1968 the volume of foreign manufactured
imports increased fourfold.[3] A more publicly dramatic symptom of what
was happening was the destruction in the early 1960s of the English
motor cycle industry by superior Japanese imported machines.

Meanwhile, the costs of playing at being a Great Power did not diminish, while these same costs did much to ensure that the reequipment and rejuvenation of British industry which the government intended had no chance of finding adequate resources or of avoiding being disrupted by the regular deflations to which the government resorted in order to sustain its central priority. That priority '... forced a government elected on working class votes to spend the bulk of its period in office attempting to undermine the industrial power, job security and living standards of its own electorate'.[4]

That priority was to maintain the position of the pound sterling as an international currency, a fetish to which ultimately everything else was sacrificed. There is no reason to imagine that this objective met with any serious dissent, at least in the earlier phase of the government, either within the leadership of the Labour Party or the trade union movement. There was some argument over the advisability of devaluation and a section of the Cabinet did favour an early move in that direction, but this must be understood as a debate about the most expedient way of maintaining the strength of the pound rather than any questioning of the basic principle. It can be viewed in one sense as a straightforward capitulation to the demands of British finance capital pursuing its sectional interest with enough muscle to force conformity from a government such as Wilson's. Wilson himself acknowledged as much:

> Was it his view, I asked [the Governor of the Bank of England], that we should cut them off half-finished – roads left as an eyesore on the countryside, schools left without a roof, in order to satisfy a foreign financial fetishism? The question was difficult for him, but he answered 'Yes'... and this discussion took place not against the background of a critical run on sterling, but in a period of calm, following his succesful swap operations.
>
> Not for the first time I said that we had now reached the situation where a newly-elected government with a mandate from the people were being told, not so much by the Governor of the Bank of England but by international speculators, that the policies on which we had fought the election could not be implemented ... The Governor confirmed that this was, in fact, the case.

Citing this passage from Wilson's memoirs David Coates comments, 'Few industrialists have that kind of leverage on governments, and certainly trade unionists do not'.[5]

An explanaton set in these terms however would be inadequate. In spite of Wilson's anecdote and although the gnomes of Zurich were eventually to feature in ministers' rhetoric, there is no question that the City, Bank and Treasury, exercising all the powers of economic blackmail that they could summon, forced their will upon a hostile Labour government. On the contrary, the government was amazed and dismayed at the refusal of international finance to behave more reasonably towards the sympathetic, reconciling administration that they perceived themselves to be. Nor, although the dilemma was naturally presented in such terms, was it a case of having to preserve a firm pound to secure the flow of imports upon which industry, welfare and survival all depended.

It is abundantly apparent that the new government and its Prime Minister, who had, after all, been an economist before he became a politician, simply took it as read that the maintenance of the tradition established under Attlee was a self-evident and correct priority. It repesented yet one more episode in labourism's long love affair with the British state. The latter's symbolisms, whether of monarchy, military display or commercial power, were embraced with as much unreflec-tive ardour as were legislative prerogative or ministerial office. The politics of the Wilson years were to be pervaded with cynicism, oppor-tunism and dishonesty, yet the initial devotion to sterling was as sincere and principled as anything his government was capable of being. Harold Wilson was a premier of prodigious vanity, complacency and deviousness and it is certain that in his direction of government policy his own reputation was his primary concern. At the same time it may be acknowledged that, in 1964, he aimed to implement the election manifesto and establish that reputation by presiding over a dramatic trans-formation of British industry, far-reaching extensions in welfare and equality and further humanisation in social relations.

Two strands emerging from the 1950s have to be distinguished in this programme. Recognition of major shortcomings in the productive economy had neutralised the force of the 'never had it so good' slogan, in spite of the continuing growth of average incomes. The ground was prepared for a strategic assault on the main claim the tories had estab-lished to political legitimacy – being the most competent managers of a welfare mixed economy. Labour propaganda had been able to present them instead as being tradition-bound, feudal, addicted to the grouse moor, out of touch with science and technology, their essence embodied in Macmillan's successor, the Fourteenth Earl of Home. Presenting Labour, in contrast, as the party of modernity and technological wizardry (with a dash of anti-EEC nationalism) had served, no less importantly, to unify the contending factions and lobbies generated by Gaitskell's endeavours to remodel the party's traditional perspectives and internal relations. CND and the New Left subsided as political forces and largely disappeared from the scene, the growth of the CP, which had been recovering since 1957, ceased. This technocratic orientation, implicit perhaps in certain of labour's ideological themes, those which had admired – albeit at a distance – the success of Soviet planning in the 1930s, certainly overcame the immediate problems of internal Party cohesion, but created a major hostage to fortune in that under a harsh publicity spotlight subsequent performance would at all times in the future be compared with the rhetoric.

The second strand simply embodied the programme of the academic revisionists and new thinkers of the 1950s. It advocated, within a technocratic matrix, a lessening of inequality and privilege, more evenness in life's opportunities (if not income and property), to be achieved particularly by improved educational provision, enhancement of welfare provision generally and removal of some of the more barbarous social residues of the past.

Only the last of these aims achieved any real measure of success. Under the pretext of a moritorium, capital punishment ceased in the final third of the 20th century to be a British institution. Homosexual acts between consenting males over the age 21 were partially removed from the ambit of the criminal law, as was abortion, albeit on fairly restrictive terms. Divorce law was humanised, the franchise conferred at eighteen. The benefits implied by these measures should by no means be underrated and indeed they probably count as labourism's last significant legislative attainments: but there was nothing there that a decent Liberal government would not have done and, in fact, the Abortion Act 1967 was the work of a Liberal private member, David Steel, and the partial decriminalisation of male homosexuality the initiative of a backbencher, not of the government. These commendable departures had no specifically socialist content, nor were they even in the labourist tradition – all the evidence suggests that the legislation on capital punishment and homosexuality was disapproved of by Labour's own electorate.

In the sphere of social reform, where resources were at stake, success was partial at most. With the inauguration of new universities and the creation of the polytechnic sector, higher education provision was substantially expanded, although characteristically the strategy was to do it on the cheap, for while the public justification of the binary principle was that the polytechnics would fulfil a different and more technologically orientated function from the universities, in fact they were inferior establishments in both funding and status. Elsewhere, in nursery and school education, in welfare cash benefits, in pensions, the Labour government's own economic policies ensured that nothing significant would be accomplished. On the contrary, it had the singular distinction among social democratic governments of making income tax negatively redistributive by lowering the income threshold at which it began to be levied. Unemployment doubled between 1966 and 1969. Commentators of the period disputed the precise degree of movement in the level of poverty during the late 1960s, yet were unanimous in their opinion that government policy had done nothing or virtually nothing to diminish it.

Such a depressing record stemmed in turn from the debacle of the government's economic policies. The course and nature of their collapse has been frequently chronicled and was itself consequent upon the perceived necessity to maintain at all costs the value of the pound sterling. 'The strength of sterling [was their] first and primary consideration' taking 'priority over all other considerations'.[6] Everything else was regarded as ultimately expendable.

With the inauguration of a government professing socially reformist objectives, the international pressures which had been building upon the British economy since the 1950s exploded into crisis. During that decade the country's balance of payments had been kept in precarious surplus by the accident of a rapid fall in commodity prices, above all that of oil. Nonetheless, on each 'go' phase of the stop-go cycle the deficit grew bigger while diminishing returns set in every time the brake was applied and every deflation produced a more shrunken surplus. The 'confidence' of sterling holders both native and foreign was disturbed by the outcome of the election. When the budget which followed improved pensions and removed prescription charges, they hastened to unload their British currency and so commenced a run on the pound which threatened its international value and became the principal focus of the government's panic-stricken attention. It was a pattern which was to be constantly repeated up to 1969.

The plans which were forthcoming, in accordance with the election manifesto, for industrial growth and technological renewal amounted in the event to little more than indicative targets derived from surveys which reflected industrial management's own assumptions. Even so they were quickly swept away and nullified in the financial tempest. Repeated doses of deflation and high interest rates intended to defend the sacred sterling parity (which was sacrificed in the end anyway) made a shambles of planning on any basis, whether public or private. In the end, all that remained of the economic perspectives of 1964 were generous government handouts to manufacturing companies to counteract the adverse effects of the government's own financial measures and especially to encourage mergers and conglomerates, on the presumption that improved efficiency must result from greater size.

Meanwhile, social expenditure was rigorously cut back and intended programmes abandoned. These retrenchments were accompanied by government-imposed wages stops and attempts at legally imposed controls on pay, actions unprecedented in the era of affluence. These were animated by a dual purpose: first, to deflate the economy overall – it was thought that retarding the inrush of consumer products would take pressure off the balance of payments; secondly, they were intended as a permanent feature of the industrial relations scene and designed, hopefully, to assist industrial modernisation by reducing wage costs. They failed, and by the late 1960s investment in key industrial growth sectors was felt by both government and employers to be seriously impeded by a crisis in profitability. In these circumstances, the trade union power entrenched on the shopfloor, which exercised considerable control over both the work process and actual pay levels, was identified as the principal obstacle to industrial renewal and sustained growth. The Cabinet set out to break this power by legislative enactment. The project failed, as did a belated decision to reverse previous stands and seek admission to the EEC, but a balance of payments surplus was at last attained – just in time for it to be inherited by the incoming Conservative administration.

Blown Off Course?

The chronic failure – from any point of view – in economic management was paralled by no less spectacular disgrace in nearly every other field of policy. The FO was absorbed in supporting the US against the Vietnamese.[7] The government was outmanoeuvered and humiliated at every point by the settler rebels in Rhodesia. The Home Secretary, James Callaghan, found himself legislating to deprive black British passport holders of their right to take up residence in Britain. The internal collapse of the Orange regime in Northern Ireland and the demoralisation of its mass support among the Protestant working and lower middle classes of the Six Counties presented an unrepeatable opportunity there peacefully to enforce the democratic aspirations of the minority community, but the opportunity was, naturally, allowed to pass.

Our concern now is not to condemn and deplore, which has been done often enough,[8] nor even to analyse the character of the pressures

which brought Harold Wilson and his colleagues to their miserable
denouement; that too has been adequately undertaken.[9] Rather the aim
is first, to understand what it was in the tradition they inherited that
caused the Labour leaders to react in the way they did to the challenges
which beset them and, secondly, to examine the effect this record
produced on the character of the labour movement and its ideologies.

Once again it is necesary to turn to the intimate, if not incestuous
connexions between the leaders of British labour and the British state.
No sooner had they assumed their titles of office than the Labour
political chiefs embraced and identified themselves unreservedly and
uncompromisingly with that state in its guise of national interest, maintaining none of the distance in attitude that would have been proper
to politicians bred in an oppositional tradition, however diluted. Instead,
at a time when 'The theatre of imperial grandeur began to be viewed
by leading politicians as an anachronism,'[10] Wilson publicised with impas-
sioned rhetoric his attachment to the overseas military commitments of
the state and an 'East of Suez' posture that was only finally ended with
the devaluation crisis of 1967. Attlee and his cabinet had behaved no
differently, but whereas theirs had been a sustainable posture in times
when state and civil society – especially the organised structures of capital
and labour – were engaged in a joint project of postwar survival and
recovery, the scene had altogether changed by the late 1960s. Beneath
a still relatively harmonious surface of industrial relations, the endemic
strain between capital and labour which resulted from the division of
the economic surplus had arrived at a state of unsustainable tension. This
represented the permanent and irreconcilable dilemma for the Wilson
Government.

Linked to this same dilemma by means of the dollar/pound relationship
but animated with a life of its own issuing from the atlanticist and imperial
obsessions that ministers shared with their permanent advisers, likewise
inherited fom the wartime Coalition and the Attlee administration, was
a foreign policy which bitterly alienated a large and vociferous segment
of the public across different social strata and was acclaimed by hardly
any, not even the establishment, so ineptly was it executed. The
Foreign Secretaries of the time, Patrick Gordon Walker, George Brown
and Michael Stewart were of particularly inferior calibre it is true but
that was no accident – reflecting with particular vividness the degeneration of Bevin's tradition and the reduction of the British role in world
affairs to that of a diplomatic and military satellite of the USA.

Thirdly, for a variety of reasons – some connected to the general
economic faltering and its impact on the labour market, some

contingent and accidental – racial tension and hostility coupled with the issue of immigration, articulated with demonic effect by Enoch Powell, moved up the political agenda. While the government's origins and traditions barred it from making a public identification with the racist lobby and its populist following, repeated evasions and capitulations, together with its inability to deal with rebellion in Rhodesia, multiplied its discredit in the eyes of anti-racists, most importantly those belonging to the Labour Party itself.

Finally, the quesion of government *style* cannot be overlooked. Wilson's administraion, and not least the Prime Minister himself, succeeded in projecting an image of vanity, evasion, shiftiness and dishonesty. Somebody once complained that the Premier seemed to combine in his own person all the worst characteristics of his 20th century predecessors: Lloyd George's crookedness, Baldwin's complacency, Macdonald's vanity and vapidity, Chamberlain's self-deception and Churchill's arrogance, features which an increasingly sophisticated and irreverent broadcasting media displayed in front of the public as never before. Any populist appeal transcending class lines was therefore out of the question.

> It was rather that he continued to behave as if he were 'king for a day', as if the trappings of office were not really meant for people like him. Perhaps this reflects one of the basic appeals of the Labour Party – not the changing of society, but a mechanism whereby, albeit briefly, 'we' can inhabit 'their' world and exercise 'their' power.[11]

Having thoroughly alienated the labour movement both union and political, unable to base itself on any alternative popular constituency, this government, isolated and trapped inside the corridors of power, had to live or die by its technocratic achievements and public relations skills.

Beneath the fluctuations and lurches of government action, the wild and desperate flailings and responses to a long succession of crises, a strategy can be identified, one wholly in line with the basic presuppositions of labourism as a political project. The essence of this strategy was to employ centralised state authority to induce or enforce a more functional (and growth-promoting) articulation between the segments of civil society, in fact to integrate some of them a lot more closely with the apparatuses of a directive state. The overall objective, in other words, can be regarded as a strengthening and centralising of the historic labour–capital–state corporatism of British society, achieving a breakthrough into high-tech, high productivity, state-guided affluence, the Holy Grail which would turn Labour into 'the natural party of government'. The spheres of arms and sterling policy would, however, remain off-limits to any basic restructuring which such objectives might have suggested.

The following elements therefore conjoined in the second half of the decade: a perceived failure in government economic strategy, a rise in social tension at various levels, a continuation of the trend towards a social climate of disrespect for traditional symbols and totems (most notably those of the Cold War), a common contempt felt by left and right from different angles for the occupants of government office; these factors resulted in an unprecedented fissure opening up within the body of labourism between that part of it concerned with the state and all the remainder.

Party versus Movement

Disillusionment and friction from the direction of organised labour was manifested well before the conflict finally crystallised round the issue of trade union constraints. Trade union leadership turnover since Attlee's time had given rise to a generation considerably more in sympathy with militant and internationalist rank and file sentiment than their predecessors had been. They were not prepared to take on trust governmental definitions of reality. Frank Cousins was initially co-opted into the Cabinet but he soon left, finding himself out of step not only with economic policy but also with the fripperies of parliamentary procedure. It was apparent before long that both the exciting plans for economic regeneration with which Labour had made its slogan, and the existing level of industrial activity, were to be made hostage to the security of the pound. From 1966 onwards there commenced an absolute decline in the numbers of the manufacturing workforce, setting in train a process never subsequently reversed. Before long, loudly-voiced complaints started to be heard from union conferences, from the Scottish and British TUCs and even the Labour Party Conference itself, all of which had the temerity to pass resolutions critical of government policy and action. In the 1968 Conference the NUM successfully moved back a section of the NEC report because it failed to tackle the question of an overall fuel plan. Nor were they content to confine themselves to grumbles about factory and pit closures or even to the overall trend of economic policy – the adoption by this government of the stop-go cycle contrary to all its promises – but paraded their insolence by concerning themselves with matters of high state mystery, the doings of the Foreign and Colonial Offices. For the first time since the Macdonald catastrophe, significant sections of the trade union movement began to appear more radical than the politicians. It was not long before Wilson's administration adopted an attitude towards the internationalist postures of the Labour movement which was indistinguishable from that of its Conservative predecessors as well as an international policy distinguished only by an even more abject compliance with US requirements.

In consequence of all such trends, the state-centred component of labourism's corporate being was divorced from the hopes and aspirations of its grassroots following in both trade union and political dimensions. The immediate result, so far as the Labour Party itself was concerned, was disorientation and demoralisation.

Individual membership, which had risen up to 1965, went into steep decline, shrinking from 817,000 in the middle of the decade to an official figure of 692,000 by 1970, although independent estimates suggest a true figure which is barely half the quoted one. Organisational structures in numerous local constituencies fell to pieces. Between 1966 and 1969 19 English seats were defended in by-elections of which, in bleak contrast to the Attlee record, 11 were lost to the Conservatives and one to the Liberals. At Dudley in 1968 an anti-government swing of over 21 per cent was recorded. In the local elections of 1968 and 1969 Labour councils throughout the country were decimated. Sheffield, for example, which had been continuously Labour for 38 years, fell to the Conservatives. To this last process however there was a positive aspect; the electoral massacre in the councils cleared out, more effectively than any reselection process could have done, many longstanding Labour functionaries who had come to take their tenure for granted and to treat their constituencies as personal fiefs.

An anecdote from 1968 – the postwar peak of upheaval, turmoil and dissension from both leftists and working class on a west European as well as British scale – will illustrate the climate which had come to prevail and the depth of demoralisation into which the official labour movement had been plunged.

The biggest oppositional demonstration in the capital's 20th century history took place on 27 October 1968. It was a protest against the Vietnam war, organised on a scale sufficient to cause nervous media commentators to speculate upon the dangers of insurrection.

The demonstrators assembled on the Embankment in London. Because the numbers were so enormous it inevitably took a long time, during which, as usual upon these occasions, the political journal sellers exploited the curiosity of the participants and the tedium of the wait.

Among the plethora of journals being proffered, scarcely anything was to be found connected with oppositional movement emerging from the traditional Labour Party left. A very small number of *Tribune* sellers were present, but they were visibly experiencing great difficulty in selling copies and were being openly and regularly mocked for the archaism which they represented. The Tribune group of Labour MPs had been formed in 1966 but had no effect on government behaviour and no significant extra-parliamentary presence. Some of its members had even accepted government office, one, it is said, as a reward for pointing out to Wilson the impropriety of launching a Polaris submarine on 6 August. Many years later Ken Livingstone was to comment that when he joined the Labour Party in the same year he felt like the rat *boarding* the sinking ship.

The collapse of the link between Labour Party and trade union leaderships, the loss of direction and confidence by the non-governmental part of the Labour Party and the fulfilment by the government of all the worst forecasts made by Marxist parties, grouplets or individuals like Ralph Miliband, prepared the ground for the emergence into the political daylight of the revolutionary sects, whether from Maoist or Trotskyist traditions, and their ability to capture an audience of significant size beyond the bounds of their own partisans.

The Revolutionary Left

Overwhelmingly the audience was drawn from the ranks of the young people whose entry into higher education had been set on foot by the educational policies of the government itself. It was, after all, the era of student occupations, of the capture of the National Union of Students by the left, of the secular canonisation of Che Guevara, of 1968. These people provided the masses which by sit-in, demonstration and manifesto created a public stir, brought revolutionary politics to national attention, and set the tone of the British left in a way which was to persist long after this particular wave had itself passed into history.[12] It represented the political face of a social process which had been proceeding in a molecular fashion since the days of the 1950s youth cultures, and now all but inundated, across all social classes, the surviving structures of Victorian sensibility among the younger generations.

It was the essence of what was to appear in subsequent Thatcherite demonology as 'the permissive society'. The terminology itself indicates a lot, embodying as it does the presumption that people's lives and choices, and especially those of youth, are *naturally* subject to authority and require *permission* from superiors to develop along autonomous lines. Its central demand was for a freely-chosen identity and lifestyle, whether as consumers, students, family members, sexual actors or even workers. It rejected all forms of tradition and social authority which could not be rationally justified (and even many which could) and contested all claims to prescriptive authority, especially in academic – and, by extension, political – institutions. For the politicised element the 1968 events in France and the Cultural Revolution in China (or their perception of it) supplied material inspiration. However, the profoundly anti-authoritarian ambience of this social phenomenon coexisted very uneasily with the organisational forms through which its political aspirations were expressed.

For the most part these were Leninist (when they were not Stalinist), hence intrinsically and committedly authoritarian in tenor. Leaving aside the self-isolated, sinister and ultra-authoritarian Socialist Labour League (later the WRP), three strands of the Trotskyist tradition contested its heritage.[13]

In terms of formal politics the International Socialists, while acknowledging their Trotskyist ancestry, distanced themselves both from Leninism and Trotskyism, finding their principles best embodied by Rosa Luxemburg among the great revolutionaries. Their outlook stressed the inherent and spontaneous militancy and revolutionary potential of the industrial proletariat and they applied very considerable efforts to trying to communicate with it and to construct their own workplace organisation. The growth of their student numbers indeed provoked considerable tension over what the nature of the relationship should be. In the end, however, ostensible ideological positions made little difference; transforming itself into the Socialist Workers' Party the IS tried to replicate in miniature the apparatus of what it believed to be a revolutionary workers' party on the model of the early Comintern, stressing, all the more as its impact declined, the values of discipline and leadership.[14]

Greater attention than for any other of the sects has been focussed upon the Militant organisation, (otherwise the Revolutionary Socialist League), and it succeeded to a much greater extent than any of the others in mobilising numbers in its support and securing concrete political objectives – not least the eventual capture of a major local authority, ascendancy over an important segment of the Labour Party and the election of supporters to Parliament. Both of these aspects followed from the success of a political tactic which Militant turned into its central principle of action, namely the insistence that its supporters must work within the Labour Party and strive to control its units for the objectives of the organisation, from which it followed that, in order to escape constitutional sanctions, Militant had to operate as a secret authoritarian society within the structure of the Party with adherents obliged to lie consistently about what they were doing.[15]

What is perhaps most astonishing about all of this is that Militant made its advances in spite of being afflicted by theoretical vacuity, an armour-plated social conservatism and an implacable cultural philistinism – quite the reverse of the trend of the times in the late 1960s. Its members consciously and deliberately aped the working class styles of a previous era – although I suppose it could be claimed that in choosing these rather than in being born into them they were exercising the privilege of seeking and selecting an identity in the best 1960s fashion. The organisation's success was based on nothing other than relentless organisational zeal, derived in turn from crude and simplistic sloganising which, against all the apparent odds, not only attracted a youthful following but inspired it as well. The compass in Militant political navigation, however, was the conviction that when social democracy had discredited itself by repeated betrayal, the working class would turn to its historic organisations for remedy, the trade unions and the Labour Party, and would find them then infused with a revolutionary consciousness thanks to Militant spadework.

The third such strand of significance called itself at the time the International Marxist Group and represented the more academic side of British Trotskyism – although some of its supporters, like Tariq Ali, were high-profile student militants and it too tried to establish an industrial base. It was also somewhat more aware than its counterparts of the contradictions in the orthodox Trotskyist model of the universe, and therefore readily accused by them of revisionism, or rather apostasy from the true church. Although much smaller than IS or Militant, the journalistic talents which it acquired as recruits or sympathisers and the connexions it enjoyed with Perry Anderson's *New Left Review* enabled it to exercise an influence quite disproportionate to its size, and to contribute directly or indirectly by its elaboration of a theoretical argument for socialist perspectives beyond the old horizons of labourist radicalism, to the outlook of the labour left in the 1970s. Deep down nevertheless, its principles remained classically Trotskyist and its expectation was of a rerun of 1917 and a resumption of the international revolutionary thread broken by Stalinism in the 1920s.

These were all organisations with traditions, albeit largely hidden ones, going back to the 1930s. The Maoists by contrast represented an entirely new arrival on the scene. They were divided into about half a dozen separate splinters, sometimes in conflict, sometimes uneasily collaborating, which had usually begun life as fragments dislodged from the CP, a by-product of the Sino-Soviet rupture, but they mushroomed in the favourable climate of the later decade. Although one of them was actually established by a leading official of the engineering trade union, Reg Birch, overwhelmingly their support was drawn from student activists, who, in the Revolutionary Socialist Students' Federation, co-operated suspiciously with the Trotskyists and with assorted leftists in the Vietnam Solidarity Campaign.

With little other perspective than a crude and abstract revolutionism coupled with distant adoration of the Chinese developments, the Maoists left behind them scarcely any political legacy, although one of their Scottish components may have contributed significantly to the restoration in socialist history of John Maclean, whose ideological descendants they purported to be. For the most part however, their impact was immediate and was to heighten the atmosphere of frenetic leftist revolutionism which, not so long afterwards in comparable political cultures like Germany, Italy, Japan, and the USA – though not Britain – was to give birth to directionless terrorism.

Though much less publicised and regarded indeed by the new revolutionaries as schlerotic and outmoded, the CP was also present in these developments. Certainly it experienced no growth and after 1964 began a remorseless numerical decline, yet its industrial base was still significant and moreover it had succeeded in establishing good or at least workable relations with the new, more radical union leaders. Very early it was in the firing line from the Wilson government when he accused it of orchestrating the seamen's strike of 1966. The libel was generally disbelieved and in any case did the Party no harm, quite the contrary. When the more general attack on the trade unionism commenced, the Party, with its renowned organisational skills, became a natural focus for resistance through the mechanism of the Liaison Committee for the Defence of Trade Unions, which it dominated.

Nor was the party absent from the student scene, where its membership grew substantially, its branches multiplied and a strong organisational framework was established. Effective links were made also with Labour Party and Liberal students, permitting the election in due course and on more than one occasion of CP members to the leadership of the NUS both in Britain and Scotland. The inauguration in 1969 of the Communist University of London, subsequently a much-copied initiative, further multiplied the contacts between the party and other leftward elements and was the starting point for much of the theoretical discussion which echoed through the following decade.

The character and evolution of the late 1960s revolutionary left (including the CP) are interesting in themselves, but our concern is with its overall significance for the future development of British labourism. During the Wilson period of government the CP and the sects occupied a field without substantial rivals in elaborating theory and strategy, the parliamentary left having collapsed and fragmented. No extra-parliamentary Labour left was in evidence and the growing resentment in the unions was focussed on immediate practical concerns of bargaining, unemployment and legislation.

In the light of subsequent history, the long-term significance of these organisations was considerable, for their political style and organisational practice infused that of the Labour Party left a decade or so later. They were able to provide a model, the only one available in fact, when the Labour left began to mobilise its grassroots strength in the 1970s and, of course, many of the same individuals were involved, while Militant was working from within the organisation. In one respect certainly, the entry of that current of revolutionary tradition into the mainstream of British labour politics was positive, if not very influential. It did wash some of the sacramental gloss of the venerable Royal-connected institutions of the British state from Labour's consciousness, albeit at the expense of shrinking its popular constituency.

However, in general terms the interaction of labourism and revolutionism proved detrimental to both partners. The facets of the revolutionary style which were handed on were those which had classically permitted small and sectarian organisations to perpetuate themselves and attract a following: intense conviction and narrowly channelled zeal. With that went an emphasis on uncompromising attachment to stated positions, regardless of how practicable they might be in particular circumstances, a readiness to identify and denounce backsliding, and a disposition to accuse leaders of faithlessness and betrayal when things went badly – irrespective of whether the 'betrayal' was real or forced by impossible odds. The CP, if more flexible and more stigmatised by its rivals for being so, was not altogether exempt from these reproaches. When, following the experiences of 1966–73, its strategic ideas and proposals started to be taken more seriously than hitherto within the trade union structures, it too proved unable to adjust its inherited thinking to the perils and potentialities of an altogether novel situation.

The influences in the reverse direction were no less significant. The British left in the 1970s, reinforced by the revolutionary impulses coming out of the previous decade, may have abandoned a number of the classic characteristics of labourism, such as the metaphysical separation of industrial and parliamentary struggles or faith in the perfection of the existing constitution; but in virtue of these same impulses it became all the more firmly attached to certain other features just as venerable, even while exhibiting them in a radical guise.

First and foremost must be noted an almost touching faith in the potency of votes and resolutions taken within the organisations of the movement. The left, assisted by a grassroots surge of exasperation with the deceits and failures of the past, learned to use the rules and procedures in a manner it had never done before and with unprecedented effect, but the other side of this coin was that it took its successes within the structures of the labour movement, and the Labour Party in particular, as equivalent to shifting public consciousness in a leftward direction. Thus they fatally neglected the need to convince millions of individuals outside the circles of activists and to whom the propositions and analyses of left-wing socialism appeared as relevant as those of theologians.

Secondly, and here with a true irony of history, a more revolutionary consciousness on the part of labour activists was accompanied by a strengthened attachment to the institutions and achievements which had marked and furthered the high tide of postwar labourism. At the top of that list stood the traditional British electoral model, the first-past-the-post system, capable of delivering parliamentary majorities on a minority vote, and total rejection of any notion of coalitionism (though a parliamentary agreement was eventually to be adopted *in extremis*). Proportional representation or commitment in principle to electoral pacts were seen as devices to hobble the socialist initiative of a future Labour government and regarded as hallmarks of the Labour right. It was the same with the notion of a Bill of Rights. Although national devolution was reluctantly accepted by most of the left, the acceptance was so manifestly insincere and unwilling that it lacked all credibility and major figures on the left, such as Neil Kinnock, continued to campaign in opposition to it.

State ownership of major economic sectors as the key to social restructuring likewise remained an unexamined premise, as did centralised bureaucratic provision of services at national or local level as the foundation principle of welfare. Behind these attitudes stood a presumption common to both Leninism and labourism, namely that undiluted sovereignty (however much these ideologies might disagree about what sovereignty was) enabled a government in possession of it to do, legislatively, whatever it liked. This notion acquired colour from the opposite end in the 1970s by Lord Hailsham's fulminations against 'elective dictatorship'. What had been wrong with the Attlee (and to a greater degree, the Wilson) governments was that they had failed to use in the proper manner the powers that were legally theirs. The Westminster system was capable of delivering such theoretical sovereignty, and for the left, once the possibility began to glimmer of gaining control of the Labour Party, the Westminster system became sacrosanct for them too. This outlook was also their primary reason for opposing British adhesion to the Treaty of Rome, because its clauses would prohibit the construction of a fully-fledged socialist economy within the confines of the British state. It is possible to identify, coupled with this, the unstated admission that the left's programme could scarcely ever hope to command a majority of the electorate, but could be imposed by a majority government elected on a minority vote and *then* hopefully go on to win broader acceptance.

The successful struggles against two governments to defend trade union rights and autonomy also undermined the left and generated its dialectical reversal, a parallel in a minor key with the earlier reinforcement of archaic state institutions in virtue of the wartime victory. The existing character, rules and traditions of the movement, which the left had vehemently denounced when they were controlled and manipulated by the right, now became sacred objects. So did the relationship of the unions with both government and the wider society. Adherence to Frank Cousins's dictum 'that if there's to be a free-for-all we have to be part of the all', left out of account the actual difficulties of continually reproducing and reconstructing sympathy and consent in the public consciousness, particularly in radically changed social circumstances. This was all the more so when the Wilson government of 1974 was widely viewed in public eyes as having been put into power by the unions and the balance of ascendancy in the traditional tri-corporate relationship to have shifted from governmnent to unions – with capital nowhere. That the government would act as a union movement puppet was in reality nonsensical, but it was the perception, reinforced with every resource of the media, which counted. Expecting the public at large to take a trade union view of trade union rights without a constant effort to instruct and enlighten it (and showing willingness to be enlightened in turn), invited an eventual bitter nemesis.

The Heath Administration

At an earlier stage nemesis had caught up with Harold Wilson and the politics he represented. He went to the polls in June 1970 having devastated the fabric of the Labour Party and demoralised the labour movement in every direction, but with the elusive balance of payments surplus secured at last and a semblance of social peace prevailing in the country. The opinion polls confirmed that such realism had worked and that electoral victory was assured.

The Conservative victory was thus wholly unexpected and represented a definite and momentous stage in the eclipse of the traditional Labour right. *Parliamentary* labourism had failed conclusively and publicly on its own ground. The discredit of Wilson's degenerate version of the Attlee tradition was complete, along with the demoralisation of its proponents, already deprived of rank and file acceptance and trade union underpinning and now even of the cachet of electoral viability.

The new Premier, Edward Heath, prepared at once to address from a Conservative direction the still unresolved basic problems of the British economy, by mixing traditional corporatism with a sound dose of free market principles and a renewed application to join the EEC on whatever terms might be available. It is common nowadays to think of Heath as a socially-conscious and consensual Tory, which, compared to his successor, is certainly true; but it has to be recalled that in his time Heath was regarded as and resolved to be an innovative departure from the exhausted postwar tradition. In his economic strategy, ratified by the Selsdon Park meeting of the Tory shadow cabinet, can be discerned the first stirrings of the Thatcherite storm. Heath wanted 'to embark on a change so radical, a revolution so quiet and so total that it will go far beyond the programme of a Parliament … We were returned to office to change the course and the history of this nation, nothing less.'[16]

Equally though, corporatism was not to be abandoned. Heath's basic line of policy can be viewed convincingly not as a reversal but as a continuation of Wilson's, with a somewhat different means and emphasis.[17] The fundamental objective remained, while perpetuating the overblown financial and military apparatuses, to strengthen their foundations by making British industry internationally competitive – which certainly did not exclude close relations with government and generous public subsidy to promising industrial initiatives. What was new was that a stiff competitive wind would be allowed to weed out 'lame ducks', in the phraseology of the Industry Minister, John Davies and EEC entry would help to strengthen the force of that breeze. Similarly, there was no intention of turning the trade union movement into an outlaw institution: its powers would be constrained by legislation remarkably similar to that intended by the previous administration, but once rank and file militancy was curbed and obdurate leaders brought to heel, the pacified movement could continue to be an acceptable junior partner in the new national consensus that the Premier meant to establish. Simultaneously, the government signalled its intended break with the weakness and indulgence of its predecessor and threw a bone to the tory right wing by reverting to the most atavistic style of tory authoritarianism in an area where that was judged to be politically feasible. In Northern Ireland, at the behest of a Stormont administration still struggling to perpetuate the Orange ascendancy in face of a mounting storm of resistance from the civil rights movement and the nationalist populace, the practice of internment without trial was reverted to without warning. Conditions of terror and torture were inflicted upon the victims, and continued systematically until it culminated in the Bloody Sunday massacre of unarmed demonstrators in 1972.

Nevertheless, the fate of the redesigned corporatist model was to be settled not in Ireland but on the British mainland, and here Edward Heath found himself caught in the same trap which no British government since 1945 has succeeded in escaping: in order to create the social base necessary for electoral success, financial policy had to be designed to stimulate a consumer boom. But once underway any such boom would stoke up inflation and lead to all sorts of uncontrollable side-effects, including wage pressures and balance-of-payments disasters. Very soon the proto-monetarism on which the government had assumed office was abandoned and the phrase 'U-turn' entered the political vocabulary; the government even felt itself compelled to indulge in nationalisation of bankrupt private industries – the Rolls Royce aero-engine division. Well it might, in the words of Lord Blake, 'cause consternation among the party faithful.' Heath's Chancellor of the Exchequer, Anthony Barber, early in 1972 received the specific commission to get consumer purchases going at unprecedented rates, and government spending shot forward. By making attacks on union power, compulsory wage controls and EEC membership Heath sought to evade the inflationary consequences of this capitulation.

It was in these circumstances that the strengths of traditional labourism – outside parliament – were effectively mobilised for the last time. This must be regarded as the dominant theme of the years 1971–73, although inputs from the newer forces and approaches foreshadowed in the 1960s were also present.

The UCS work-in had been an indicator. It had shown that an entire community and a whole nation could be mobilised around the labour movement and its demands when these were seen as being in accordance with popular conceptions of democracy and social justice. The work-in transcended the long-established labourist forms of politics, organisation and public presentation. Its impact, in its successful outcome, on morale and self-confidence was incalculable.[18] The following confrontations were in a more classically labourist mould, conducted through the traditional movement organisations and not seeking public involvement on a large scale – even though they were conducted with overtones not met with in Britain since the days of near-revolutionary conflict following World War I.

Now, for the remaining life of this administration, wherever the movement faced the government it prevailed. The centrepiece of the intended new corporatist structures, the Industrial Relations Act, was passed in August 1971 and was immediately challenged by industrial action now illegal. A government-appointed court jailed five dockers, the TUC threatened a general strike and there was enough evident outrage and indignation among the workforce to make the threat a real one. The government was forced to arrange for the dockers' release and to suffer the utmost humiliation. There seems little reason to doubt that it was this episode above all which coalesced the Tory right and ultra-right together in the conviction that Heath was not up to the demands of preserving the existing balance of socio-economic forces, let alone of shifting it against labour – not that his standing with conservative ministers, MPs and activists was helped by his personal inadequacies.

Facing a disorganised and demoralised opponent and with the wind of at least tentative public approval in their sails, the unions now went on the offensive. Substantial wage demands were made by the National Union of Mineworkers. The government's fall was helped along by severe tactical misjudgments and growing public alarm at an unemployment level which had passed the million mark and – by previous British standards – roaring inflation, spectacularly fanned by the oil supply crisis brought on through the Egypt–Israeli war of 1973. The Labour Party was only beginning to recover numerically, organisationally and morally from the decrepitude of the Wilson premiership and, although it had at least backed the industrial wing of the movement in parliament since 1970, it was no more of a campaigning force outside election times than it had ever been. Consequently its electoral victory in February 1974 was narrow, achieved on a lower percentage vote than any before and owed more to the government's unpopularity than to any perceived merits of its own. The discredit of the established right, however, had allowed new currents to flow and the left, fortified by what was happening in the industrial arena, to gain the initiative. In 1973 the policy document *Economic Policy and the Cost of Living* committed the party to redistribute income and power to working people and impose rent and price controls along with markedly increased social provision. The 1973 election manifesto was the most radical since 1945, if not since 1900. The balance of strength on the NEC was shifting towards the left.

What had happened was that a Tory administration unexpectedly elected, which aspired to follow a new line of policy but was still unsure of its ground, which still carried with it many of the assumptions and traditions of the Butskell era, and was distracted with personal animosities and rivalries, encountered a trade union movement still in the glow of its postwar boom confidence, still growing, organisationally intact, undefeated, the victor over Harold Wilson and the offensive he had launched against it.

The events of these four years thus revealed the latent strength still to be found within British labourism – but likewise underlined its limitations. The success had been gained almost wholly on the industrial terrain, the political and *a fortiori* the parliamentary wing, busy with their internal realignment, had contributed very little. Nor had any dramatic alteration in popular consciousness taken place outside the confines of the movement. The election results of 1974 unmistakably indicated, for all the shortcomings of the British system as a true measure of public feeling, no more than a tentative and sceptical preference for the policies and programmes of Labour over those which were offered from other quarters. The only way forward for labourism at this point was therefore to transcend itself, to use the respite it had got to work for the construction of a new popular consensus and a new kind of hegemony to replace the broken-down one of Butskellite social democracy. It was a project which would require a novel approach: the united determination and relentless endeavours of parliamentarians, activists, union leaders and rank and file, something equivalent to what had transpired during the 1940s but in in a far more diverse, consumer-orientated and sophisticated society and without gruesome external menaces to concentrate the effort. Even so, there would be no guarantee of success, but if the change in social climate was ignored and the venerable practices and institutions of labourism continued unchanged, then the victory of 1974 surely contained the seeds of its own ruin.

4 Left Ascendency 1973–81

Structural Contradictions

From one point of view the Labour government taking over following Wilson's election victory in February 1974 faced an absolutely hopeless position that would have been scarcely improved even by a comfortable Commons majority. In that sense the fact that it turned out to be a minority government may well have counted as the least of its problems.

More potentially destructive to any Labour administration with ambitions to re-establish the social balance of the 1950s or even the 1960s (let alone to attempt anything more far-reaching) was the interlocking complex of international and domestic crises and disabilities ready to undercut any initiative requiring a high degree of popular mobilisation or dramatically new ways of thinking.

Heath's own debacle was connected with the drastic oil price rises following the Yom Kippur war of 1973, which was the immediate cause of the policies of economic stringency imposed upon the workforce in the last phases of his government. Labour inherited the consequences, a double blow to the British balance of payments, for the fuel price rise triggered a world depression which greatly worsened the prospects for British exports while, before North Sea oil came on stream, shoving up the import bill to unequalled heights.

So by 1973–74 all the major indicators of a growing capitalist crisis were to hand: the reappearance of a generalised trade cycle, monetary instability, a significantly higher rate of concentration and centralisation of capital, a growth in the intensity of international competition, the exhaustion of the industrial reserve army, a falling rate of profit, calls for the intensification of labour, and working class militancy.[1]

During the 1960s investment as a percentage of Gross National Product was consistently lower in Britain than in any major capitalist competitor and, in Coates's words, 'international competitiveness was persistently dwindling.'[2]

Even a much healthier economy would have faced serious problems in circumstances such as these, but in the Britsh case the chronic decay of her international competitiveness, which had not been arrested under Wilson during the 1960s, had continued in the years of the Heath administration. The manufacturing base was even further eroded, more obsolescent, its share of world trade still more shrunken than Wilson's 'technological revolution' had left it. The economy's central orientation preferred as much as it had ever done the direction of financial manipulation and capital export, with unprecedented inflationary pressures destroying the indispensable foundation of any long-term social consensus on hitherto established lines – the expectation of steadily rising or at least securely comfortable standards of living.

A further obstacle confronting any potentially innovative government was an apparatus of state that was totally unreconstructed – in both senses of the term. A full revelation of what the Civil Service bureaucracy really felt about the state of the country and the economy and what ought to be done about these things will have to await the exposure of the relevant documents,[3] although we do know that the higher civil servants constantly and forcefully urged the government to change its voluntary incomes restraint policy into a compulsory one. In spite of that circumstance, there is no suggestion that the Civil Service had any more concrete and defined goals than the politicians of either party: its leading personnel seem to have been just as dismayed and uncomprehending as anybody else – but they were wedded to the procedures and compromises of the tradition-encrusted British state and anxiously concerned to block significant changes even in the organisation and management of their own caste.

In relation to the military and the secret state the position was a good deal more sinister. The repressions which they had been sent to conduct in Northern Ireland during the Heath years had led rapidly to their exemption from any legal restraint and their more ideologically aggressive elements were not disposed to tolerate interference with their objectives from anything so despicable as an elected government. They soon collaborated with Orange terror gangs to abort the fragile power-sharing agreement between majority representatives of Ulster's nationalist and unionist communities. Middle-ranking elements, paranoid about the government's socialist label and regardless of its practial feebleness, took to using their media conduits to disseminate smears upon individual ministers and in due course to plotting the government's overthrow.[4] Their role, using Airey Neave as intermediary, in advancing Margaret

Thatcher to the Conservative Party leadership remains obscure but was probably not inconsiderable.

The demands of the *official* sphere of state coercion, the traditional military commitments, in spite of the rationalisations and cutbacks previously undertaken both by Wilson and Heath, still vacuumed up resources at a prodigious rate, imposing yet more strain upon the creaking economic supports of the postwar settlement. There is no evidence, however, that this was regarded by Labour ministers at the time as any kind of a central problem.

The staple hostility of nearly all the British print media to labour politics and Labour governments entered a new dimension at this point with the flowering of the journalistic style associated with Rupert Murdoch. When he bought the ailing *Sun* in 1969 and transformed its presentation, a promise was made to preserve the Labour-inclined stance it had inherited from its previous incarnation as the *Daily Herald*, and in fact the original Murdoch paper was very different from what it subsequently became. By the late 1970s though it was exhibiting the full force of its proprietor's neanderthal politics combined with a panache and flair in plumbing masculine atavisms that were to carry it to the top of the circulation charts.

The pervasive sense of anxiety, the public belief whether unspoken or clearly articulated that the postwar settlement was in deep trouble, could have motivated either increasingly despairing endeavours to hold it together or else the determination to remodel it completely. Clearly the tendency of labourism, a defensive ideology in all its essentials and organically linked to the existing state system, would be towards the former alternative.

For Marxists of all shades the longstanding assertion that British welfare capitalism was inherently unstable were confirmed and forecasts of its terminal sickness had finally come to pass. In conditions like these, their expectation was necessarily of an advance of class consciousness and its development towards the left, as the bankruptcy of ruling class solutions became unmistakably apparent.[5] From that expectation, the militancy displayed in the closing episodes of the Heath administration were no more than the first ripples of a rising wave capable of smashing into oblivion the rotting timbers of the capitalist state. It was no accident that the SWP reorganised itself according to its image of a Leninist party in anticipation that the day was at hand.[6]

Perspectives of this sort took no account of the specific characteristics of British political culture nor of its ingrained patterns of response. They discounted such peculiarities of tradition and expectation in favour of a universalist conception of how class relations *ought* to operate. The ruling class were no longer *able* to rule in the old way, it was true, but the people in general were only too willing to go on *being ruled* in the old way (which after all represented their era of greatest good fortune) and most of all wanted to find their way back to it. The political definition of what the 'old way' was, became therefore a major instrument of ideological mobilisation, capable of being used to affirm the welfare consensus or, given the right developments, to overthrow it.

The Social Contract

The first act of the incoming minority government was to calm the political storm it had inherited by making a set of agreements with the trade union leadership which was christened the 'Social Contract'. The phrase was stolen from Rousseau but given a fundamentally different meaning, and the difference is revealing. Rousseau's social contract was an imaginary agreement between sovereign individuals to constitute Society, Wilson's a real agreement between two of the partners in the corporate polity of Great Britain – government and trade unions, to abate their conflict, and an interesting public acknowledgment of the reality of that corporatism, contradicting, in reality if not explicitly, the official constitutional version of a sovereign Crown-in-Parliament.

The Social Contract was effectively a treaty reflecting the balance of political forces that existed in Britain in 1974. The parties to it each had its own very different idea of the significance of the agreement. Jack Jones presented it as a socialist document, Callaghan as justifying an incomes policy, Harold Wilson as the key to national economic recovery.[7] For the government it was a necessary, though perhaps not very palatable, price that had to be met in order to get the postwar consensus back upon the rails again. It is an open question how seriously the Labour leaders took the commitments they had accepted to far-reaching economic and social intervention or, if they did, did they understand them in an exclusively technocratic sense, as a basis for resuming the white heat of technological revolution interrupted a decade earlier, whose failure they interpreted as an accidental misfortune, oblivious of the structural constraints which hemmed them in? At the 1973 Labour Party Conference Denis Healey had been so bold as to promise tax policies which would produce 'howls of anguish' from the rich, but there was almost certainly no recognition that a crisis of completely new dimensions was now upon them. Most probably there was a lingering hope that the immediate economic difficulties might clear up of their own accord and allow the advance to be resumed according to the prescriptions of 1970, realising the dream of a modernising industrial base without prejudice to capital export or military spending. A permanent incomes policy was still viewed as intrinsic to such a project, although events since 1968 had persuaded Wilson and his government colleagues that it could not be made legally compulsory but must be atttained on the basis of consent: another pressing argument for strengthening the corporate bias present in British society and accentuating the labourist tradition of government/union-magnate deals. From this angle then, the Social Contract very much fitted in with the traditions of British politics since 1940, indeed could be seen as reasserting them against the break represented by Heath's administration and as another phase in the quest for the equilibrium which was continually threatened by deteriorating economic relationships.

For their part, the union leaders almost certainly did not appreciate the novelty of what their movement had accomplished since 1968: they too were thinking in traditional terms. They had, after an arduous struggle, expelled government interference from what they saw as their own legitimate sphere of industrial relations and wage bargaining but, altogether contrary to the hysteria of Conservative propaganda, they had absolutely no aspiration to run the state. They regarded government as the province of elected administrations and were content to let them get on with it so long as they respected the corporate interests of trade unionism. The union leaders of 1974 were different individuals from those who had occupied the same positions in 1951 and most of them may have indeed had a more left-wing slant to their politics than did their predecessors, but there is no reason to believe that they had a different vision of the British constitution from the men who had extended a reserved but loyal greeting to Churchill's incoming government.

Thus on neither side was there a conception of the Social Contract as a strategic lever, a political instrument which a government in office could use to give British economic and social policy a radically different direction from that which it had pursued over the previous 30 years. It would of course be entirely utopian to imagine that a government dominated by Wilson and his political colleagues could ever have possessed such an objective, it would have been contrary to their whole political experience and outlook. But equally there was no conception that the Social Contract could be used to maintain and expand the high ground that the trade unions had won; that here to hand was a means of mobilising public consciousness to impose upon government the demand for intervention in particular directions and according to a coherent socialist strategy that took account both of the potentialities inherent in the situation and the constraints that were unavoidable. The unions, or those charged with the responsibility for leading them, should have been far more interventionist in their approach to government: and if it is objected that this would have been quite incompatible with the traditions of union leaders the objection is acknowledged – which brings into focus the question of political leadership and of where such strategic vision might be expected to be found.

Surely the answer to that question could only be found upon the left which, whatever its shortcomings and fragmentation, at least put into question the structure and character of British society and its polity. It had been declaring for nearly 30 years the fragility and ephemeral nature of the social democratic settlement; the fulfilment of that prophecy was now upon the nation. The window of opportunity had opened at last. The bankruptcy of past courses was publicly visible while simultaneously a prodigious and wholly unexpected new resource in the shape of North Sea oil was about to make its appearance.

The Impetus for Change

By the left here we mean the left wing of the Labour Party, (accepting that this was in itself a very diffuse entity and became progressively more so), the CP, certain individuals not identified with specific organisations and the proliferation of sectarian and ultra-left groups. It would be an historical injustice to suggest that the left entirely failed to engage the challenge of the times and remained stuck in traditional and blinkered courses. On the contrary, from the early 1970s onward a stream of new thinking and initiative emerged both in the intellectual and organisational dimensions.

In the forefront of the first was the book which appeared in 1975, written by Stuart Holland, *The Socialist Challenge*. It constituted a coherent and systematic argument for socialism in British terms such as the parliamentary left seemed to have been incapable of producing since the days of the wartime Coalition and can be regarded in some senses as a riposte to Crosland's celebrated volume written two decades earlier. It made its impact in the light of the breakdown of the 1950s vision of a British mixed economy capable, through modest levels of central guidance and a public sector limited to the boundaries of 1951, of delivering Swedish levels of prosperity and welfare while maintaining

the state as a nuclear great power and exporter of capital second only
to the USA. A central component of that vision, a tamed and acquies-
cent capitalist class wielding social and political power considerably
inferior to that of organised labour also looked pretty threadbare in the
light of the experiences of the Wilson and Heath governments. Holland's
work made a considerable public impact and pointed in a direction that
was to be pursued assiduously on the Labour left for more than another
decade. It called for major extensions of public ownership, strict controls
upon capital movements in the private sector to compel investment in
the priority areas and major extensions in the welfare system. Moreover
The Socialist Challenge argued that these things could only be accomplished
by a Labour government prepared to ignore the screams of agony and
outrage emanating from capital and to rely instead on mass extra-parliamentary support and on honest public explanation of its aims.

At roughly the same time and complementing these developments,
the CP had evolved the concept of an Alternative Economic and
Political Strategy. The similarities to Stuart Holland's perspectives were
probably not accidental, for the discussions which had gone on round
this theme since the late 1960s must surely have influenced his own
thinking. However, the AEPS was more narrowly conceived than *The
Socialist Challenge*, but it likewise proved influential and went on to find
considerable favour in sections of the trade union movement. Doubtless
part of its attraction was that it was deliberately presented as being
unrelated to, if not quite repudiating, any revolutionary perspective. It
was not envisaged, or at least not advocated, as opening the way to
socialist transformation but instead as having the more modest objective
of dealing with the endemic structural crisis afflicting the British
economy. Central to its case was the demand for import controls and
withdrawal from the EEC as the only manner in which policies hostile
to transnational capital could be enforced; policies which would include
a far-reaching programme of nationalisation and greatly enhanced
welfare expenditure, all of which, though it might stop short of a
socialist transformation, would achieve the shift in the balance of wealth
and power towards working people to which the government of the
day was formally committed.

At the same time, while government and the Party leadership
continued to be dominated by the most traditional of labourist politicians, the left began to make organisational advances on a scale never
previously experienced. In 1974 Ian Mikardo secured the chairmanship
of the parliamentary party, albeit only briefly, and along with Tony Benn
chaired the two most important committees of the NEC. The following

year the parliamentary left began to try to construct an organised presence in the party at large with the formation of the first extra-parliamentary Tribune Group in Bristol. They had already been anticipated by the Campaign for Labour Party Democracy, which came into existence at the 1973 Conference and was essentially an initiative by extra-parliamentary activists, although it also had the backing of ten MPs. Five years later a body concerned with ideology and policy development as much as with the inner-party organisation arose among the labour left. This was the Labour Co-ordinating Committee, which owed its initial inspiration to Michael Meacher and Frances Morrell and subsequently went on to publish a mass of material on all aspects of the left's strategy and perspectives.[8]

As dissatisfaction with government performance began to grow, elections to the NEC began to swing in a leftward direction and in two instances of public and sensational challenge to the leadership the left triumphed. In the reselection battles at Newham North East and Sheffield Brightside, constituency organisations rejected sitting MPs notorious for their right-wing politics and their arrogant postures towards their local activists. The case of the Sheffield constituency was particularly interesting, for the facts entirely contradicted the press stereotype of the middle class academic left infiltrating a moribund constituency organisation, as was alleged to have happened with Reg Prentice. Brightside was a very working class constituency and had for generations been under the control of the right. The character of the revolution that had occurred here is demonstrated by the fact that Eddie Griffith's replacement was Joan Maynard. The case of Newham was still more sensational for the MP in question was a Cabinet minister, Reg Prentice, and the Party leadership made strenuous efforts to avert his disgrace, not to speak of the intense media support which naturally came his way. For all that, the deselection stood in both cases and put on the agenda the question of a regular procedure whereby MPs would cease to have automatic tenure unless specifically removed as these two had been, and instead be required to compete for their constituency party's endorsement at stated intervals.

Evidently, fundamental and unprecedented developments were in process. The old dream of a Labour Party with the left in control at the top and hegemonic throughout the party structures, a party which would adopt a left-wing programme, would argue for it publicly with all the resources at its disposal, would fight for it electorally and strive to implement it once in office: all that began to seem perhaps not to be so visionary after all. The conviction of writers like David Coates and Ralph Miliband[9] that the Labour Party was unreformable and its left a permanent and structural minority, now looked distinctly compromised. The left appeared to be on the march, both in theory and practice, even if the contingents found it difficult to keep in step and the number of sects upon the scene multiplied by division even while some of them, such as the Socialist League, successor to the IMG, formally dissolved themselves in order to send their members back into the Labour Party. As Patrick Seyd expresses it, between 1973 and 1979 groups were formed which were not bound by the older Labour left's conventional parliamentary-centred methods but developed their skills in tactics and procedures for winning votes in local Labour Party and union branches.

Without doubt a crisis of social democracy had begun to manifest itself and the labourist framework started to break down. The disjunction between government action and rank and file attitudes was hardly less severe than it had been in the 1960s and the corresponding bitterness nearly as vehement. The major difference was that the leadership was no longer able to maintain its control over the structures of the party. Its supersession and replacement was imagined as being only a matter of time once its performance in government had finally and irretrievably discredited it.

Unhappily, the perceptions and perspectives of the left, all sections of it, were no less tradition-bound and enslaved by the past than were those of the Labour leaders and the mainstream of the Party. Left advance was conceived wholly in terms of securing and consolidating the classic objectives of the left as inherited from whichever element of the tradition a particular left tendency happened to adhere to – and within the Party (or at best the labour movement) at that, rather than within the wider public consciousness.

In reality, the left fought the wrong battle on the wrong terrain. There was a general failure, from the Tribune Group leftwards, to recognise the real significance of the developments in the union movement which had occurred since 1970. The industrial actions between 1970 and 1974 were applauded – except where efforts to broaden their scope and and attract non-movement support, such as the UCS were denounced as pandering to the media and middle-class sentiment – but regarded only as defensive battles against capital's state-supported intrusion into the traditional network of workplace defences. Their political potential was viewed by the revolutionary left as no more than the raw material which the Leninist party might hope to process into a revolutionary consciousness.

So naturally, when the TUC negotiated with the incoming Wilson government 'the promise of a large-scale redistribution of wealth, permanent price control, expanded social services, extended public ownership, and other concessions' sufficient to alarm the tory media, these pretensions were simply not taken seriously by the left. Perry Anderson in his much discussed article, 'Figures of Descent' in *New Left Review* 161, generally speaking a perceptive analysis of the origins of the structural crisis, (see Chapter 1) summarises the typical left response:

> At the crest of an industrial upsurge that had toppled a government … the major union leaders showed no interest in planning powers … They contented themselves with marginal improvements in social insurance and greater equity in the tightly controlled nominal pay rises[10]

Even in terms of fact this is a distortion in a number of respects (the pay rises, for instance, were far from being tightly controlled at first), but it is the implied judgment which is essentially faulty. To suggest that the trade union leaders could in principle have been a lot bolder – not taking into account the real character of the movement they led or considering the distance they had moved in five years – is abstract and mechanical. It also ignores the nature of the British political and cultural environment and presumes that the union offensive had been solidly based on conscious majority support, a shaky premise even for the labour movement, let alone other elements of the population. In reality, the masses were far from being as fully politicised as the sectors of the movement which had organised the victory. When Heath fought and lost on the slogan 'Who rules Britain?' he was making a perfectly sober and reasonable calculation.[11] It was his bad luck to underestimate the degree of human sympathy the miners' case aroused – on the basis, as they sensibly presented it, of 'a fair day's wage for a fair day's work' not, by any stretch of the imagination, 'abolition of the wages system'. The constitutionalist, traditionalist responses endemic to British political culture had not disappeared (Labour's share of the vote was still declining) and lay waiting to be evoked as soon as the labour movement or Party could be convincingly portrayed as wanting to exploit their victory beyond the limits of moderation.

No potential whatever was visible to the left in the original Social Contract. All denounced it as a pernicious cloak for wage restraint and 'shifting the burden of the crisis onto the backs of the working class'.

It was counterposed to free collective bargaining as the proper form of British trade union practice regardless of specific circumstances. In effect, what had occurred was that the consciousness of the British left itself had become a militant labourist one, while its political perspectives remained stuck tight in unreal dogmas of various sorts, such influence as it was able to exert within the movement only had the effect of reinforcing labourist prejudices. 'The evidence of Marxist publications is that instead of raising the political consciousness of the movement above the level of wage demands, the Marxist left was intent on raising the wages question above the political issues.'[12]

All this is not to argue that the trade unions and the left should have rolled over and accepted whatever the Wilson–Callaghan governments wanted to impose – on the contrary. But is it unreasonable to suggest that it would have made better sense to have campaigned around the objective of holding the government to its Social Contract promises than to have hoist the banner of a labourist principle which, in the economic climate of the mid-1970s, had lost any public credibility it might once have had? By the end of the decade the unions had abandoned the effectively political perspectives they had evolved prior to 1974 and, after being 'consulted on a scale, and with a degree of publicity, never before seen in peacetime',[13] had relapsed into economic defencism. Perhaps if they had acted otherwise it would have made no difference and maybe if the left had been more in tune with the situation the outcome would have been the same in any case, but at any rate the practical problems of political power under the British *ancien regime* would have come under scrutiny and debate.

Instead, the final breaking wave from the turbulence of the decade was the process of internal constitutional reform effected within the Labour Party itself in the aftermath of the 1979 election defeat. This was a process which, by its assault, if only implicit, upon the ratbag proprieties of the political tradition evoked a frenzy of fear and loathing among the establishment, both inside and outside the Party.

But by then it was too late. The greater part of the left had collapsed into militant labourism, a posture based upon the expectation that if only traditional practices and forms of struggle were applied vigorously and uncompromisingly enough and adopted by other disadvantaged minorities and groupings, they would mobilise the labour movement into an irresistible political force and win over, by force of example, further elements of the masses as well. The Militant sect represented the epitome of this trend: myopic philistine labourism masquerading as a revolutionary conspiracy.

Traditional Policies

The Labour government of the 1970s adhered to the same essential priorities as its Labour and Conservative predecesssors had done: the defence of the pound sterling as an international currency and the pretension, so far as it was able, to play at being a Great Power. In respect of the first of these, it was not long before the specific undertakings on the government side of the Social Contract, let alone the general commitment to 'an irreversible shift in wealth and power...' were jettisoned in favour of public spending cuts and a counter-inflation policy designed to satisfy financial capital rather than the sufferer-in-the-street. From 1975 onwards the Labour Chancellor, Denis Healey, began to implement programmes of expenditure control and money supply reduction which would be recognised later as a foretaste of Thatcherism. These reached their climax in 1976 when these restrictions were tightened unashamedly at the behest of the IMF to meet the conditions of an emergency loan. By then the index of industrial production (1970 = 100) had scarcely returned to 1974 levels, while investment abroad was over two-thirds more than the domestic figure.[14]

With regard to the second objective, however scarce resources might prove to be for purposes of enhancing public investment or welfare, they were found readily enough for the Chevaline programme to upgrade the Polaris nuclear missile fleet. The fleet was rapidly becoming obsolescent at this juncture, a process whose continuation would have caused Britain to cease being a nuclear weapons power without the Labour government having to lift a legislative finger. So unthinkable was such an outcome to the establishment elite's self-perception of their world role that the preservation of the sacred symbol became an absolute priority. In a manner reminiscent of the way in which secret treaties were concluded prior to 1914 and the British atomic bomb was developed under Attlee, the Chevaline programme was concealed from public scrutiny, from the House of Commons and even from the majority of the Cabinet, its funding hidden among the general military estimates.[15]

This administration was loyal, in traditional labourist fashion, to the fundamental principles of the British state. But it was unable, even at a period when the space for manoeuvre was much less than had been the case during the years of the long boom, to control the social and political consequences of its actions. This generated on the part of the tabloid press a level of hysteria formerly unthinkable even by their standards, and provoked on the part of the demented right entrenched in the security services plots first of all to discredit the government and its ministers in the public eye by means of a disinformation campaign, and latterly even to scheme for its overthrow on Greek or Chilean lines.

It is a far-reaching distortion of reality, which has gone on to acquire the dimensions of an historic myth, that the trade unions and their leaders systematically reneged on their 1974 bargain with the incoming government, exploited their industrial strength to the utmost and presented an immoderate series of wage claims culminating in the morale-shattering 'winter of discontent' of 1978-79, the principal cause of Labour's loss of office in the 1979 election.

What really happened was, if anything, nearer the precise opposite. The leaders of the major unions appear to have been genuinely convinced that Wilson and his colleagues were sincere in their intentions and, in collaboration with a union movement working in partnership rather than rivalry, could be genuinely expected to commit themselves to the Manifesto programme. As Len Murray expressed it at the time, 'The Chancellor will be able to count on a good response from the mass of working people in combatting the effects of worldwide inflation'.

Events soon demonstrated otherwise. As early as the beginning of 1975 the Treasury was showing where its real priorities lay: the severities of its deflationary and cost-cutting protection of the exchange rate reflected them and were only minimally abated by inadequate and opportunist gestures towards particularly sensitive social issues, such as the pensioners' £10 Christmas bonus. In the face of Wilson's effective abandonment of the Manifesto perspectives, followed by his and his successor's grasping at any available expedient to maintain themselves in office regardless of principle or direction, the trade unions continued to accept policies of wage restraint from a government that was patently incapable of protecting their members' jobs or incomes, let alone enhancing them. As David Coates remarks:

> ... union leaders did not use their position inside the Party to embarrass the Cabinet, even on issues directly relating to the living standards and job security of their members; nor, with very rare and quickly withdrawn exceptions did they even apply pressure on their sponsored MPs.[16]

Indeed, corporatism, as defined by Middlemas, briefly touched its high-water mark and assumed the *appearance* of a government-union partnership excluding the collective organisations of industrial capital, to a greater extent than ever before. Policy consultations were frequent and regular, with the unions themselves left to implement the details

of incomes policy – at least in the earlier stages. Various items of legislation conforming to trade union demands were instituted, including
ones on equal pay and sexual equality. The Manpower Services
Commission, ACAS and the Health and Safety Commission all made
their appearance at this time 'and leading trade union figures played a
prominent part in the design and running of each'.[17]

It was only from late 1977, following repeated disillusionments and
against a background of escalating unemployment and a government
shrouded with an atmosphere of demoralisation over its parliamentary,
devolutionary and Irish entanglements as much as its economic ones,
that the unions finally lost patience. Wage militancy broke through in
a cascade of claims by industrial and public service personnel whose recent
experience had been of the sharp end of government incomes policies
– the combination of circumstances which enabled the media to portray
a Britain on the verge of anarchical collapse.

David Coates in his examination is concerned to emphasise that the
Labour government succeeded for nearly four years in keeping trade
union leaders in line with its increasingly restrictive economic policies
and in restricting rank and file militancy as well. What it could not
prevent, however, was the control of the party machinery itself slipping
away from the traditional right wing. As Seyd notes, the left wing groups
formed in this period were not limited in the way the Labour Party left
conventionally had been in earlier periods to parliament-centred
methods but developed skill in tactics and procedures for winning
votes in local Labour Party and union branches. The successful dese-
lections of Eddie Griffiths and Reg Prentice were a portent of things
to come. The failure of the Wilson–Callaghan governments to
implement the Party's programme reinforced the left's adherence to it
and the left now concentrated on bringing about constitutional restructuring in the Labour Party. This aimed to secure the future accountability
of leaders so as to ensure that next time round such a betrayal could not
recur. The possibilities that appeared to be opening up convinced
many members of leftist sects, or of social movements that had held aloof,
that the time had arrived to add their weight to the Labour Party's
putative transformation. The women's movement supplied numerous
new recruits at the same time as trade union membership expanded
among women generally. In 1977 the debacle of the traditionally
labourist administration in the Greater London Council, which was
succeeded by a tory regime that marked a foretaste of Thatcherism,
enabled the left to win control of the London Labour Party.

They were people who had often acquired political skills from outside the administration of local government – through feminism, community politics, the student movement, the Vietnam campaign or wherever. Their view of local government had been radicalised by writings like those of Cynthia Cockburn on the local state and *Red Bologna*.[18]

But in fact the left, all sections of it, Labour, communist, the unaligned and the sects, had already squandered its opportunity and the apparent progress and accession of strength was thoroughly deceptive, for by the end of the 1970s the social and cultural ground was shifting under its feet.

With a few individual exceptions which weren't taken seriously, all the left's presumptions reflected its governing premise that political advance had to be within the tradition of classical left formulae – stated succintly, elegantly and authoritatively by writers such as Coates and Miliband. This meant enhanced state control through further nation-alisation measures, particularly of financial centres, controls on capital movements and transfers, greatly increased levels of state investment in publicly owned industries, withdrawal from the EEC, but above all an unremitting attack by workers' industrial power upon the allocation of the surplus product between labour and capital, ie the use of unrestricted freedom to engage in wage bargaining upon the terms which had been set in 1945 and reinstated, if not improved upon, in 1974. The implied strategy here was to exploit the terms of the victory of 1974 and the political weakness of the Labour administration *vis-à-vis* its party activists to institute a more left wing government – or a progressively reddening series of them – which would employ the sovereign powers of the British state in the manner indicated above while simultaneously using it in support of labour against the remaining sector of private capital – in short a combination of left–labourist and syndicalist perspectives.

In such a context the Social Contract, in concept no less than in operation, was denounced and damned. It was the CP's industrial organiser who coined the phrase 'social con-trick'. The voluntary restraint on free collective bargaining which it embodied was identified as its detestable essence, a device to solve the problems and dilemmas of capital at the expense of its workforce and a blind to impede the political consciousness of the working class from developing in a leftward direction by setting the answer to the national economic crisis in capitalist terms. It was argued that inflation could in no sense be attributed to rising wage costs and that it was no more or less than a device for redistributing income from wage earners back to property owners. Left wing speakers asserted that they had no objection to an incomes policy which aimed to advantage labour and penalise capital rather than the actually existing one which was creating an unmistakable drop in real wages – as indeed it was.

What never was contemplated because of this was a strategy which took the Social Contract with all its limitations as a starting point, accepted that in a 'mixed economy' an unfair, centrally monitored wages policy (with special concessions for the lowest income groups), as in the time of the Attlee government, was the only alternative to long-term inflation, and seeing that was in place on a voluntary basis, then went on to mobilise and organise around the demand that the government should keep to *its* side of the bargain and implement the terms to which it had agreed, as it manifestly failed to do after November 1974. This would have represented, in Gramscian terminology, a war of position as opposed to the war of movement in which the left tried to engage, thinking the terrain favourable but running instead into suicidal defeat. Such a strategy, if tried, would probably have failed, at least in its primary objective. It is most unlikely that the Wilson–Callaghan governments, faced with unremitting pressure from British capital, from the IMF, from the media, from the tenuousness of their parliamentary majorities and not least from the secret state, could have been persuaded by grassroots pressure, however ably deployed, to adhere to their side of the Social Contract. What *might* have been possible would have been to give a very different colour to the image of the left and the labour movement within British political culture, in short, to have built upon and expanded into the movement as a whole the popular sympathy the miners enjoyed in 1972 and 1974.

The precondition of this was that the movement's position should be seen as constructive and, in the original sense of the term, 'patriotic', so that even immediate defeat could have left behind a legacy of popular consciousness that might provide a springboard for subsequent advances. But in the event decisive sections of public feeling were alienated by the terms in which the left allowed itself to be portrayed, by the impact of the strikes which followed the breakthrough in wage militancy and by the presumed weakness of a government buried under its collapsing policy foundations and unable to deal, it was made to appear, with sinister and subversive forces to its left. And it was not only the character of the existing labour government which was called into question, but the nature of the whole postwar settlement, depicted as responsible for the status of the trade unions as overmighty powers and the economy as being bled white by profligate handouts to welfare recipients.

Tory Right-wing Resurgence

Early in 1978 Eric Hobsbawn produced the analysis, later published in
Marxism Today as 'The Forward March of Labour Halted?'[19] which noted
the falling-off in the numerical growth of working class organisation and
political response during the previous generation, and noted the growth
of sectionalism at the expense of solidarity among the workforce and
the likely impact on the consciousness of consumers created by strikes
in the service industries. Hobsbawm did not have any comment to make
on the strengthening position of the left in the Labour Party organisation, but poured cold water on the triumphalism being expressed on
the left over the industrial militancy of the early and late 1970s (which
ignored the quiescence of the middle years) and what it might mean for
the movement's long-term prospects. The analysis turned out to be
percipient, not to say prophetic.

When Margaret Thatcher replaced the discredited Heath as Conservative Party leader, the first reaction on the left and among Labour
supporters generally was to rejoice that the tories had chosen an
apparently unelectable politician to lead them. Although in no way as
dreadful as what the actuality was to prove to be, the view of Thatcher
even at that juncture was of an extreme and strident authoritarian, an
enemy of labour and of welfare – therefore a guaranteed electoral
turn-off.

What the left failed to appreciate, though Hobsbawm's article had
hinted at the posssibility, was that the electoral mood was turning in a
fundamental and epochal manner. The bankruptcy of social democracy
was manifested not solely in the government's incapacity to fulfil any
of its economic objectives, but in a range of structural breakdowns and
deadlocks. The existence of that state of affairs, however, did not
generate a popular mood which, prompted and guided by revolutionary Marxists, recognised the inadequacies of the social democratic
framework and demanded advances along the road to socialism. The
welfare state and the mixed economy remained the horizon of social
achievement, but the events of the late 1970s, interpreted through the
prism of the popular media, radically called into question in the consciousness of large swathes of Labour's natural constituency – particularly
skilled manual workers – that state's foundations in the corporate
balance of trade unions, industry and government.

The country was beginning to appear ungovernable and the labour
movement to be identified as the source of its instability. Prodigal
public expenditure, multiplying bureaucracy and excessive trade union

power appeared more and more convincingly to be the true explanation of the country's wretched economic performance. The government was seen to lack *authority*, reliant on a shabby deal with the Liberals in parliament even to preserve its majority, blown around with every vagrant political wind, beset with Irish terrorism (to which the Home Secretary's Prevention of Terrorism Act appeared a panicked and belated response), bleeding with self-inflicted wounds from its devolution quarrels. The political and the moral climate altered in favour of the new right, whose representatives and spokespeople had advocated from the margins of political life ever since the mid 1950s principles of economic liberalism and social authoritarianism. The new right had extended of late their network of propagandist centres and enhanced their weight within the Conservative Party. The Labour Chancellor's own acceptance of a variety of monetarist policy under IMF supervision could be read as a reluctant and unintended tribute to the correctness of their analysis.

Margaret Thatcher was a leader after their own heart. She represented in her own person and outlook the new times into which the British polity was being drawn by the weight of its southern English electorate. Her government was to shatter the pillars of labourism, overturn the postwar settlement and initiate a transformation in the public mentality. Her statistical record as the longest-serving Prime Minister of the 20th century and the only one to win three successive general elections is symptomatic: her significance is enormous and derives from the circumstance that she was riding an historic wave. Her success is certainly not related to any exceptional individual attributes – possessing as she does a personality that is as contemptible as it is odious.

By 1979 the government's credit was exhausted, in the political if not in the monetary sense. Ironically, in a replication of one aspect of 1970, the worst of the economic crisis was over, temporarily at least, and a more convincing administration might have succeeded in convincing sufficient of the electorate that its intelligent utilisation of North Sea oil would permit the labourist consensus to be rebuilt on more secure foundations.

Economic tribulation, however, was not the only weakness of this government and possibly, for all its apparent centrality, not even the most important one. No doubt the outcome of the election was indeed determined primarily by perceptions of economic incompetence in a very broad sense, but Callaghan's administration did not fall because of an economic issue but over an entirely different matter, one intrinsic to the very soul of labourism – its symbiosis with the British state and the latter's archaic constitutional forms.

The Constitutional Issue

A modest restructuring of these forms appeared on the political agenda during the 1974–79 government. The government tried to grapple with that agenda, but the leadership did so with manifest reluctance and no appreciation of the potential significance of the proposed changes; major sections of the party resolutely opposed them and the left, itself divided inside and outside the party, altogether failed to provide any effective lead.

The proposed remodelling was not in all conscience terribly far-reaching and involved no more than the establishment of devolved assemblies with limited powers in Scotland and Wales, only diluting very marginally the concentrated sovereignty of the Westminster Crown-in-Parliament. Nonetheless, like the franchise reform of 1832, it would have marked a beginning – and an irreversible recognition that the sovereignty was no longer sacrosanct.

Instead of seizing, with foresight and vision, upon an unrepeatable opportunity, the Labour Party and government succeeded only in discrediting themselves. Devolution became official policy as soon as Harold Wilson re-entered office in 1974 but it was evident even to the most imperceptive observer that the British leaders had adopted it with clenched teeth and the utmost reluctance; more, that they then had to compel the utterly unwilling Labour Party in Scotland to come into line.

No principle animated the Labour cabinet's half-hearted acceptance of devolutionary arrangements. Not even the most superficial analysis of the structure of the British state and the necessity of amending it underpinned the decision that assemblies with certain legislative powers were to be established in Scotland and Wales. The move was inspired solely and exclusively by the continuing electoral advance of the Scottish National Party and Plaid Cymru, together with reluctant acceptance on the part of Wilson and his main colleagues that unless concessions of a sort were to be made to national sentiment the Labour strength in these strongholds of its electoral power could be irretrievably damaged.

In the election of February 1974 the SNP won seven seats; in October it took eleven and 30.4 per cent of the vote, less than six percentage points behind Labour and eating massively into the hitherto solid Labour electorate in the peripheral big-city housing estates, a point underlined in subsequent local elections.

The Scottish Executive of the Labour Party resisted bitterly and fervently, taking its stand upon the assertion that the Scottish problem in all its dimensions was one of economic inadequacy and that questions of constitutional restructuring constituted a diversion from the real world. In 1970 it had given evidence (contradicting the position of the Scottish Trades Union Congress), which rubbished devolution to the Royal Commission on the Constitution:

> ...it was stated that although the only solution to Scotland's problems was a Labour Government at Westminster, it was prepared to tolerate a British Conservative Government which did not have a Scottish majority because it feared the creation of a Frankenstein's monster, a body which it might be unable to control.[20]

A veritable caricature of labourism in its stolid, banal and unimaginative economism, its inability to appreciate that the form of the state, so long as a democratic gloss was preserved, could ever be a problem, the Scottish EC's pronouncements were echoed by part of a divided left which viewed nationalism as no more than a weapon in the armoury of the class enemy, and constitutional debate as a distraction from the serious business of nationalising the principal monopolies.

Encouraged by the mediocre SNP performance in 1970 and undeterred by its subsequent revival, the Scottish EC went on to reaffirm its opposition in the most intransigent terms during the course of 1973. A few days later the SNP sensationally overturned a 16,000 Labour majority in Glasgow Govan, a rock-solid working class constituency in the heart of what had once been red Clydeside.

Determined arm-twisting by the leadership in Westminster finally brought the Scottish Executive into line, although it by no means convinced the members of that body. A Special Conference on devolution was convened in Scotland in August 1974 and met '...with its Scottish Executive Committee opposed to the concept, a Government pledged to legislate on it, a NEC favouring a Scottish Assembly with legislative powers and a Party membership split down the middle.'[21] A large majority at the Conference backed devolution and an elected Assembly 'within the context of the political and economic unity of the UK'.

The manner in which the commitment had been arrived at generated doubts, not surprisingly, about its sincerity: these reservations were scarcely dissipated a year later when one of the leading Scottish pro-devolution MPs, Jim Sillars, went to the length of breaking with the Labour Party and setting up another of his own to pursue socialism and devolution together. The enterprise was provoked by his frustration and exasperation at the foot-dragging speed with which the promised devolution bill was being advanced and the limitations inherent in the powers which were intended for it. The new Scottish Labour Party generated a lot of media attention and attracted a number of significant figures from the apparatus of the Labour Party in Scotland but no actual labour organisation – not even Sillars's own constituency party. Neither did it achieve much impact in numbers (it never exceeded a thousand members) or in the elections which it contested. Nevertheless, its existence and the circumstances of its formation represented a further blow to the morale and confidence of the mainstream, pro-devolution element among Scottish labour.[22]

The progress of the Devolution Bill through parliament was scarcely an episode to inspire conviction or confidence in the Labour leadership's determination to recast the foundations of the British political system. On the contrary, it was a bumbling and inept performance, motivated solely by fear of the consequences of *not* undertaking it and only partially excusable by the absence of an overall parliamentary majority and the existence of determined opposition within the PLP's own ranks. The government accepted an amendment from a Labour member by which, in the referendum that was to follow the passage of the Bill, an abstention would effectively count as a 'no' vote and in the subsequent campaign around the referendum Labour politicians in opposition to devolution were allowed a free hand to oppose it vociferously. Perhaps that was unavoidable given the precedent of the Common Market referendum and the strength of the feelings involved, but what *was* a matter of choice was the refusal of the Labour Party to co-ordinate its own campaign with those of any of the other pro-devolution elements in the field, so that there were no less than three separate central organisations promoting a 'yes' vote in the early months of 1979, contributing thereby to the image of disorganisation, ineffectiveness and half-heartedness around the overall campaign.

While the Welsh referendum vote resulted in unmistakable rejection of the form of devolution on offer there, in Scotland the worst possible outcome came to pass. A majority of those voting cast their ballots in favour, but their numbers fell well beneath the 40 per cent of the electorate required to pass the hurdle of the Cunningham Amendment. The Devolution Act, however, had still gone through and only awaited the implementation which could have been put in hand by a Commons vote overriding the Amendment. The vote was taken, but the Callaghan government, in a suicidal gesture, refused to make support for implementing the Act a matter of confidence. Had it done so, any Labour MPs daring in such circumstances to defy the whips would have been more than counterbalanced by votes in favour from Liberal and Nationalist members. What the administration can be most justifiably blamed for on this occasion was its blindness to the centrality of the issues involved: Callaghan and his ministers gave every impression of still treating devolution as an inescapable nuisance which they only wanted to get off their hands, and the preservation of the Labour Party's tattered unity as the only consideration of moment, at the expense of everybody else's welfare and regardless of the immediate danger of allowing a Thatcher-led Conservative Party to gain control of the unreformed state apparatus. Their attitude made certain the prospect of Parliamentary defeat, for the embittered Nationalists, not to speak of the Liberals, could now be guaranteed to vote against the government in the forthcoming vote of no confidence on the industrial issues. The Labour government fell, the first party to be defeated on a vote of confidence since its predecessor in 1924, needlessly, but not inappropriately, on account of its paralysing indifference to issues outside the classic span of labourist concern: the economy, welfare, and the traditonal state: a fitting conclusion to eight decades of subordination to the hegemonic assumptions which pervade the governing structures of the United Kingdom.

The fact that it was destroyed by a constitutional issue deserves to be remenbered better than it is. While the economic record and the winter of discontent may have been decisively influential in the resultant general election, they were not the matters which provoked it – a point that commentators frequently overlook. David Coates's *Labour in Power?* though subtitled *A Study of the Labour Government 1974–79* deals only with economic policy and industrial relations, with no discussion of foreign issues, or nationalism in the UK. Its title is therefore highly misleading, although symptomatic.

The 1979 Election

The 1979 general election continued the long-term trend of a declining Labour vote both in percentage and absolute terms. It recorded too a more specific shift in the voting patterns of skilled workers towards the Conservatives. Nearly one-third of trade unionists voted for them, and they concentrated their campaign skilfully and mercilessly upon the unhealed sores and bruises of the labourist inheritance and summed it up brilliantly in the slogan which their advertisers superimposed upon the photograph of an immense supposed dole queue: 'Labour isn't working.'

The Conservative appeal was double-edged, indeed contradictory, which is a common enough feature of populist right-wing initiatives which need to find a rhetorical stance which reconciles inherently opposed interests and programmes into an electoral bloc. Overtones of repentance and chastisement (greed, material over-indulgence and moral relaxation had provoked their nemisis in economic breakdown and the people deserved an overdue penance) combined with implicit promises to make everybody better off and further to expand a consumer paradise fuelled by self-interest and strenuous rapacity if only the obstacles to growth, such as trade unions and their restrictive practices were done away with. The Conservative pitch is perhaps best viewed as the advertising and public relations version of the assertion that lower wages will produce more jobs, yoked with the endemic strain of Victorian moralism in British culture that was overlaid but far from extinguished during the boom years and the permissive society.

In the long term the shape of the Thatcherite project was to correspond pretty closely to the anti-consensus and confrontationist rhetoric of the initial message, but more immediately this was obscured by the appointment of a government containing many representatives of old-guard conservatism, and there was no reason to expect that once more, as soon as the difficulties of governing against the grain of the postwar settlement became apparent, this administration, like its predecessors, would not be brought round by a series of U-turns, to consensual corporatism.

Appearances were never more misleading. In retrospect there is a brilliant simplicity to the Thatcherite strategy for dealing with the crisis which her government inherited: it was to avoid being impaled upon the hook which had entangled all governments since 1945, namely the problem of achieving with organised labour a long-term *agreement* capable of holding the rise of earnings below an inflationary threshold while accumulating a surplus sufficient simultaneously to finance capital export, military pretensions and technological refurbishment.

Reliance upon market forces, unmediated so far as possible, to restructure and reshape the contours of the British economy was therefore as much a central principle as an ideological slogan and initial pronouncements about social harmony were no more than a public relations sedative. Incomes policy was out and macro-wage agreements were no longer sought. It was a policy which favoured materially sections of the workforce that were favourably situated in the labour market, while others would be obliged to submit to its discipline. To make that discipline effective, trade union power had to be curtailed dramatically, indeed the whole culture of capital–labour relations as it had evolved for over a century put into reverse. Nevertheless, the government would refrain from launching the kind of immediate all-out frontal assault which would be likely to unify the trade union movement and possibly lead on to a repetition of the Heath scenario. Instead, it would proceed by stages and always on ground of its own choosing.

Nor was it only the labour market that was to be freed from institutional restrictions and supports, but those for capital and commodities as well. A measure of deep strategic significance, in appearance so technical as to evoke no vehement or widespread reaction, was to lift all remaining foreign exchange controls and thereby remove any last restrictions upon capital export. Moreover, the Heathite 'lame ducks' rhetoric would now be taken wholly seriously, and decrepit enterprises (or whole industries) in trouble were never again bailed out by public funding, regardless of the social cost involved. This was certainly a good deal more contentious than the arcane mysteries of exchange control, but it was felt to be within the government's strength to enforce. Meantime a strict deflationary policy would put an additional squeeze upon companies which were incapable of controlling their labour costs or too profligate in other respects. The implications for the industrial economy were foreseen and accepted. Whole swathes of it that were not fully competitive in terms of the world market would have to disappear, in the same way and for the same reasons that major sections of British agriculture had been devastated a century earlier. In their place a smaller but efficient low-wage industrial sector, based to a great extent upon imported capital, would compete dynamically in those divisions of the international market where a comparative advantage could be secured, while indigenous British capital concentrated upon doing the things it did best – operating financial services and making loans.

The project of large-scale denationalisation was no less a brilliant initiative – even in such a detail as the term invented to define it, privatisation, which sounded at once both more positive and less bureaucratic. As with the macro-economic strategy, it was in principle a simple and straightforward move with multiple payoffs. At a stroke (to recall the phrase which had come to haunt the luckless Edward Heath) it relieved the government of ultimate responsibility for these enterprises and, above all, for their losses and their customer dissatisfaction. It provided a very welcome financial killing for the institutions, the banks, advertising agencies and suchlike, which handled the details of

the transfers and eventually bought most of the shares; especially it represented a tremendous propaganda coup in the aggressive marketing of
shares to the general public, the person-in-the-street who could afford
to buy them, as a much better version of the football pool, a cost-free
investment that could not fail to be profitable, perhaps hugely profitable.
In this, as the eventual uptake of the share issues demonstrated, the
Thatcher government impressively mobilised in its own interest the
acquisitive responses inculcated by the consumer society of the previous
three decades.

These same responses, combined with anti-bureaucratic longings, were
witnessed in the no less successful project of selling municipally owned
houses at a discount to their owners and compelling the local authorities to accept offers to buy. Undoubtedly, the policy proved to be widely
popular. It appealed to whatever resentments might exist among tenants
about council housing administration, from slowness of repair work to
enforced uniformity of outside decor; it appealed to a very widespread
sense of injustice (however unjustified) that a tenant could pay rent for
a working lifetime and have nothing concrete to show for it in the end;
it appealed to simple acquisitiveness and to status ambitions. As with the
notion of 'people's capitalism' represented by the privatisation share issues,
it was intended to create an enlarged Conservative constituency, to
generate a popular vested interest in the continuance of Conservative
rule, to cut the social root of labourism.

In the face of a well articulated and cunningly devised social assault,
the Labour Party and the left especially, concentrated on its internal constitution and machinery, together with the question of its leading
personnel. The Wilson–Callaghan debacle and the discredit of the
right which accompanied it inspired the conviction that the time had
come to take the movement away from its habitual betrayers, entrench
the left in control, and begin to campaign for and educate the electorate
in the socialist objectives which the movement now prepared to
embrace. An unrepeatable opportunity was at hand.

The right in the party was on the defensive: their loss of the initiative,
their unfamiliarity with that situation and their resentment at finding
themselves in it, betrayed them into severe tactical misjudgments which
the left used to good advantage. Disconcerted by the turn of events,
leading right-wing personalities exhibited publicly their elitist and
administratively-orientated postures, displayed their arrogance and
disdain for constituency activists, whom they plainly regarded as unrepresentative of public opinion and not to be taken seriously. Evidence
from Labour Party activists to an internal commission in the course of

1979 revealed a very strong majority for constitutional reform, a 'groundswell of support'.[23]

Finally, the left managed to coalesce in order to seize advantage of the opportunity. The Rank and File Mobilising Committee was established in 1980 as a front uniting the Socialist Campaign for a Labour Victory, the Campaign for Labour Party Democracy, the Labour Coordinating Committee, Independent Labour Publications, the Institute for Workers' Control, the National Organisation of Labour Students and the Clause 4 group, to be joined subsequently by Militant, the Labour Party Young Socialists, Labour Action for Peace and the Socialist Educational Association.

The front was unified by five specific objectives, all of them internal to the Labour Party and all of a constitutional nature. These were:

• defence of mandatary selection procedures;
• defence of the NEC structure;
• the control of election manifestos by the NEC rather than the parliamentary leadership;
• the election of the Leader and Deputy Leader by the Party as a whole;
• the accountability of open and democratic decision making by the PLP.

In the runup to the 1979 Labour Party Conference, the RFMC organised 20 rallies around the country to mobilise support for the proposed reforms. Behind them all stood the principle of a single objective, namely to deplete the constitutional power of the distrusted parliamentarians and transfer it so far as possible to the rank and file. The combination of a political tide set in their favour combined with skilful strategy and intelligent tactics brought to the Labour Party left the greatest successes it was ever to achieve, but, in the words of Patrick Seyd:

> ...concentration on political advance through these internal structural reforms was at the expense of developing a radical programme which combined intellectual credibility, practical application and popular support.[24]

The essence of the left's error was in the presumption that a left wing programme would be self-validating with the electorate, that it only needed to be put before the voters to generate spontaneous acceptance, thus that its viability could be taken for granted. On the part of the traditonal Labour left that assumption could be made in the expectation that the moral superiority and attachment to community values embodied in a socialist programme would carry self-evident conviction.

For the newer, Marxist-orientated or explicitly Marxist tendencies, the conviction was rather different, although it had the same practical consequences. In these circles it was supposed that socialism represented the inherent natural consciousness of the working class (who of course constitute the overwhelming majority of voters), and if this was unhappily overlaid by a trade union, sectional or even deferentially reactionary mentality, that would soon be dissolved by the enlightenment carried on the wings of a socialist Labour Party campaigning with socialist slogans.

> ...objective, or structural class position is the primary determinant of social and political identities and alignments ... there are structural tendencies towards unification of the working class ... as compared with other radical forces it has a special ... connexion with the struggle for socialism.[25]

Geras is far too subtle a thinker to be convicted of economic reductionism and his formulation is one that would have been acceptable prior to the mid 1970s to anyone who regarded themselves as a Marxist. The problem with it is that experience confers no warrant for believing it to be true to the dominant realities of working class history in the world during the past century – instance the USA, let alone Northern Ireland – and certainly not in Britain. There is no intrinsic reason to expect the working class in this country to have developed a hegemonic consciousness, the peculiarity requiring explanation would have been if (like the Russian in 1917) it had actually done so.

The exposure of these weaknesses however was still a matter for the future. The struggles of 1979–81 marked the climax of the long contest which had been waged between right and left since 1945, and for a lengthy period the left triumphed everywhere. The success was spread over the autumn Conference of 1980 and the Wembley Special Conference in January 1981, where the essence of the constitutional changes being demanded were endorsed, above all mandatory reselection and the election of Leader and Deputy Leader by trade union and constituency representation as well as by parliamentarians. Shortly thereafter, in the Greater London Council elections, Labour not only evicted a proto-Thatcherite administration of the capital but elevated to the leadership of the new Council a radical left-wing caucus presided over by Ken Livingstone. As it turned out, they were to pursue a far more sophisticated and less 'economist' strategy than the character of the Labour left at large would have suggested. In fact, the GLC under Livingstone was to achieve the most significant transcendence of labourism to which the Party was ever to rise. Regrettably, the strategic collapse of the Party itself ensured that this local government would become one of the most celebrated Thatcherite victims and exist for no more than a further five years.

Even as the left were acclaiming the outcome of the Wembley Conference, the local government victory, and opinion polls recording an unprecedented depth of government unpopularity, the signs were already clear of a fatal disposition to give priority to internal party considerations as against serious engagement with a deeply conservative popular culture and sentiment. The election of a new leader in succession to Callaghan proved indicative. Michael Foot, whatever his personal qualities, was a wretched choice to undertake such a responsibility. To be sure, Foot was elected solely by the Parliamentary Labour Party, the last election to take place on such terms, but the outcome would probably not have been different if the new system had been in operation. Seyd's comment that the decision was '... saddling the Party with a Leader who lacked the necessary communicative skills to appeal to a wider body of voters than the Party activists'[26] is a masterpiece of restrained understatement. The elevation of Foot as Leader made only too plain that labourism was incapable of *understanding*, let alone resisting, what the Thatcherite offensive entailed, for he was an individual about as manifestly ill-equipped as it was possible to be to lead a life-and-death defence of the imperilled postwar consensus against a government determined to destroy it. The only rationale there could be for selecting him was to be found in terms of the Party's own predicaments – he could be seen as a potentially unifying figure (one is tempted to say figurehead) – a stopgap solution in the form of a former leftwing wildman who had never renounced his outlook but had shown himself in practice to be politically harmless and anxious at all costs to placate the warring factions and to paper over the yawning rifts within the movement. It can be said to his credit that he could never be mistaken for an authoritarian, but that was not the reason for his election.

Conflict within the PLP

The defection in March 1981, after several months of consciously prolonged suspense, of three Party eminences, either current or former MPs, to join up with Roy Jenkins as the Gang of Four and launch the Social Democratic Party, was a more ambiguous development, though no less disastrous. All were graduates of the school of Gaitskellite atlanticism and totally out of place in a Labour Party which was cate-

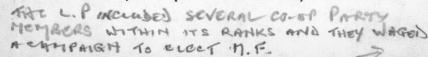

THE L.P INCLUDED SEVERAL CO-OP PARTY MEMBERS WITHIN ITS RANKS AND THEY WAGED A CAMPAIGN TO ELECT M.F. →

gorically abandoning that position and writing unilateral nuclear disarmament into its policy objectives. One of them, David Owen was an unreconstructed worshipper of British great power fetishes who had disapproved of the Labour Party's stance over the Suez invasion. Neither were they people with any popular base among trade unionists or constituency activists; they were utterly dependent for their high positions upon the maintenance of the Party's traditional structures of hierarchy and patronage. It is doubtful whether they could have been reconciled on any basis to the constitutional and policy changes which were occurring, being as they were frustrated and disgruntled careerists, with an outlook best summed up in the words of one of their forerunners and subsequent adherents, Dick Taverne:

> Why then did I not join the Liberal Party? Because I could never quite see the Liberals breaking through on their own. They had a smell of failure associated with them. They had been in Opposition since 1920. So the Liberals were no longer associated with power. And that still holds true today. If there is a difference between Social Democrats and Liberals it's not in philosophy but in attitude. The Liberals are less realistic in formulating policy and the Social Democrats, having had experience in Government, are more practical and realistic.[27]

It is a most revealing passage, for it displays a politician animated by no smidgeon of principle, only a raw appetite for office and the best tactics to pursue it. It is not, however, the personal shortcomings of the founders of the SDP, blatant though these were, nor the even more repulsive sight of minor labour politicians speeding towards its embrace when threatened with deselection or loss of other assured privilege, that was centrally important, but rather the fact that for many thousands of honest and concerned people, inside or outside the Labour Party, it arrived as a new dawn, which should have been a warning to the left. The response to the declaration of the SDP's establishment, the flood of recruits, the enthusiasm, commitment and sincerity which its rank and file displayed in the early days, highlighted the extent to which the Labour Party had succeeded in alienating one of its natural constituencies, the conscience-motivated lower middle class who had *not* identified with one or other variant of revolutionary tradition and in whose eyes the Party had become identified with sectional selfishnesses, militant dogmatism or squalid political manoeuvre. The Party leadership, conscious of the electoral implications rather than of the social meaning of what was happening, tried to persuade the defecting parliamentarians and councillors to remain, but the attitude of the left, even

THE CAMPAIGN WAS BOTH NAT^L & LOCAL
AND WAS PURSUED AGAINST LABOUR TO SEE
THE SOCIAL DEMOCRAT PARTY FORMED & L.P DEFEATED

more shortsighted, was to wish good riddance to traitors and renegades, to feel gratified that the purge was happening of its own accord rather than needing to take place against entrenched resistance and opposition.

The classic fabric of labourism, as constructed in the early years of the century and consolidated during the postwar consensus, was splitting apart and the advance of the left was the consequence rather than the cause of the party's debacle. Within the body of the leaders and activists who remained committed to the Labour Party, both on the right and the left, the quality of classic labourism that was most in evidence was sectarianism, the inability to imagine or to accord legitimacy to any form of progressive politics outside the corporate institutions of the labour movement. Institutional loyalty, on the right, remained the focus and the overriding concern. While there might be sympathy, more or less overt, for the sentiments of the defectors, the permanence of the two-party system was viewed to all intents and purposes as a law of nature, the loyalties of the voting public assumed to be fixed and no change in the traditional parameters regarded as even imaginable. The safety of the authority, recognition and status enjoyed or anticipated from a career in labour movement politics was preferable to the gamble of staking everything on a new political formation, even if that were more ideologically compatible. It was an outlook in which principle coincided with calculation. On the left too, sectarianism was as much, indeed more, in evidence, although its form might differ. Here the commitment to a closed mental universe prevailed, the inability to appreciate or respond imaginatively to the fears and concerns of people who failed to share the left's interpretation of the world. As Seyd puts it:

(the left's)... concentration on political advance through these internal structural reforms was at the expense of developing a radical programme which combined intellectual credibility, practical application and popular support.[28]

The crippling presumption continued that a left programme only required to be advanced confidently and unhesitatingly by a Labour Party leadership for its logic and rightness to become as evident to the electorate at large as they already were to the left itself: it displayed a touching if unreal faith in the powers of rational persuasion. If these policies were only *campaigned* for energetically enough, they could not fail to win. In the triumphalist atmosphere produced by the collapse of the right's organisational supremacy the more sceptical, less embattled approaches generated during the previous decade in the women's liberation movement, expressed in the 'Beyond the Fragments' conference and literature, and embodied to a degree in the GLC administration, were submerged if not swept aside.

The Deputy Leadership Election

The fatal concentration on internal organisation, the emphasis on winning positions and resolutions as the key to political change and ideological success, became an ailment which assumed fever proportions in the campaign during the summer of 1981 to elect Tony Benn as Deputy Leader of the Labour Party in place of Denis Healey.

In concrete terms the issue at stake might appear fairly secondary, one individual as against another for a subordinate and largely honorary position. Yet it proved to be the most divisive and embittered of all the conflicts within the Party since the left had begun to assert itself. Its importance was of course symbolic, and a titanic struggle over the meaning of the labour movement's history and the perspective of its future was concentrated into this electoral battle. Healey was easily the most able and charismatic of the old-guard Labour politicians, an atlanticist and cold-warrior in the mould of Ernest Bevin, if a far more intelligent one; just that bit too aggressively right wing to achieve his designated place as Callaghan's successor in the leadership.[29] Benn had, in the course of the 1970s, declared himself the standard-bearer of the left, both in its older form of parliamentary caucus and also the quasi-mass movement which had emerged since 1974. He spoke the language of traditional moral radicalism at the same time as that of class politics and the labour metaphysic in a manner which made him more than acceptable to the greater part of the Marxist left even while he avoided specific identification as a Marxist. Even those fully-fledged Leninists who, distrusting Benn's past and moral discourse, regarded him as a centrist, still viewed his election as major index of transformation within the Labour Party and passionately supported his campaign.

It would be unhistorical to heap retrospective blame upon the left for going down this road, even if its outcome was ultimately disastrous and nearly terminal for the Labour Party. The Labour right was disintegrating. The party leader was self-evidently a provisional stopgap; the left, however shakily, was united in the meantime. Catacalysmic changes had taken place at the constitutional level amounting to an internal revolution. Few obstacles remained to drafting an election manifesto of a properly socialist character and ensuring a draft of parliamentary candidates who were prepared to take it seriously. It seemed natural, inevitably, to want to consolidate this position by putting into the Deputy Leadership a person who had been in the forefront of the process, who might then reasonably expect to inherit Foot's position and so give the party a Leader who was totally identified with the new dispensation, or who at least owed everything to the extra-parliamentary left.

Benn only just failed to win. Supposing that he had done so, what outcome could have been expected in that event? The morale of the left, already high, would of course have expanded prodigiously. It is more than probable that Foot, having backed Healey, would have found his position impossible and resigned shortly thereafter and that Benn, well in the ascendant, would have succeeded to the leadership without much difficulty. It is no less probable that the flow of Labour MPs and members into the SDP would have taken on flood-like dimensions as those opposed to the trend of events for either principled or opportunist motives saw their worst political nightmares irreversibly realised. The rifts in the trade union movement produced by the contest would inevitably have widened and even those unions most loyal to the Labour Party connexion could not have failed to find themselves in difficulties so far as they were obliged to reflect the feelings of a membership far from committed to the left. Notoriously, some of the union executives at the 1981 conference had cast their votes for Benn in the face of good evidence that the bulk of their membership thought otherwise. The likelihood of Labour being reduced to third-party status after the subsequent election would have been high.

It is possible that out of such a trauma might have emerged a Labour Party that would have reversed the wrong turn of 1900 when the decision was made to concentrate on parliamentary representation as *the* priority and which would have gone on to fulfil the classic dream of the left, a Labour Party which set out to address as a long-term project the construction of an hegemonic socialist consciousness within British society – possible, but not very likely! Any such scenario omits the realities of the interaction, which existed in the early 1980s, between the left and the audience it had to win outside its own ranks. Once again Seyd sums it up:

> The Labour Left also needed to recognise that the manner in which it conducted its debates within the Party was crucial to its long-term success. The Labour Left needed to create a Party in which there was trust of Party leadership, there was respect for the views of the individual Party member, and in which intra-party debate was tolerated. There should have been a respect for minority points of view and a recognition that paper majorities were inadequate. Arguments

needed to be won by the strength of the case and not by the strength of the vote. There also needed to be no place within a democratic socialist party for the practice of democratic centralism.[30]

In fact, the transitory unity of the left was unable to survive Benn's defeat, not a good prognostication for what the future would have been if he had succeeded. In the months which followed however, it was not the factional struggles and manoeuvres (though these continued, in a lower key, to dominate the Labour Party's existence) but rather dramatic events on the public world stage which were to set the character and direction for the culminating stage of labourism's decline.

5   The Thatcher Period 1981–87

A New Approach to Government

If the defeat of the Labour government in 1951 marked not the eclipse of labourism but rather the beginning of its consolidation in the consensus regime of the 1950s, a very different outcome succeeded the fall of the 1974–79 administration. A marked degree of opportunism, pragmatism and sensitivity to the main chance certainly characterised the incoming Thatcher administration, but there can be no doubt that the leading circles of this government, and in particular Thatcher herself, had in mind a conscious and deliberate project of undoing not merely the corporatist measures and the consensus institutions developed under her immediate predecessor, but the whole direction of civil society in Britain since World War II at least.

The Thatcher period which followed was one of fiercely interacting contradictions, not least within the collective consciousness of the British masses themselves. The contradictions between expanding wealth and deepening poverty, between north and south Britain, between England, particularly southern England, and the subject nationalities, are only the most evident and glaring. No less significant are the contradictions between a majority, or at least very widespread, endorsement of the Thatcher programme and even more emphatic dislike of particular major elements within it, between acquiescence in the project and sympathy for its victims; within the government's own discourse an appeal to democratic concepts and tradition contrasted with its implacable confinement of power and decision-making to Westminster and Whitehall, emphasis on family values and sexual constraint indissolubly connected with attitudes which made a billion pound business out of pornographic phone messages. Between these sets of contradictions, the upper and nether millstones of the Thatcher era, labourism was ground to powder both institutionally and ideologically.

The Labour governments of the 1960s and 1970s had, in their different ways, destroyed the moral consensus around labourism. In both decades these governments had been suspended on the hook of the relative competitive disadvantage suffered by British manufacturing industry and the priority accorded to capital export. In the 1970s it faced a world economic recession in addition. The first two Wilson governments had tried to institute a corporatist solution against the trade union movement, the latter two (and Callaghan's) in concert with it. Both had failed. In the process, the moral capital of the postwar settlement had been badly overdrawn, not least because both these administrations had never hesitated to call upon it to underpin their corporatist rhetoric, Wilson's attempted evocation of the Dunkirk spirit being only the most notorious instance. In consequence, the community as well as the corporatist values enshrined in the settlement had become devalued so that, well before 1979, labourism was ceasing to be the commonsense of British society – although certain elements of the settlement did continue to retain their popularity, like islands surviving after an inundation.

With a long-term ideological preparation extending over two decades, from the isolated and quixotic Thorneycroft of 1957 through Powell in the late 1960s to the right wing think tanks of the 1970s, the reactionary ideologues had found growing resonance with significant elements of the popular mood[1] as well as with strategic sections of the Conservative leadership. The incoming Thatcher government was therefore well equipped, both ideologically and temperamentally, to initiate a comprehensive break in British social and political history, with labourism as the principal victim. The centrepiece of the strategy was systematically to destroy the power of its adherents in their major social strongholds – the central government machine, local government apparatuses and the trade union movement. The corporate polity was henceforth dead, with even the authorised spokespersons of organised capital – especially manufacturing capital – being kept at arms length.

The attack within the central government machine came first and ranged comprehensively, embracing everything and everyone from leading Conservative politicians who clung to a consensus outlook – the 'wets', through promotions in the senior civil service – 'is he one of us?', to the advisory and fund-allocating bodies concerned with every manner of social issue and practice, the quangoes. These latter, stigmatised as unaccountable and irresponsible, were subjected to a rhetoric threatening their total abolition although in practice what was more likely to happen was the redefinition of their responsibilities, the restructuring of their organisation and the alteration of their personnel to make them more compliant with central government direction.

For the local government structure there could, of course, be no
question of abolition. The objective here was drastically to curtail the
independent powers, both financial and otherwise, of these authorities,
to reduce or eradicate their ability to respond to their electorates'
labourist aspirations, and to compel them to exercise such powers they
were allowed to retain under the direction and for the purposes
prescribed by central government. Local authorities were to be made
primarily responsible to Westminster and the courts rather than to
their electors. The pre-election commitment to some form of devolution
in Scotland was, of course, abandoned forthwith.

The Conservatives had learned from the dramatic confrontations
during the 1960s and 1970s of the trade union movement with both
Conservative and Labour governments. Two vital government strategies
of these former times were recognised as counterproductive and
abandoned. The first of these was the attempt to bind trade union leaderships more intimately to the government and to induce them to
take responsibility for government industrial strategy and measures.
The second was trying to make individual trade unionists responsible
in their own persons for breaches of labour legislation. This could
result in leaders or rank and file members ending up in prison for civil
disobedience in the name of democracy, with consequent bad publicity.
Instead, the long dreamed of aspiration of the tory rank and file activists
was to be made a reality; the unions would be stripped of their legal
immunities in the field of industrial action and permitted to operate there
only under the most restrictive and tightly-defined conditions. These
were of course designed to make effective action as difficult as could
be or even altogether impossible, while trade unionists who defied the
courts were not to be punished individually and given the opportunity
to appear as martyrs but would render the collective property of their
unions liable to unlimited legal confiscation. The strategy had the
secondary advantage of allowing the government to disclaim responsibility for actions by public employers, police or courts which it was
in reality directing. In the belief that union militancy was essentially a
product of leadership and that trade unionists at large were more sympathetic than their officials to the government's direction, ballots were
made compulsory preliminaries to any decision to initiate industrial action
or establish a political levy as well as for appointment to certain executive
offices.

There is every likelihood that these measures, especially those designed
to curb strikes in public services, were viewed with general public
approval. As one commentator expressed it, 'the commuters waiting on

a crowded railway platform for a train delayed or cancelled for the umpteenth time by industrial action finally began to listen to the saloon-bar loudmouth declaring that strikes ought to be banned and shop stewards shot.' The sharply accelerating unemployment that followed from the government's financial policies of restricting the money supply was certainly less popular, especially when inflation did not at first retreat significantly, and by late 1981 the government's poll ratings were beginning to plummet. Undoubtedly they would have sunk even further if the Labour Party had not been perceived at the same time to be in such disastrous shape.

The disaster did not relate only to its frenzied disorganisation and internal catfight, bad as these were for the public image, but even more detrimentally to the paralysis of thinking which overcame the labour movement, the Labour Party and its left wing above all, in the early 1980s. The fatal incapacity was manifested in several dimensions but especially the inability to cope with Thatcherism as a qualitatively new phenomenon in British politics and the inability to identify, let alone respond to, the crisis of labourism that was overtaking the movement itself and all its formations.[2]

Instead, traditional responses were deployed in the face of new issues constantly being thrust forward by an aggressively innovatory and hostile government and labourism bypassed and isolated even as it struggled fumblingly to engage. The dialectic of regressive modernisation and reactionary populism simply could not be grasped within the political terms in which the labour movement had been schooled. The slogan 'the personal is political' was one which had achieved a certain popularity among the left, or some parts of it, in the later 1970s, especially under the influence of the feminist movement. The Thatcherites may not have used the phrase as such, but their approach was one which embodied the concept, giving it a reactionary twist. Against the increasingly threatened consensus of collective provision and community protection they launched a moral rhetoric of individual choice and responsibility integrated through market relationships, drawing upon and appealing to deeply buried elements in the national psyche which had never died even in the years of the welfare state: attitudes of hatred and contempt towards scroungers and able-bodied or undeserving recipients of welfare, a national heritage from the era of the Poor Law of punitive social authoritarianism, stigmatising any individual unable to take full economic responsibility for themselves and their families as morally reprobate. It was an ideological posture which had as a corollary positive enthusiasm for the erection of the strong state needed to protect the respectable against the victims of revived Victorian values. As the logic of a consumer society eroded the foundations of the postwar settlement from within, Margaret Thatcher renewed on her own terms an ancient compact between market acquisitiveness and traditional prejudice and expressed the aspirations of her social constituency in tones of strident authoritarianism which terrified where they did not enthuse. On the field of ideological conviction, where its strength might have been expected to be most in evidence, the labour movement was hopelessly outmanoeuvered and the left was never even in the contest.

Even so, it might not have been enough, for the strategy of solving the perennial problem of enfeebled British manufacturing industry by simply letting it die through government non-intervention and tight monetarist policy generated such mayhem, with rocketing unemployment and consequent social distress, that for all the Labour Party's concurrent tribulations, the polls indicated a public verdict of great unpopularity. The Thatcherite economic strategy was both simplistic and incoherent and the Thatcherite moral–political rhetoric might well have died along with its failure. What it needed was time to realise the enormous assets of North Sea oil and asset-stripping in the public sector. That time was made available to the Conservative government by the opportunity to exploit another set of traditional English atavisms.

The Falklands War

The Falklands War is generally considered to have been the turning point in the initial phase of Thatcherism and to have changed a very insecure political entrenchment into a virtually impregnable one, not because of the reality of the war of course, but its presentational handling. Two sorts of popular tradition and memory were mobilised together: the nostalgia of imperial sentiment and contempt for lesser breeds, and the recollection of World War II and mortal conflict with dictatorship. For the first time in decades the popular press began to remind its readers of the existence of Fascism and the fact that the Argentine regime was of that sort. Just to make certain however, an unprecedented degree of governmental control and even intimidation was imposed upon the broadcasting media and even the press so far as possible to ensure that these institutions did not falter in their patriotic duty. The government spokesman, Ian Macdonald, was certainly be mocked for his dalek-like delivery, but there was no audible challenge to the content of what he had to say. There can now be no serious doubt that the ruling circle fully appreciated the potential political asset such a war could be, was determined to pursue it and deliberately sabotaged peace initiatives that could have avoided it. A *Private Eye* cartoon published in the aftermath summed it up: it showed a gravestone in the Falklands topped with a bust of Thatcher and the legend, 'They Died to Save Her Face'.

Nonetheless it was an enormous gamble. If the war had been lost, as could easily have happened given the scale of logistical problems and the usual level of military incompetence, Thatcher's political career would have been abruptly over. A scenario of government failure, either before or after the commencement of hostilities, undoubtedly existed in the minds of the Labour leadership, but it does them little credit, for their words and behaviour suggests that what they foresaw was themselves implementing the military option more effectively than the government could. They too were haunted by the ghosts of the past, in this case one of the supreme as well as most dramatic moments of labourist achievement, April 1940. In such a vision, Margaret Thatcher stood for Neville Chamberlain, disgraced by his handling of the Norwegian campaign, and Michael Foot for Attlee – or possibly even Churchill. As Anthony Barnett puts it,

> Foot was Churchill and Foot was Bevan, rolled into one. He was the John Bull of the Labour movement; the world statesman confronted by the forces of evil; righteous and determined he spoke for the whole, united House. Foot called for action ... Only 30 [tory] fanatics would be needed to march into the lobby behind Michael Foot and Douglas Jay to bring down the appeasers.[3]

In the event the Labour leadership committed itself just as enthusiastically as any Conservative to the dispatch of the warfleet and the military campaign. During the crucial Commons debate of 3 April, presumably in collusion with the Speaker, none of the dissenting voices were allowed to be heard. The Labour front bench had to live with the consequences, a tide of English nationalist hysteria and the deification of Thatcher so that subsequent attempts in a more sober mood to question some elements of government behaviour during the crisis carried no conviction, apart from Tam Dalyell's isolated crusade – but he was only a backbencher and Scottish at that! The general indifference of public feeling in the non-English nations to the mighty conquest was a pointer to the extent to which Thatcher was in the course of constructing her regime upon a foundation of the deliberately cultivated sentiments of English nationalist irrationalism.

The General Election campaign of the following year represented the payoff for a strategy of risktaking which had proved to be extravagantly successful. In spite of the fact that unemployment stood at an all time high and none of the other main economic indicators were particularly favourable, the worst depths of the early 1980s recession were by then in the past, offshore oil production was beginning to make its mark and sufficient people were feeling an improvement in living standards or had hopes of doing so, to establish a solid electoral base for the Conservative Party that reached far into the manual working class and the ranks of trade unionists. Institutional loyalty among large swathes of their membership was insufficient to make the attack which the government had conducted upon their rights and organisation into a serious electoral liability. So far as government-directed economic stringency persisted, it could be and was presented in Crippsian terms as the necessary purgative for overindulgent and flabby lifestyles and standards of work.

For the labour movement it was the political nadir. The ability of a government not just to survive but to record huge electoral gains in the face of unprecedented unemployment rates made it only too clear how far the postwar settlement, to which labourism was indissolubly bound, was disintegrating and ceasing to accord with the unreflecting conceptions of the electorate. There was in addition the circumstance that organisationally, strategically and politically the Labour Party itself was in hopeless disarray. Reflecting the ascendancy of the left, still very considerable even after its high tide had passed in 1981, the specific proposals and promises contained in its election manifesto made it probably the most radical document ever issued by this party; but it was only too obvious that they constituted a mere catalogue of objectives, incoherently assembled. Lacking any unified strategic conception or notion as to how they could be achieved practically other than by employing the sovereign fiat of Parliament, they amounted to a most unconvincing presentation.

Central to this list was the manifesto commitment to nuclear disarmament by the British state within the lifetime of the next Labour government, sensible enough in itself, but not advanced in a manner that could hope to overcome the by now ingrained prejudice in favour of nuclear weapons in the majority public mind. No plausible overall policy for armaments accompanied the commitment. Party spokespeople on this issue were particularly bumbling and inept, often not bothering to conceal their unhappiness with it and frequently contradicting each other. It was combined, moreover, with an assertion of continuing attachment and loyalty to NATO but without any stress on the fact that the majority of NATO members are non-nuclear powers. In short, there was no sense of perspective, either in explaining why a break with the bipartisan foreign and defence policies of the previous 40 years was required, or else in demonstrating that they could be intelligently continued under a non-nuclear dispensation. Not unexpectedly either, internal war over this question broke out again between the wings of the party in the very course of the election campaign. The official defence spokesperson, Denis Healey did his best to play it down and avoid discussing it – and it showed; the former leader Jim Callaghan, went so far as to denounce it, and was in turn vehemently denounced by the left.

Under the pitiless glare of the television lights all Michael Foot's personal virtues became public disasters, the quirks in his appearance, comportment and speech were mercilessly exposed before the national audience, so that he emerged looking like a well-intentioned idiot who didn't have the first idea about running a government and who, should he have the misfortune to be elected premier, would be quickly devoured by the left-wing fiends surrounding him. Many a left-winger who would have been appalled at the prospect three years before, was heard fervently wishing that Denis Healey had succeeded in the leadership election.

As it happened, these crippling drawbacks combined with the peculiarities of the British electoral system to further disadvantage Labour. All its confidence in 'moderate' consensus, in the ability of ethically motivated experts to bring about administrative solutions on an agreed basis to social problems – the Fabian-Keynesian tradition in other words – seemed to have been transferred to the Alliance parties, together with the elan and determination springing from such confidence. Perhaps it was appropriate that the SDP stole the name of R H Tawney for its theoretical think-tank. Facing a divided, discredited, stigmatised and demoralised Labour Party, the Alliance sponged up the vital middle class vote in the marginal constituencies, particularly the southern ones, thereby hopelessly dividing the anti-Conservative majority where one existed. The eventual outcome was an electoral triumph parallel to that of 1945, only for a different party and one that marked a shift in public consciousness nearly as profound as the earlier one.

The tories at least, following their catastrophe in 1945, were united under the leadership of a charismatic and world renowned figure, apart from all the other advantages which tories habitually possess. After the debacle of 1983 Labour had no such security. It is not unimaginable that the political bitterness and rancour within the party, combined with the

Alliance capture of a large part of its electorate and the shambles inside its organisation, could have finally torn it apart and sent the pieces spinning across the breadth of the political spectrum.

Attacks on Labourism

That did not happen, because in the crisis another labourist instinct asserted itself more strongly, that for survival. Michael Foot, as was inevitable, stepped down and a right/left ticket was constructed which was capable of attracting the thankful votes of the overwhelming majority both inside and outside Westminster as well as definitively marginalising the irreconcilable left, increasingly grouped around Tony Benn. The person of Neil Kinnock embodied the gains that the mainstream left had made since the 1970s; his dissociation from Tony Benn and vote against him in 1981 signalled its self-restraint. Unhappily, the events of the four years that followed were also to reveal his short-sightedness.

The sweeping electoral victory they had gained and what it suggested about the popular mood gave the Thatcherites the consolidation of strength they needed to embark on the second phase of their governmental project, the eradication so far as possible of the labourist universe and the dismemberment of its institutions. The sapping operations, so to speak, had taken place during the first term: the central strongholds were now subjected to frontal assault.

This undertaking brought out the real character of the British state in a manner not previously seen for centuries, an unaccountable and quasi-absolutist concentration of sovereignty which offered no constitutional impediment to a government, so long as it commanded a Commons majority, from forcing through any measure it saw fit, regardless of its unpopularity, provided there was sufficient determination behind its intentions. This form of government means that only the next general election brings a reckoning, by which time the government can hope that public indignation will have abated and acquiescence in the controversial measure taken root. On paper, a Labour administration could have followed the same kind of practice and the perennial hope of the left was to find one which would do so. However, the two situations are in no sense comparable. Margaret Thatcher's government was cutting with the grain, whereas an imaginary Labour counterpart would have been cutting against it. Unpopular though Thatcher's particular actions might be, in their general direction during this parliament they did not contradict the mood of the times and more importantly, if the comparison with Labour is pursued, did not offend the centres of non-elected power inside and outside the country. Since the undiluted and unconstrained sovereignty of Westminster is likewise the central fetish in the labourist metaphysic, its representatives could not attack the legitimacy of parliamentary omnicompetence and were rendered helpless by the legislative offensive; reduced to issuing plaintive appeals to their mass support to observe the properly instituted law, not as a tactic of necessity but as a dogmatic principle.

The three spearheads of the offensive were directed against the unions, the local authorities and the nationalised industries. It was not confined to legislative enactments, though these were certainly included to further undermine the power to resist. The central and, as it emerged, definitive battle was joined in resistance to a simultaneous all-out attack on the most sensitive element of the union movement and the nationalised sector together.

Coal mining and miners have occupied a very particular place in the history and traditions of the British labour movement. Their legend represented the most dramatic and spectacular class confrontations of the 20th century and what the NUM had done to Edward Heath was well remembered in government circles as much as by its opponents. It was here first of all that the Conservatives chose to test their mandate, and all, regardless of the quality of their toryism, were united in confronting the ancient enemy. Peter Walker, the archetypal 'wet', was dispatched to the Department of Energy for the occasion in order to superintend the campaign.

A scarcely disguised intention to mutilate the industry, sunder the cohesion of the communities linked to it and make its remnants fit for ultimate privatisation provoked the strike the government sought on the terrain least favourable to the miners and their supporters. The NUM was a large, decentralised and federal union made up of areas with sharply divergent social and political traditions, often in uneasy relationship with each other. The CP, for example, was more strongly entrenched in the Welsh and especially the Scottish areas than in any other sector of trade unionism; the politics of the Nottinghamshire area by contrast, were of the most far-right labourist kind. The areas represented previously independent local unions which had come together only in the course of World War II when the likelihood of postwar nationalisation had provided the incentive. Constitutionally as well as in practice each possessed a large measure of independence.

The NUM Strike

Early in 1984 the NUM leadership found itself faced with an open provocation, ostensibly from the National Coal Board, in reality from the government, by the unilateral closure of a pit contrary to agreed procedures. It also found itself in the position of having parts of its membership straining at the leash for strike action and others just as adamantly opposing it. It was a state of affairs which would have challenged the most politically adept and tactically sensitive trade union leader. Unfortunately this was exactly what the NUM did not have.

Instead in Arthur Scargill it had a President of enormous energy and ability – and equally enormous vanity; who allowed his strategic ideas to turn into obsessions and strove to surmount the material weaknesses in his position by exercises in willpower.

Three essential aspects can be identified for the year-long strike which commenced in March 1984. First, and most prominent in the public media, there were the set-piece confrontations between NUM pickets and the machinery of the state, where the force of mass picketing was deployed to try to enforce the shutdown of mines, depots and coal-using industrial plants and was combatted by even greater degrees of violent coercion on the part of a government co-ordinated police force assisted by the services of the intelligence agencies.[4]

Secondly there was the development of strike-connected community initiatives, particularly those of the women's support groups, in the mining areas which were committed to the struggle. It generated quite exceptional feelings of social solidarity and in some places developments amounted almost to a mini-social revolution. Thirdly, there was the dimension of relations between those directly involved either as NUM members or through the support groups with the general public outside, whether in the shape of the labour movement or the citizenry at large.[5]

The first of these aspects marked what will surely be recorded as the climax of militant labourism in Britain. It was cast entirely within the terms of traditional industrial action raised to an unprecedented peak of intensity; forceful and authoritarian. Military analogies and metaphors abounded. It was force against force and undoubtedly there were many who gloried in the opportunity for the display of masculine qualities. The news sheets of the Leninist sects especially, which interpreted the strike as a quasi-revolutionary event, exemplified this intoxication.

Although doubts were known to exist within the NUM's leading bodies, the official line was one which reflected Scargill's own outlook – mass picketing if applied strenuously enough for long enough would win, and it was a line that was continued even beyond the point when the strike was visibly collapsing. One recalls E P Thompson's comment on 'Orator' Hunt, a charismatic mass leader from an earlier era:

The demagogue is a bad or ineffectual leader. Hunt voiced, not principle or even well-formulated radical strategy, but the emotions of the moment. Striving always to say whatever would provoke the loudest cheer, he was not the leader but the captive of the least stable portion of the crowd.[6]

In the second of those dimensions however, the innovative qualities, the transcendence of gender barriers, the manner in which communities united their members in a common purpose and themselves took responsibility for their social living, rose far above the level of any labourist conceptions, whether subservient or militant. The distribution of food parcels, the organisation of entertainments, the allocation of donated Christmas presents, the welcome given to gay and lesbian support groups – the people involved spoke later of the depth of emotional experience which had accompanied their participation, a new birth of their consciousness.

Something of that was apparent too in the relations which the mining communities and the support groups succeeded in establishing with other, less defined, communities and with major sections of the public at large irrespective of occupation or status. Unquestionably a widespread and profound feeling of sympathy for the miners' position and their case was present among other sections of the workforce and far beyond it:

I shall never forget the response of the people of Hackney; it left a deep impression on me ... the effect of collecting for the miners for the first time made me feel proud of people in this country. It wasn't just the extent of the support, it was also the way people identified with the miners' struggle and how much they wanted to make a positive contribution. In particular, the support in the ethnic and black communities was tremendous. For many of us it came as something of a surprise to see the extent of the concern in those communities for the miners' struggle ... when the miners themselves came out on collections with us ... their amazement at the response of black people was very noticeable. It was talked about endlessly, they marvelled at it.[7]

But what the sympathy did not extend to was willingness to undertake massive industrial sympathy action in defiance of the anti-union legislation implemented since 1979 and the dire consequences its terms implied for the resources of any defiant union. The effectiveness of these laws was quickly demonstrated against the miners themselves, when attempts to ignore restrictive court rulings were answered with exhorbitant fines and sequestration of assets. There can be little doubt either that the strategy and tactics identified with Scargill's leadership helped to ensure that sympathy remained passive rather than active or was even actually alienated. The government was able to derive great propaganda advantage from Scargill's implicit and sometimes even explicit encouragement of violence on picket lines and his refusal to use the obvious tactic of telling his pickets at all costs to avoid violent response to violent provocation.

The fact that the NUM was unable to bring out all its own members, that the coalfields in Derbyshire and Nottingham were overwhelmingly opposed to the strike, represented a major disincentive to sympathetic action by other unions, most vitally by NACODS, the safety technicians' union, whose withdrawal of labour would have stopped the industry forthwith. The refusal of the NUM leadership to hold a strike ballot, especially in the summer of 1984 when all indicators suggested that it would have been won, was a further weapon handed to the government. The argument against a ballot on principle, on the grounds that it would contradict the democracy of action and that those who might oppose the strike did not have the right to vote their fellow workers out of a job, was not one calculated to win over those whose conviction might have been strengthened by a successful vote. Scargill's insistence on prolonging the strike when any observer, let alone participant, could see that it was beaten, was in line with the same style of leadership, or rather non-leadership, for the decision to end a hopeless position was the result of an internal revolt on the executive which the President acquiesced in but still formally opposed. His subsequent determination to describe a total and comprehensive defeat as in fact a victory, reflected perhaps on the sense of reality with which he had conducted the strike.

As a result of his conduct, enormous reserves of loyalty, determination, imagination and initiative were recklessly squandered and a devastating blow received by the NUM, the nationalised coal industry and the trade union movement in general. Thatcher's victory here marked a most significant stage in the consolidation of her political hegemony. But if the ultimate calamity was in a large measure the outcome of Scargill's leadership – and it has to be emphasised that it was his prestige and dynamism that ensured, against considerable reservation, the undeviating pursuit of a particular strategy – the question that has to be asked is how it was possible for one individual to wield such influence within a democratic and decentralised trade union. The answer points back towards different aspects of the labourist tradition; first the formal structures of authority and decision-making which ensured that an extraordinary deference would be paid to the President and his way of seeing things as the sanctified representative of the union's collective being. Secondly, Scargill proved to be a master at deploying for his own perspectives the narratives of struggle, solidarity and sacrifice inherited from the country's history of industrial and class confrontations, the struggles pre-eminently of male skilled workers, in which militancy, strength and resolution were at a premium and where the participation of womenfolk or outsiders, though welcome, was acceptable only in subordinate and peripheral roles.

But if a heavy responsibility lies with Scargill, his partisans and those who backed him in spite of their better judgment, the leaders of the labour movement who dissented from the conduct of the strike scarcely covered themselves with glory, and the other side of the labourist coin, its incestuous relationship with the state (even a Thatcherite state) and fetishistic obsession with the British constitution, was here much in evidence. The TUC leadership offered only the most pallid and platonic support – which is not to say that they ought to have called out other sections of the workforce, for such a call would not have met with a convincing response – but their dislike of the strike on principle and reluctance to give it any endorsement was palpable; in the event only the most minimal backing was received from this source.

As a collective body the attitude of the Labour Party leaders was worse if anything, although in individual capacities many of them did not spare their energies. But the supposed collective political representative of the British working class offered no leadership or guidance. Neil Kinnock is supposed – and he has never denied it – to have regarded the months of the strike as purely wasted time, a distraction which only made it impossible for the party effectively to develop its electoral presence or to start formulating policies for the next general election. It is possible to imagine a scenario in which a powerful body like the TUC or the Labour Party had proclaimed its unconditional support for the principle of the miners' action, than bent all its efforts to making that effective so far as circumstances allowed and used that position as a basis for relentless criticism of mistaken strategy and tactics. But such an approach would have been wholly in contradiction to the character and tradition of labourist politics. It has to be said that the far left, inside and outside the Labour Party, while certainly meeting their obligations in terms of solidarity and support, did not dare to criticise either.

Local Government Under Siege

The unbridled power conferred upon central government by the nature of the British constitution emerged clearly as the regime moved on from its triumph on the industrial battlefield to subjugate recalcitrant local authorities and compel them to defer to the government's notions of retrenchment, privatisation of services and sound financial management, quite regardless of any preference that local electorates might have. The confrontation had already been building up in the course of the previous year, but during 1984 the government, preoccupied with its offensive against the NUM, had been wary of entering another major conflict which might coalesce to its disadvantage with the more central one, or at least divide its energies. Consequently, in July 1984, the Environment Secretary, Patrick Jenkin, had struck a financial deal with Liverpool city council in order to avert an immediate crisis and confrontation over an illicit deficit budget in circumstances where the militant (and Militant) new council would have enjoyed solid local labour movement and popular support. The agreement could be interpreted as a major government climb-down and was so presented by the Liverpool councillors as well as the Conservative press. The hapless Jenkin was sacked after a decent interval and the ground prepared for the enforcement of centralised authority.

The events which followed in Liverpool provided an illuminating test case, for in that city control of the new Labour council had been secured by Militant, a leftist sect which combined in itself all the worst elements of both Leninism and labourism and which followed a strategy of concealing its existence as a distinct entity in order to operate within the Labour Party.[8] It was indeed no accident that this success was achieved in Liverpool, for the Labour Party in its previous incarnation there had been especially renowned for political racketeering and machine politics, the most disreputable aspects of unchallenged control by the traditional Labour Party right. In the debacle of right wing Labour during the late 1970s Militant had been able to lay hold of that machine and direct it to its own purposes, all the more effectively in combination with the political and organisational discipline exercised by a Trotskyite faction over its adherents. Having won control on the council by means which enabled less than a dozen Militant councillors to dominate, through a series of caucuses, over 40 labour ones, it used its position to distribute municipal resources to its own front organisations, employ sympathisers in council positions, and marginalise the official leader of the council so that its affairs were effectively in the hands of the deputy leader, Derek Hatton, an authoritarian and self-indulgent publicity-seeker who strutted like a cock on a midden.[9]

The Liverpool episode was, however, only one aspect of the offensive conducted by the government against local authority power, with a central thrust directed against their financial autonomy and accompanied with compulsion to make them farm out numerous municipal services to private bidders and sell off quantities of municipal assets, especially housing. Curtailment of the share of direct government funding in council budgets forced substantial rate increases by councils which treated the maintenance of services as their chief priority. When this proved insufficient to alienate local electorates and so induce them to throw out Labour councils, the governemnt resorted to rate-capping, the legal limitation of the extent of rate increase.

In response to the challenge a number of large Labour authorities, including Liverpool and London, adopted early in 1985 a tactic of defiant illegality in refusing to set a rate. It did not prove to be a very formidable response for in face of threats of surcharge and disqualification (and, to be fair, genuine worries over the consequent chaos in local administration) the plan collapsed amid bitter recrimination as the local authorities capitulated.

The reaction of the Militant organisation in Liverpool was indicative of a wider and extremely important consideration, for it was this debacle which finally wrecked the increasingly strained cohesion of the far left and the tacit, if fragile, co-operation that had existed between certain of the self-proclaimed revolutionary sects and the most left wing elements within the mainstream Labour Party such as the Campaign Group. Barely-suppressed sectarian antagonisms erupted as the irresistible temptation to find traitors to blame was supplied by the surrendering councillors. The leftward momentum that had existed since the late 1970s, founded on a real if ambiguous degree of mass mobilisation within the labour movement and at the grassroots of the Labour Party, was now wholly dissipated. Inside the Labour Party the left conclusively lost the initiative; inside or outside it the sects resumed their marginality.

The Liverpool Militants had gone along with the refusal tactic though they had been openly critical of it. They now tried, in an extremely opportunist fashion, to continue the campaign out of considerations of publicity, by advancing a deficit budget. According to Michael Crick, even this was a manoeuvre, not seriously intended at first. They had hoped and expected that their own proposal would be defeated in full council and allegations of right wing treason would then relieve them of responsibility but when, against their intentions, it was passed, they had no alternative but to pursue and exploit the strategy for all the publicity it was worth, proclaiming themselves to be 'the city that dared to fight!' Again according to Crick, the national leadership found themselves extremely disturbed by the incapacity and erratic behaviour of their Liverpool subordinates. Certainly the combination of pseudo-revolutionary rhetoric with labourist patronage, intrigue and manipulation turned out to be an especially deadly mixture, culminating in September 1985 in the distribution of redundancy notices, in particularly farcical circumstances, to 31,000 members of the council workforce. Once again there was no actual intention that the workers in question should be dismissed, it was meant to be a gesture which would force the government's hand. The resulting union outrage however, exacerbated by the spectacle of Militant-supporting shop stewards delivering the notices by taxi because other trade unionists had refused to handle them, discredited Militant's militancy and provided a superb opportunity for Neil Kinnock to strengthen his grip on the Labour Party organisation, and on public regard, by denouncing them in the spotlight glare of the Labour Party Conference rostrum.[10]

Thus what had up to that point been the most successful of the leftist organisations committed effective political suicide. The government had not of course backed down over Liverpool's finances nor even suspended local government there and put in a commissioner, which would at least have been a propaganda achievement for Militant. Instead, the councillors ended the financial crisis themselves by extensive borrowing – from Swiss bankers. Apart from the fierce antagonism aroused from the beginning in certain trade unions, the loyalty and comitment extended to the Militant leadership by other sections of the council workforce and their trade union branches was dissipated irresponsibly and replaced in many cases with embittered disillusion. The behaviour of the council leaders – patronage and strongarm methods of control degenerating into ultimate farce – confirmed for the general public all their worst prejudices about the character of Leninist organisations and proved enormously valuable both to the Conservative propaganda machine and to the right wing within the labour movement. Although Militant was not extinguished on Merseyside, the events of 1984–85 ensured that it would never again exercise a predominant influence there, far less nationally.

The one thing that does emerge clearly from the Liverpool affair, however, is the similarity of Militant's methods and policies with those of the people most determined to expel it from the party – the Labour right. Militant's corrupt use of patronage and exclusion of rank and file community groups from the decision-making process has an obvious affinity with the city boss long established in the Labour right … Militant became exclusively preoccupied with the sort of policies which could make headway in a Labourist milieu.[11]

The central weakness is not hard to define and was at one and the same time the source of Militant's temporary strength. The exploitation of a combination of both right and left labourist traditions permitted a revolutionary sect to attain control for a time of a large local authority along with a substantial measure of mass support. Once it had that advantage, however, it refused to consolidate a general leftward shift among the Liverpool public by conducting any sort of dialogue with potential allies, let alone as yet uncommitted sections of the electorate. Instead, the leaders, cocooned in their revolutionary rectitude, preferred to employ the classic techniques of right-wing labour control to abort debate and assert their unconstrained supremacy.

By contrast, the GLC campaign against its own abolition showed what could be possible when an imaginative and flexible style was adopted,[12] and was all the more effective in that no single group with a revolutionary theology dominated the GLC. Not that the GLC's own performance since the Labour accession to power there had been impeccable by any means; along with the routine press distortions and slanders of extravagance, partiality and mismanagement, a degree of justified resentment was evoked by cases of leftist posturing, inefficiency and overzealous interference with established local government procedures, sometimes even authoritarian practices and misapplication of resources. The difference with Liverpool however was that in Ken Livingstone and his colleagues the GLC, working in a far less socially homogenous environment, had a leadership that was capable of learning from its mistakes and, though not always successful, genuinely tried to involve local communities, whether geographic, ethnic or sexual, not only in dialogue but in actual formation and direction of the Council's policies. In consequence the 'Say no to no say' campaign, which had the further advantage of a brilliant presentation by the Council's publicists, secured overwhelming public support among the London electorate and was successful in attracting the adherence even of many who disliked the GLC's specific policies and actions. Its strength was in the fact that it broke with the traditions of labourist appeal and campaigning. Livingstone's professed aim, to found socialist politics on an alliance of the dispossessed and by empowering them, where necessary at the expense of those comfortably situated in the labour market – whatever its actual merits or deficiencies – pointed in a similar direction and indicated at any rate an approach wholly at variance with the outlook of traditional labourism.

However, none of these things could prevent the government with its unchallengable parliamentary majority from ignoring popular sentiment in the metropolis and abolishing the GLC regardless. But it was a victory which, in terms of public perception, probably did the government more harm than good, a loss in credibility which was nevertheless from the government standpoint compensated to some extent by certain after-effects of the abolition. Although this aspect was probably not foreseen and calculated by the government's strategists, in fact a valuable propaganda tool fell into their hands. With the removal of the city-wide framework represented by the GLC some of the Labour-controlled London boroughs became more prone to indulge in leftist gesture politics, sometimes of a largely symbolic nature, sometimes with considerable material implications, which provided copy for indictment of the 'looney left' councils, naturally retailed through the media with the utmost hysteria and exaggeration.

The Effects of Consumerism – the Rich and the Poor

The basic trend of social development in the course of the decade continued to favour the regime. After the depth of recession in the early 1980s, growth was resumed, albeit on a much shrunken manufacturing base, inflation slackened and the tide of unemployment started to abate, helped by an official manipulation of the statistics unprecedented since the time of Mussolini. Nonetheless, though much overblown and wholly dependent on the uncontrolled exploitation of an irreplacable natural resource, North Sea oil, the degree of recovery was still genuine and served as the foundation for the opportunity to continue personal improvement in living standards among those members of the public fortunate enough to retain secure employment and thereby access to an expanding range of consumer products. As the labour market became increasingly segmented the favourably placed sectors of it, from well-qualified secretaries to motor workers, experienced a scarcity value which exerted a steady upward pressure upon the incomes of employees within them, a ghostly echo of the unofficial wage-bargaining of the 1950s. At the same time, the advancing public squalor which accompanied this renewed private affluence, from the deterioration of sewage and transport infrastructures to the loss of adult education opportunities, had not yet progressed far enough to constitute a serious liability for the government. In a sense, Thatcher can be seen as using up at this stage of her career the last social capital inherited from the consensus era.[13]

The extent and depth of poverty grew as well. It intensified in particular among those, overwhelmingly single, women who were excluded intrinsically by age, parenthood, or other family responsibility from the restructured labour market and were therefore entirely dependent upon state benefits which declined remorselessly in value and availability. It was prevalent too, if in a marginally less grinding fashion, among people in the overstocked segments of the labour market — again women were particularly affected, as were ethnic minorities — where plenty of takers were available for unskilled work and competition was fierce; among cleaners, home workers, the catering trades. As vertical integration between manufacturing and retail proceeded in the consumer goods industries and was integrated by information technologies to tune output and ordering to fluctuations in demand, the scope increased for the introduction of a 'core/periphery' pattern, a corps of permanent, usually skilled, employees with high pay and career prospects responsible for the ongoing and irreducible operations of the firm, and an expanding or contracting payroll of short-term or part time employees, normally unskilled, often working from their own homes and hired or fired according to the state of the consumer market. This principle proved to be capable of application in the most unexpected situations, not only in multinational supermarket chains, but among the most highly qualified labour forces, in higher education for example. Here, as the government time and again forced the reduction of these institutions' budgets they were forced, when permanent posts fell vacant, to freeze or abolish them and replace their holders with part-time or short contract staff who moved from appointment to appointment with little hope of ever securing permanent tenure, an academic sub-proletariat. A superfluity of highly qualified candidates enabled (and enables) the system to operate.

For the first time in many decades beggars, often in their early teens or younger, began to appear on the streets of major cities. In a radio interview, one boasted that he could make a comfortable living out of it and maintained a bank account, echoing sentiments expressed by the more fortunate members of the trade in other eras, such as the early 19th century, where deep and massive poverty had made begging into a routine profession. The comparison is instructive, for the conclusion to be drawn from the existence of these affluent beggars is not the one that official society assumed in both eras, that begging was a fraudulent lifestyle indulged in out of choice, but that the presence of abysmal poverty has become so taken for granted that the necessity for widespread begging has become a public assumption.

Despite the rise of begging as a growth industry and the state of affairs which this reflected, the spread of deep poverty did not constitute a central threat to the Thatcherite hegemony, for poverty was more effectively ghettoised than it had been in the 1930s when it afflicted entire populations in the heartlands of traditional industry. Although the north–south divide of the 1980s certainly resumed the trend which had been even more sharply visible in the 1930s but obscured since then by the prosperous decades, the line of division this time was on the whole more social than geographical and the relative invisibility of misery more a construct of its official presentation, of being viewed as a form of distributive, not to say retributive, justice rather than as a disgraceful scandal.

When the Prime Minister asserted with passion her commitment to Victorian values it may be surmised that the one she had chiefly in mind was the Victorian moral practice of blaming the victims – certainly not that of the total responsibility of Ministers, including Prime Ministers, for all the actions of their government. The notion of the 'two-thirds, one-third society' may be something of an oversimplification, but it undoubtedly expresses an essential truth about the character of social division in the era of late capitalism. The notorious Thatcher remark that 'society does not exist, only individuals and their families', reflected only in an extreme form the official line that the life situation of any individual was that person's own sole responsibility and that nobody else, least of all the public authorities, was under any obligation to secure to them anything more than the barest starvation-line existence; perhaps not even that. Naturally the Ministers said other things, like 'targetting benefits' and so forth, at each new curtailment, but the subtextual message was plain enough to anyone who had ears to hear, especially when interpreted through the popular newspapers. If the deterrent workhouse had not already existed in the past and become a folk bogey, Margaret Thatcher would probably have found it necessary to invent it.

Changes in Political Culture

To what extent then was there, as the Prime Minister never tired of asserting, 'No Alternative'? Certainly in the sense that no creditable political force was offering one, she was quite justified. The Labour Party was hardly in a position to claim, as they plausibly could after 1951, that their previous government's record had been a great social accomplishment unhappily cut off in its prime,[14] and to call upon the electorate to enable them once again to pick up the thread. On the contrary, that record was a source of odium not least to a very large segment of the Labour Party itself. Some still attributed it to the individual or collective failings of the people who had led that government, but more evident was a widespread, if poorly articulated, recognition that the factors which had ruined and brought down the Wilson/Callaghan administrations were structural rather than accidental or personal, a realisation that the social democratic postwar settlement had indeed run into the sand and that fundamentally new directions were required in the British economy and the tripartite corporatist system if a long-term secular decline was to have any hope of being stopped and reversed. But the Labour Party offered no convincing model of how that might be done, the only line of argument it could deploy referred to the social injustices being wrought by Thatcherism and particular isolated items of government policy. It was quite insufficient, and the shortcoming was reflected in the public perception constantly reiterated in the opinion polls and which Labour could do nothing to shift, that the tories might be harsh and uncaring but were far better managers of the economy.

Even so, fewer than half the electorate voted for them, and the sense that other alternatives might nevertheless exist, that the Thatcherite programme was never intrinsically popular but accepted in a spirit of resignation only because nothing more convincing appeared to be on offer, even among those who had lost hope of the consensus and were appalled by the Labour Party's character and behaviour, is reflected in the vote that the Alliance parties were able to attract. But since they too had little to offer beyond pieties and pious hopes, they were generally perceived in the labour heartlands as middle class, renegades and nest-featherers, and being so manifestly committed to parliamentary opportunism at all costs, their chances of making a really decisive electoral breakthrough were slight. In fact, ignoring socialist possibilities and strategies, an alternative *capitalist* programme for tackling the endemic crisis was imaginable in principle. It would still have involved severely weakening the entrenched social power of the workforce and its organisations, for the international division of labour decreed that, until that took place, investment in British productive industry must continue to stagnate, but that could have been traded off against a programme of a Japanese style *dirigiste* renewal of the manufacturing base, a genuine youth opportunities and training scheme, and conservation or even enhancement of the communal infrastructure and the social wage and, not least, a transformation of the political and constitutional structure – all resourced, as it well might have been, by North Sea oil revenues. It is even conceivable that a government of Labour, Conservative or for that matter Alliance character could have mobilised genuine popular consent around such a project.

All that however is a matter of imagination. In the real world the intended economic restructuring was tightly yoked to extremist *laissez-faire* principles and relentless assault on the welfare system. It is hard to judge with any certainty the extent to which the government was riding a socio-economic trend that operated quite independently of its own actions, or how far it itself created the climate of which it took advantage to impose certain dogmas about the appropriate role for market forces and private initiative in preference to public direction and provision. It is true that contemporaneous governments in the USA and in Europe – even ones which called themselves socialist – were adopting broadly similar economic programmes and that Thatcherism can be reckoned to be the specifically British-conditioned form of response to a general crisis of the expansionary postwar world economic structure founded on the strong dollar and cheap energy. It is also true that the government's strategy was a good deal more pragmatic and less rigid than its ideologists liked to pretend. What were initially presented as two cardinal principles, reduced government spending and a more tightly controlled money supply, were both quietly abandoned once their unfeasibility became plain. At the same time it is hard to imagine that without such ideological zealotry at the head of the government there would not have been a more or less rapid slip back towards a consensus outlook, with the unions once again discreetly admitted to government counsels, economic intervention to save crumbling industrial sectors and the search for an agreed incomes policy.

Most likely it was a tacit recognition of such a reality that helped to numb both arms of the labour movement and render it so inept during the middle years of the decade. So closely adapted had the unions become to the corporatist system that its extinction deprived them of any sense of direction or confidence in their social role. Their division and general helplessness in face of determined aggression by the government against the miners and by Rupert Murdoch against the print unions shortly afterwards was the outcome. The movement splintered, some like the NUM adopting postures of quasi-syndicalist defiance, others like the electricians committing themselves wholeheartedly to the principles of the new judicially regulated labour market individualism, negotiating favourable single-union deals with employers at the expense of less compliant organisations and being expelled from the TUC for their pains. Most remained unhappily stuck, paralysed and pulled in different directions. In essence they awaited the restoration of the vanished relationship with government and the return of consensus resulting from a shift in government direction or else the electoral success of the Labour Party.

Labour's Unavailing Opposition

The Labour Party for its own part had little effective sense of purpose or conception of strategy to bind its antagonistic components or the disparate policies which it had inherited. It combined a commitment to the dismantling of British nuclear weapons and the removal of US ones from British territory with continued adherence to the NATO alliance and diplomatic junior partnership with the USA. In the abstract the two stances might not have been incompatible, but in terms of the role which Britain had come to serve in the alliance they certainly were. So far as an economic strategy was concerned, this cannnot be said to have really existed. No assessment was made of the lessons of the 1970s and no real appreciation of the sources of Thatcherism's ideological strength and popular penetration. So far as political strategy was concerned it amounted in essence to no more than the hope that the Government would destroy its own credibility by outrageous error or scandal while the Alliance vote evaporated. The Labour Party leaders pinned their hopes on the prospect that the Conservative government would win the next election for them. Not surprisingly, the Conservative propaganda machine concentrated upon and pitilessly exposed these confusions, contradictions and shortcomings. Labour was not helped either by its new leader's personal style, his use of long convoluted sentences, lack of confidence and impression of querulous subordination in his parliamentary confrontations with the Prime Minister.

More serious still perhaps was the failure represented by a continuing uncritical adherence to all the sacred norms of British parliamentary tradition and the institutional apparatus of government constructed on top of it, including the secret state. Consequently, in the erection of a constantly stronger state to contain the social tensions unleashed by government action, the Conservatives found no serious or very forceful barrier presented either by the parliamentary opposition or the labour movement in a more general sense. Labour's performance in defence of civil liberties certainly counts as the worst item in its record during the second Thatcher administration. The arbitary powers assumed by a centrally directed police force at the time of the miners' strike were not in any way made the subject of a vehement public outcry, at least by the organs of official labour. In the legal persecution of the civil servant Sarah Tisdall for exposing the duplicity practiced by government departments; in attempted similar action against even more highly placed bureaucrat Clive Ponting for a comparable offence; in the further restriction of immigration rights and nationality entitlement; in the legal stigmatisation of homosexuality by Clause 28 of the Local Government Act the Labour response was abject, amounting in fact either to token objection or none at all.

Worst of all was the posture which the Labour leadership chose to adopt, in spite of very considerable unease among its own party ranks, over the affair of the Zircon spy satellite. This constituted one item, compiled by the journalist Duncan Campbell, in a television series on various aspects of the secret state, made for the BBC and centred at its Scottish headquarters. The very existence of this object was a matter of deep concealment, at least from the British public, for there is no doubt that the intended object of surveillance, the USSR, knew all there was to know about it. Since the secret was out anyway, the action the government then took – not only stopping the broadcast but sending the police to raid the Glasgow premises of the BBC – must be interpreted as having no connexion with actual military secrecy but only as threat and intimidation against citizens and journalists who got too nosey about these kind of things. Neil Kinnock's reaction was lamentable: not only did he fail to challenge the government on the principle of its unaccountable powers and its arbitary exercise of them, but went so far as to attack Thatcher for not having acted more promptly and effectively against the programme, aligning himself unhesitatingly with MI5 definition of reality in the hope of exploiting the fetishes about security that were believed to lurk in the popular consciousness. In a similar manner Michael Foot had thrown the weight of parliamentary Labour behind the Falklands War, and with the same result – outrageous and self-serving action on the part of the government received endorsement from the opposition because these acts were done under the cover of patriotic virtue or necessity. The ability of the tories to monopolise definitions of the national interest was demonstrated once again.

The labour movement and party was admittedly less compliant over another instance of arbitrary spite, namely the prohibition of trade unionism at a major high-tech communication spy centre, GCHQ at

Cheltenham. Once again this was a thing which had been concealed for decades, of prodigious importance, that the public wasn't supposed to know about, although when it came to light eventually nobody noticed any shift in the balance of the superpower conflict. However, the cabinet was intent on having its revenge and did so by attacking the trade union rights of the centre's employees. Bitter protests followed, but the terms in which they were phrased in no sense questioned the moral legitimacy of GCHQ or what it was doing. On the contrary, the TUC strove to emphasise the patriotic zeal of its members engaged in this work and even offered a no-strike deal in return for the government's concession of a right to exist. So long as the agenda continued to be set by the inheritance of Great Power militarism being taken for granted as forming the central purpose of government, the labour movement could only be at a disadvantage when it came to disputes over the resolution of particular items on it. Throughout its history labourism's record on civil rights has been mediocre if not positively wretched. This should not be attributed to a taste on the part of its leaders for arbitrary government, but to its relationship, constantly strengthened in the course of the present century, with the British state as the centre of its political universe and thereby lacking any coherent standpoint to set against reason of state as proclaimed or practiced by government ministers. It was only necessary for a premier, foreign or home secretary to utter the magic words 'national security' for the parliamentary opposition's leadership to collapse in a heap of quivering jelly. Even the intimidation of the BBC by Norman Tebbit in his role as Chairman of the Conservative Party for alleged political bias in its news reporting brought only a halfhearted response from the Labour Party leadership.

In the course of 1986, however, the government ran into serious difficulties and the electoral outlook for Labour did appear to improve. The affair of the Westland helicopter firm was important in several ways. First, it vividly highlighted the expanding gap between the government's nationalist rhetoric and the realities of a world market and technological structure which presented no other options except a European or a US takeover of a centrally important British firm.[15] Secondly, the internal Conservative Party conflict over which of these options to pursue exposed the unaccountability of the Prime Minister, her sidelining of the Cabinet over matters in which she took a personal interest and the petty lying and cheating endemic to her political style. Two leading ministers, Michael Heseltine and Leon Brittan, resigned or were forced to resign from the Cabinet.

The Westland affair also revealed however the degree to which the standards of public life had become corrupted. This scandal would certainly have brought down any administration before 1979, but in this case it only resulted in a closing of Conservative ranks around the Premier as soon as the threat of a government debacle leading to loss of office and the possible undoing of the Thatcher revolution became apparent.

It showed up too the inability of the Labour Party, whether in parliament or more broadly, to take advantage of the situation or to exploit it effectively. The set piece debate in the House of Commons proved to be an anti-climax which underlined Thatcher's capacity for survival and recovery, largely because the opposition's veneration for the Westminster conventions made it incapable of pinning down or discrediting a prime minister who, obedient to their form, was ready to violate their substance at every turn to secure her party's advantage or to gratify her personal prejudices. It has been a cardinal principle of labourism always to play the game and generally to lose it.

The government's embarrassment therefore brought Labour no profit other than a small temporary lead in the opinion polls, which soon evaporated. This was partly because the consumer surge founded upon Thatcher's asset-stripping operations upon the material economy was still running strongly and its full destructive consequences not as yet matured. The MORI economic optimism index – an essential tool for party managers – which measures the relationship between public expectations of economic improvement or decline, indicated that confidence was high, and a militant reassertion of Thatcherite values and programmes at the Conservative annual conference in the autumn gave the tories in the following months once more a firm command over the political agenda.

The other principal reason for their rapid recovery was that among that portion of the electorate which needed to be won back to Labour the party continued to be seen as incapable of effectively exercising power. The successful cultivation of this presumption was Thatcher's primary asset. In terms of what was traditionally expected of a party aspiring to government, cohesiveness, self-confidence and authoritarian leadership, it was seen to fail badly, in spite of Kinnock's conference assault upon the Militant tendency and subsequent expulsions. The Party was still perceived as politically fragmented and torn with factional rivalry. Its continuing commitment to nuclear disarmament – on paper at least – contradicted the now deeply embedded sentiment which associated these weapons with the preservation of national security if not identity.

Above all, Labour continued to be stigmatised as adhering to economic principles which, if implemented, would bring the economy into bankruptcy and breakdown. Certain Labour local authorities, particularly in the London boroughs, were effectively smeared by the popular press as insanely dogmatic squandermaniacs.

A left wing worldview, however expressed, has been an alien element in British political culture since the miiddle of the 19th century and its seeming advance in the 1970s, its potential breakthrough in the power structure, had been received with the utmost fear and alarm. Mobilising every layer of social, economic and cultural prejuduce inherited from the eras of *laissez-faire* capitalism and imperialism, Thatcherism strove with considerable success to delegitimise the left even as a minority ideological position, and then to taint the Labour Party as such with the guilt of that association, continuing the tactic remorselessly as the general election drew close,[16] even though by that point the left was more nerveless and impotent than at any time since the 1960s.

The general election called for June 1987 confirmed all of these trends. Reflecting the improving grip that Kinnock and his lieutenants were starting to get upon the party's organisation and decision-making channels, both the left and the unreconciled pre-Kinnock right avoided making disruptive or embarrassing interventions. The publicity campaign was generally rated as very competent, even a presentational triumph in terms of advertising technique – although also pretty vacuous, reflecting the Conservative Party's continuing domination of the political high ground. It was this in the end which determined the outcome, in association with the widely-held expectation that the Thatcherite economic recipes were actually working, strengthening the basis of productive capacity by enforcing a leaner, fitter manufacturing industry, expanding an enormously profitable financial sector and compelling value for money in the public services. It confirmed too the extent to which the substance of the tory appeal was English nationalism, and southern English nationalism at that, for in Wales, the north and the midlands Labour did improve its standing, while in Scotland the Conservative representation was reduced to a rump of ten MPs.

Subsequent comment was fairly unanimous that in the election campaign Labour had performed as well as could be expected and that its maximum efforts fell far short of anything needed to return it to power in the foreseeable future, at least without some sort of electoral pact or alliance with other anti-tory forces – which would imply constitutional restructuring as part of any such bargain. The prospect loomed of permanent minority status, and that, in the context of the Thatcher revolution and dismantling of the tripartite corporatist system, meant exclusion forever from government councils while the social power of trade unionism and local government was steadily and irreversibly whittled away. In those circumstances, the basis of classic labourism, internally defeated in its left version, impotent in its right, ceased any longer to have viability. If the labour movement was to have any hope of surviving the demise of labourism it was going to have to address the questions which had been pressing for an answer with increasing insistence in one form or another for three decades – the end of the traditional corporate, exclusivist and patriarchal culture of the skilled workforce (or labour aristocracy), which had given its tone to the institutions of the entire movement, and the character of the centralised, omnicompetent quasi-absolutist Westminster state.

Conclusion

Revision of Labour Policy

Following the General Election of 1987 the Labour Party, defeated for the third successive time, instituted a comprehensive policy review. In truth, it was not merely policy but the Party's whole tradition and practice which was up for reconsideration. Very typically the debate, such as it was, proceeded through the 'usual channels' and no particular effort was made to involve the individual members individually or to seek any alternative modes of expression to the entrenched forms of the Party machinery.

The essential features of what emerged from the review, directed by the parliamentary leadership, are easily recounted. The perspective now placed before the electorate was emptied finally of any vestige of recognisably socialist content. The structures of late 20th century British capitalism, both industrial and financial, were acclaimed in their entirety and a hands-off policy promised from the state so far as overall direction was concerned. Privatisations, with very few exceptions, were accepted as *faits accomplis*. The EC was embraced with more fervent passion than the rival party was doing at that point.

Nearly all the trade union legal rights and privileges lost under the Thatcher regime were abandoned and written off, since the electoral liability of promising to restore them was all too clear. Nuclear unilateralism was buried, interred deep under layers of shifty rhetoric, the central presumption of which continued to assert Britain's central role as a major nuclear power.

No significant resistance occurred. Its absence, considering what had happened under Gaitskell, the battles against Wilson and the nearly hegemonic position the left had attained less than a decade earlier, was anti-climactic, but perhaps not very astonishing. Whatever flights of rhetoric the left might develop to the contrary, especially from Conference platforms, there remained a general appreciation at large throughout the Party, whether unstated or plainly articulated, that the more socialist and class conscious the programme, the more difficult it was to convince the electorate to back it. It was an intuitive perception of the British, or at least English, political culture (thoroughly understood also by right-wing demagogues) which the outcome of the two previous elections had reinforced and underlined. Thatcherism had hardened the generalised presumption that business – though not, as it turned out, social provision – was best left to businessmen. The days were long past when EC membership could be envisaged as the last obstacle to confident measures of socialist advance upon a British terrain. Now it represented more of an obstacle to Thatcherism's social inflictions. And there was no avoiding the reality that the single biggest turn-off for voters was a future Labour government's commitment to abandon nuclear weapons.

To explain the social and cultural roots of the public's false consciousness was one thing, to explain it away or deny its existence was quite another, and the left had discredited itself by too frequent recourse to this form of bad faith. It was, in consequence, unable to mount throughout the Party any significant resistance to the new turn of events and its organised networks were in the process of shrinking and dissolving. The TUC, despite Scargill's best efforts, was unable even to commit Labour to reversing the restrictive Thatcherite legislation. Its weakness stemmed only partially from the ravages which her government had inflicted upon the union movement; more important was the fact that, in view of what Conservatism had become, the union leaders had nowhere to go apart from the Labour leadership, which was therefore in a position to make its own terms. However unsatisfactory the Labour programme might be it had to be accepted because the alternative was so grisly.

Within three years the Labour Party had recovered its political credibility to the degree that the electoral danger induced the tories to sack their leader, despite her record and regardless of the trauma involved. Certainly Thatcher did more than ever the Labour Party could to destroy herself: the hope sustained by her enemies ever since she had become tory leader was at last fulfilled. Under the pressure of events and its leader's intemperate zeal the Thatcherite bloc started to crumble. The National Health Service was identified as an area of public dissatisfaction. The Prime Minister determined that the government should respond with a stronger dose of market principles rather than an input of additional resources. Medical opinion was alienated, as was public feeling, which refused to disbelieve the evidence of its own experience in place of the strident pronouncements that consumer choice was widening and everything improving.

To a certain degree the industrial relations legislation which had crippled the unions backfired, for when strikes did take place, after the secret postal ballots which the new laws prescribed, it became impossible to condemn them as arbitrary and unrepresentative. The requirement for unions to vote on the political levy only had the effect of demonstrating unquestionably, by overwhelming majorities, the strength of their members' attachment to the Labour Party. Thatcher's distaste for having her authority limited in any manner by the country's EC commitments, and her obsession with mythical sovereignty – attitudes enunciated even more provocatively by her acolytes Tebbit and Ridley – began to generate intensifying friction with her senior cabinet colleagues.

The focal point for popular rejection and discontent, however, was the innovation in local government proclaimed as the flagship of the third term. In general the public had watched without too much adverse reaction as the powers of councils were progressively whittled away between 1979 and 1987. It was a different matter altogether when the government imposed a spectacularly regressive method of financing what was left of it – the Community Charge, immediately and universally christened the Poll Tax.

The Poll Tax was the offspring both of discontent on the part of the tory electorate at the level of local rates and the dogma of tory think-tanks anxious to assimilate public services as far as possible to the form of a cash transaction – if everyone paid the same, regardless of income, for commodities off the shelves, then they should do the same for municipal services and facilities. The fact that large households with low incomes found their payments mount to stupefying levels was only part of the reason for the popular fury and loathing which the measure aroused: its shameless injustice was no less pertinent.

The End of Thatcher

For the first time in her premiership, Thatcher failed to ride along with a popular mood or to express and reinforce unarticulated but widespread feelings. Instead, ideology overreached itself and she set her face, despite the warnings of colleagues and backbenchers, in diametric opposition to public sentiment. There followed a great reflux of voting strength to the Labour Party, the beneficiary at last of a calamitous error on the part of its opponent.

The response to the Poll Tax issue on the part of labour movement officialdom exhibited all the classic features of labourism. In the declarations of the Labour front bench and the resolutions passed at various levels under their inspiration, the law was accorded its customary metaphysical sanctity. Extra-parliamentary activity might be permissible, but only in the form of authorised, legal, peaceful protest: unruly non-violent demonstration outside these boundaries was absolutely forbidden, as was passive resistance in the form of refusal to pay. The result of the official movement's refusal to channel the protest,[1] was that it became identified with the organisations on the far left, which eagerly accepted the challenge; in consequence the protest demonstrations became anything but non-violent.

It remains an open question to what extent the Poll Tax revolt and Thatcher's ruin is to be attributed to the meticulously constitutional objections of the Labour Party as against the uninhibited mass and occasionally violent street protests promoted by the Anti-Poll Tax Federations. Given my own profound dislike of the political forces which led the Federations – Militant and to a lesser extent the SWP – I would prefer to deny them the credit. It seems more likely though, that while they could not have hoped to defeat the legislation without the existence of the constitutional Labour Party as an electoral alternative, it was their action, rather than the subdued opposition of the PLP, which kept it as a live issue that got no chance to settle down into the sediment of popular consciousness.

European, local and by-elections measured the degree of public disenchantment and alienation, while senior ministers, their patience exhausted at last by endless browbeating and humiliation, fell from the ranks. This silent rebellion among her own MPs finally overthrew the impregnable leader. The prospect was not greeted all that eagerly by the Labour front bench, for they had been geared up to fight Thatcher at the forthcoming general election and had come to believe that she now represented a significant electoral asset for them. Naturally they did their utmost to portray the new premier, John Major, as being cast in essentially the same mould as his predecessor in spite of his utterly different style and personality.

The Labour Party also benefited from the eclipse of what had for two elections looked like a serious electoral rival, namely the Liberal-SDP Alliance. In 1987 it had come within striking distance of equalling the Labour percentage of vote, but once again could not achieve the breakthrough in terms of parliamentary seats. Strains within both membership and leadership were coming to the surface. David Owen's arrogance and egotism had been apparent even on the joint electoral broadcasts made by the two leaders and Owen for his part found the

Liberals much too left-wing for his taste. Following David Steel's proposition for a merger of the parties, Owen was outmanoeuvered and faced with an effective Liberal absorption of the bulk of his membership, leaving only a marginal SDP rump, which soon fell to pieces.

Economic recession, stagnation in the housing market, unemployment and fears for the future of the NHS combined to keep Labour ahead in the polls and scoring by-election victories during the course of 1991, which induced Major's government to permit the 1987 parliament to run its complete five-year term. By the TUC and Labour Party conferences of that year the Kinnock triumph was perfectly accomplished. Neither conference was really a forum for debate or discussion, but a presentation designed for their public relations impact, avoiding all controversy, at which the bland new orthodoxies were swiftly and smoothly endorsed. Changed times were symbolised by the appearance of the Labour leaders themselves: scrubbed faces, orthodox haircuts and double-breasted suits had become de rigueur.[2]

Even as the tide of British affairs ran more strongly against it, the left suffered further blows from the revolutions in eastern Europe and the Soviet Union between 1989 and 1991. In strict reason this was wholly unjust, for only a marginal fragment of the left still identified in any fashion with the barrack socialism which collapsed so spectacularly during those months. The fall of those regimes, however, and the economic mess which it uncovered, helped to discredit in public discourse and political commentary not only neo-Stalinism but also any version of economic planning and direction, centralised welfare or socialist rhetoric. Further persecution by the Labour NEC of Militant during the year evoked hardly a ripple of protest outside the sect's own ranks.

Return to Liberalism

In certain visible respects the tumultuous passage of the 1980s left the traditions of labourism intact and indeed strengthened. These, above all, were the symbolic postures and rituals performed around the shrine of the State; the theatre of State Openings, Black Rod, Remembrance Day Parades and suchlike. As election time approached the Labour leaders' devotion to the most regressive totems of popular feeling grew the more fervent and could scarcely have been exceeded by Ramsay MacDonald's insistence that his Cabinet wear knee-breeches for their presentation to the King.

But much more important was a trend summed up in the guarded approval certain former SPD luminaries were prepared to extend to Kinnock's remodelled party. This tendency did represent a growing rupture with classical labourism, in that what remained of the Labour Party's self-image and perception as a specifically class party was being systematically erased, above all in the acceptance of Thatcherite industrial relations legislation. Official Party discourse focussed solely upon Labour as the representative of the general public good in terms of economic management, infrastructural protection and efficient welfare delivery: not at all as the voice of the working class suffering a particular form of social injustice, let alone as aspiring to political and social hegemony. The Labour Party was increasingly taking on the features of what the Liberal Party might have become had it survived as a contender for office beyond 1918; the labour movement's roots in liberal politics were increasingly asserting themselves, more than a century after its beginnings. The disposition to keep its programmes within the limits of liberal traditions had, of course, been an ever-present side of the labourist outlook. What was new from the late 1980s was the fact that such orientation became steadily more dominant and unchallenged.

Perhaps it was as well that this should happen. The rejection of socialism by the labour movement and Party and their settling down into a liberal ideological framework revealed clearly the limits and reality of this formation, making clear the level of fantasy in the expectation that it might hope by some political alchemy to be transformed into a socialist mass party drawing mass support for a programme of social revolution. If standing under liberal colours was the only way to present an effective answer to Conservatism and hope to gain electoral victory, then it was best that it should do so openly rather than covertly.

By 1991, therefore, deferential British labourism was well advanced in the process of transformation into pragmatic British liberalism under another name, but in the process other things were happening to it which, in combination with its continuing mass electoral support and trade union base, raised the prospect of interesting and novel developments rather than a simple relapse into stagnant affirmation of its worst traditions.

The trauma of Thatcherism and the disorientation which had followed from it among all shades of the left had pushed the Labour Party, reluctant and unwilling though it was, into accepting the inevitability of basic constitutional change. Proportional representation and a Bill of Rights were only promised an examination, but devolution at least had become a firm commitment. A Scottish Assembly, by creating an alternative centre of legitimacy, would finally break the log-jam of the ultra-centralised British monarchy. Political and economic integration within the EC, now embraced by Labour, was likely to have a similar tendency. That same process, combined with the end of the Cold War, might also be capable of solving the classic postwar Labour dilemma of satisfying simultaneously the demands of organised labour, transnational capital and the Great Power atavisms of the British establishment. The economic options and instruments available to a future Labour government would be greatly restricted but so, correspondingly, would be the expectations laid upon it. At the same time the modernisation of what remained of British productive industry might be enforced from outside, while its social costs were funded by the EC. There were of course much less inviting alternatives to this happy scenario (ones which, at the time of writing, look more likely to be realised), such as that of irreversible decline and impoverishment, but whatever the outcome, the traditional state polity in which labourism was nurtured and operated has gone forever.

The 1992 Election and its Results

But by the spring of 1992 the Conservative government too found that its room for manoeuvre was diminishing rapidly and its chances of winning the election, now falling due, looked desperately precarious. The economy continued in immovable stagnation, with the promised revival, always just around the corner, never showing any sign of putting in an appearance. Interest rates remained punitive, producing a steady fallout of company collapses and consequent unemployment growth. As job security diminished so did consumer purchases, further tightening the cycle of depression. Even more seriously from the macro-economic viewpoint, the housing market remained stuck stubbornly at the bottom of the curve, with shattering effects upon the construction and consumer durable industries.

Opinion polls and by-election outcomes suggested an irrecoverable Conservative disadvantage. John Major's ministerial team was suffused with an air of incompetence and lack of direction in contrast to the array of dynamic talent facing them across the floor of the Commons. Even the tories' own partisans made the unfavourable comparison. The smell of defeat hung around their administration.

When the election was finally called therefore for early April 1992, a widespread if not universal expectation existed that even if Labour did not secure a working majority the Conservatives were certain to lose theirs, and that the liberalisation of the Labour Party over the preceding decade was on the point of paying off in terms of office.

But although the party had become electable, it was not elected. Even in Scotland the tories experienced a degree of resurgence. The redistribution of a few thousand votes would have turned out the government, but Labour could not complain on this occasion about the unfairness of the electoral system: for once, first-past-the-post favoured it. It got a lot more seats than was warranted by its percentage of the overall vote, which was in the end not a dramatic improvement on the 1987 position. The postmortem showed that, while the party was no longer feared among the electorate as being in the hands of ultra-left headbangers, and while its specific policies in regard to welfare issues were generally better regarded than those of its opponents, the transformations it had made still did not convince enough voters that Labour's handling of the economy was more likely to be more effective than that of the Conservatives, despite the government's lamentable performance over the recent period.

Defeat was rendered the more bitter in that the opinion polls, as they almost always do, had greatly overstated the Labour position. Tory voters, it was confirmed, were less inclined than Labour ones to give a true indication of their voting intentions; a fact which provides an interesting insight into British political culture and reflects upon the divided and contradictory attitudes noted above. There is a general feeling that Labour stands for a more selfless outlook – if you want to benefit the community and the disadvantaged then that is the party to vote for, but if you are already a solid citizen, the tories are more likely to maintain and enhance your income and prospects. If they are manifestly failing to do so it is due to the world recession and circumstances beyond anybody's control. It is, despite everything that has happened since, the contrast between the 1940s and the 1950s. Labour is viewed as the party of austerity, restriction, and dubious financial management: the Conservatives as that of economic realism and consumer affluence.

Hope deferred yet again cost Neil Kinnock his leadership. It was a question of style. In spite of his achievements – the tories had a majority of nearly 150 when he took over, 21 when he departed – he was inescapably associated with two failures to attain office. Moreover, his personal style was judged to have contributed to the failure: the impression of vagueness and long-winded garrulity, the fact that whatever the reality may have been he was unable to project the aura of an effective leader. He was also associated with the triumphalist style in which the election had been fought and lost, particularly the premature chicken-counting exercise of the much-hyped rally in Sheffield. No secret was made of the fact that his successor was chosen, whatever his political virtues might have been, primarily for his ability to evoke a more emollient and self-confident image than Kinnock's, combined with an impression of greater gravitas and competence than John Major could aspire to.

The morning of 10 April brought a sense that something very consequential had taken place, more portentous than just another return of government. In terms of contemporary Britain it could be regarded as a turning point at which history failed to turn: all sorts of expectations were confounded,[3] from devolutionists to cabinet ministers-in-waiting, not to speak of nurses and educationists. It marked the final exhaustion of the labourist tradition, whether right or left; the eclipse of a labour movement which was incapable either of resisting the Thatcherite momentum or of adjusting to it and mitigating its worst consequences.

The newly-planted Thatcherite or quasi-Thatcherite institutions, the hospital trusts, the opted-out schools, the marketisation of health and education generally; the recent privatisation of water and forthcoming privatisation of coal, rail and the post office; the impending destruction of what remained of independent local authority – all of which would have been uprooted by a Conservative defeat, could now look forward to a secure bedding-in, a further and probably irreversible alteration to the social landscape of the country.

Such developments would mean the final eradication of the ground on which labourism had stood for nearly a century: a coherent and purposeful labour movement co-ordinated between its union, local government and parliamentary wings to deliver, largely through non-market, bureaucratically-administered mechanisms, in the framework of the ancient constitution, a range of services to its members and supporters. That ground had been substantially eroded by material pressures: the shrinkage of British manufacturing industry, the decline in the strength of manual trade unions, the creation of a permanently unemployed underclass, all accelerated by the deliberate government policies adopted since 1979. It was eroded too by the sustained attack mounted against local government and, probably most important of all, by the cultural changes occurring in the developed economies of the late 20th century.

Overall these marked a trend towards a weakening of community cohesiveness and strengthening of individualisation – privatisation of the soul – but seen almost exclusively in market and consumer terms. This is not to join in lamenting a supposed healthier and more human

working-class culture of an earlier age, which could in its own way be
no less debasing and obscurantist. It is simply to note the fact of transformation. Reinforcing the expansion of consumer choice – for those
fortunate enough to possess adequate incomes – has been the impact
of the tabloid press and of television – or rather of the kind of
programmes the latter transmits. Under conditions of this sort the uni-
fication of disparate oppressed groups into a class and the pursuit of a
politics based upon it, becomes overwhelmingly difficult if not altogether
impossible.[4]

That the fragments of such an older political discourse were still around
was being demonstrated at that point in Glasgow. In the blighted
housing estates surrounding the city the formerly entrist Militant organisation, under the name of Scottish Militant Labour, was making an
electoral impact, returning several councillors and securing a creditable
parliamentary vote. The development was only partly attributable to the
personal charisma of the organisation's leading spokesperson, Tommy
Sheridan, who had built up his reputation in the anti-Poll Tax campaigns.
It was even more due to what one local observer described as 'the sound
of doors closing' all throughout the area as shrinking unemployment
opportunities, benefit cuts and a collapsing education system cut off the
sources of hope which had formerly existed, creating a mood of extreme
social desperation. With the rock-solid Labour administration in
Glasgow and in the Strathclyde region helpless to do anything to allay
it, an opening was created for a reassertion, by organisations and individuals capable of channelling the mood, of traditionalist styles of
militancy: the promise to mobilise and fight. There are evident parallels
with the earlier experience in Liverpool, but what is equally evident is
that such eruptions can have no more than a local significance. They
depend upon a combination of traditions and circumstances which
will only ever apply to a narrow percentage of the electorate. The desperation from which they spring is as likely to be expressed elsewhere
in undirected anti-social violence or neo-Fascist outbreaks.

Remarkably, the Labour Party conference in the autumn following
the general election defeat was a relatively optimistic one. The unexpectedly sanguine mood, however, had nothing to do with any change
occurring in the Labour Party itself or its relations with the electorate,
but purely to the uncontrollable debacle and split that was overtaking
the newly elected government. Something like £20billion had been
wasted trying unavailingly to keep sterling within the ERM;[5] the
British government and the Bundesbank were hurling insults at each
other; the Tory Party was fighting itself in almost traditional Labour style

over the consequences of the devaluation and over its stance on the Maastricht treaty for greater integration of EC currencies and governments. The fact that David Mellor, a cabinet minister, had also just been driven from office over sexual and personal scandal and by the tory tabloids was almost a minor irrelevance in the circumstances.

Yet the 1992 conference was incredibly decorous, in spite of the fact that the EC dispute was reflected in the Labour ranks as well and Brian Gould, a shadow cabinet member, resigned over an issue of principle. The government was condemned – not that that was formidably difficult – for incompetence and mismanagement, and Chancellor Lamont's head demanded. Yet in spite of a manifest current in public feeling that could have been appealed to, no major alternative was presented to what had been proven, in the most emphatic manner possible, to be a grotesque and catastrophic economic strategy. The point was made, correctly enough, by Gordon Brown, that the pound could not be expected to compete effectively in the currency markets if the economy lacked an adequate productive base, and that could only be secured by government intervention and guidance. Nonetheless, the Labour leadership had been as committed as the government to an overvalued pound, and while speculators might be blamed in an abstract sort of way, no suggestion followed that profound alterations were needed in the structure of currency markets which encouraged such episodes to take place.

It was the same with the question of the Maastricht treaty. The crisis of 1992 in EC structures and within individual states illuminated a range of shortcomings and contradictions in the very nature of the institution. The EC was established on the presumption of a Cold War Europe and the indefinite political, military and even economic coordination of the west by the USA. The original drive towards European political unity was framed within that context. It was never designed to cope with the disappearance of the eternal Soviet antagonist, German reunification, real or incipient civil war in the former Soviet bloc and a cascade of east European refugees. The defensive response of the EC governments and bureaucracies, in the shape of the treaty, was to tighten bureaucratic structures and to weaken yet further the remaining ability of national governments or anybody else to regulate the operation of unconstrained market forces within the Community. The Europe envisaged by Maastricht has indeed some parallels with Hayek's vision of a two-tier legislature, where the purpose of the upper authority is to stop popular pressure bringing about any interference with market relations.

The Labour leadership advanced no objections to the Maastricht principles, indeed they embraced them unquestioningly. Their only quarrel with the government in this regard was over its refusal to accept the meagre concession to popular welfare which the treaty incorporated, the Social Chapter. Again, the objection was valid enough, but scarcely embodied a dramatically different vision of the future from that of the Conservatives. It is possible to envisage, and some did envisage, a wholly different perspective; one in which the Labour Party opposed the Maastricht Treaty, not in the name of atavistic nationalist sentiment but in that of a different kind of EC, a federal and democratised one in which the European Parliament assumed real sovereign powers.[6] Any such notions were brushed aside without difficulty in favour of the unadventurous, but safer, strategy of measured criticism of the government's failure to progress along what the received wisdom of the establishment's more enlightened sections took to be the route to national recovery and prosperity. Two decades of oscillation between what was, in the British context, near ultra-leftism and the most dilute reformism had left the party, as one commentator noted, exactly in the position that the Bennites had feared it would arrive at: dull and respectable but still out of office. Not only had a recent recruitment drive proved a total washout, but membership was in calamitous decline and the financial position was desperate. Only the torments that the Conservative government was undergoing at that point made the Labour situation in late 1992 appear relatively healthy and saved it from an impression of terminal decay. With the political strength of its local authority and trade union bases pulverised and with its electoral credibility in deep crisis, the only significant asset that remained to the Labour Party as a challenger for government was a comparatively able-looking leadership team: a somewhat narrow foundation on which to win office and go on to tackle the endemic deficiencies of the British state and society. The stagnant swamp of the party's worst traditions seemed to beckon irresistibly.

In an historical perspective there can be little reasonable doubt that the labourist tradition has turned out to be a disaster – if in a less spectacular fashion than the Leninist one – and that its very achievements had the effect of prolonging a political outlook and practice which became more ruinous the longer it survived. Its immovable presence worked to prevent the rooting or development of alternative radical traditions within the British political culture. Like the revolutionary left, it was stamped with an authoritarian mark, the more detrimental in its case insofar as it was nearer the sources of state power and from time to time formed the government. Other presuppositions, in relation to the *forms* of authority, it shared with the right. From this, in a large measure, arose the fact that it did not have the political or moral resources to resist when it came under an unrelenting attack from the right which ignored the hitherto accepted rules and conventions. The culmination, under the Thatcher regime, was the dismantling of its social base in the economy, trade union movement and local government and the debacle of its political tradition. With the simultaneous fall both of labourism and neo-Stalinism, a new though difficult potential has opened up for the redevelopment of a socialist tradition cleared of its authoritarian accretions from the cultures in which the original one emerged.

Such a renewed tradition will have to be capable of coping not only with the difficulties of its inheritance but also with the even more intractable issue of reconciling the demographic and environmental limits to growth with the seeming inescapability of market mechanisms in mass societies. It will be starting under exceptionally unpropitious circumstances, but if capitalism is really an inherently unstable, murderous and planet-wrecking system – and all the historical evidence suggests that it is – then there is no alternative but to try.

Notes

Introduction

1 See for example the hard-left journal *Labour Briefing*, which runs a regular feature entitled 'Class Traitor of the Month'.

2 The American revolution, with its specifications of 'life, liberty and the pursuit of happiness' was certainly influential in the formation of the new outlook. But the Founding Fathers, aiming at political independence from the British crown, did not envisage far-reaching alterations in the internal character of colonial American politics; neither the suppression of slavery nor even a universal franchise for white males.

3 See A O Hirschman, *The Rhetoric of Reaction*, Harvard University Press, Cambridge, Massachusetts, 1991, for an analysis of the manner in which the themes exploited by reactionary publicists such as Edmund Burke, writing in opposition to the French Revolution, have formed the continuing staple of right-wing propaganda.

4 Persistent advocates of a feminist standpoint were liable to end up at the guillotine. See Joan Wallach Scott, 'French Feminists and the Rights of "Man": Olympe de Gouge's Declarations', in *History Workshop* No 28, Autumn 1989.

5 See G E M de Ste Croix, *The Class Struggle in the Ancient Greek World*, Duckworth 1981.

6 E Pagels in *Adam, Eve, and the Serpent*, Weidenfeld and Nicolson, 1988, demonstrates how the social theology of the Christian church – in its origins a militantly oppositional movement within the Roman empire – was systematically adapted, once the church had entered into close association with the imperial state, to serve ultra-authoritarian purposes.

7 J de Maistre, the most vehement denouncer, on the Continent, of the French Revolution and all it represented, is notorious for his obsessive stress upon the fully employed hangman as the champion and guarantor of social order and stability.

8 See E P Thompson, *The Making of the English Working Class*, Gollancz, 1963; J Foster, *Class Struggle and the Industrial Revolution*, Weidenfeld & Nicolson, 1974; R J Morris, *Class and Class Consciousness in the Industrial Revolution 1780–1850*, Macmillan, 1979.

9 Geoffrey Foote traces its initial theoretical expression to the economic writings of Thomas Hodgskin in the 1820s. G Foote, *The Labour Party's Political Thought*, Croom Helm, 1985, pp 8–11.

10 See E J Hobsbawm, *Industry and Empire*, Weidenfeld & Nicolson, 1968, for an outline account.

11 In this respect, the question of what constituted the 'working class' and who was doing what kind of consuming is particularly important, and in no respect more so than that of gender relations. In spite of the large number at any time of women wage earners, for only a very small minority was their primary economic relationship the one they entered into with capital. For the overwhelming majority, employed or not, it was with men of 'their own' class. During the period of the formation of the modern labour movement a large minority, if not a majority, of male wage earners inflicted additional deprivation upon their wives and families in order to finance their own leisure pursuits, such as alcohol, tobacco and gambling. The 'Andy Capp' image would scarcely have attained the notoriety it has if it had not once represented a widespread reality. For an analysis, see N Hart, 'Gender and the Rise and Fall of Class Politics', *New Left Review* 175. It is her view that these realities go a long way to account for the fact that the Labour Party has consistently been less electorally popular among women than men.

12 The example of Henry Sidgwick, a leading late Victorian intellectual, is instructive. According to Robert Skidelsky, 'In his own person he symbolised the conflict between the ... good life and the useful life ... he could not bring the private and public life into a rational relationship.' R Skidelsky, *John Maynard Keynes: Hopes Betrayed 1883–1920*, Macmillan, 1983, pp 33–35.

13 See R Gray, *The Aristocracy of Labour in Nineteenth-century Britain c. 1850–1914*, Macmillan, 1981.

14 See G Stedman Jones, *Outcast London*, OUP, 1971, for discussion of the 'respectable'/'residium' distinction – as well as the marginal and patchy degree of improvement in real incomes during the second half of the 19th century.

15 Most notably in T Nairn, *The Enchanted Glass: Britain and its Monarchy*, Radius, 1988.

16 The contrasting fates in parliamentary politics of two leading trade
    union figures Ernest Bevin and Frank Cousins, (both T&GWU
    chiefs and both brought into the House of Commons in exceptional
    circumstances) is striking. Bevin was able to adapt splendidly to the
    parliamentary ritual and achieved inflated renown as one of the
    greatest of 20th century statesmen. Cousins was unable to take it
    seriously and his parliamentary career was short and inglorious.

17 Corelli Barnett's influential text, *Audit of War: The Illusion and reality
    of Britain as a Great Nation*, Macmillan, 1986, attributes the
    experience of chronic difficulties in the postwar economy to over-
    generous welfare provision, trade union obstructionism and an
    academic distaste for industrial concerns on the part of the governing
    elite. The thesis, however, has been the object of destructive
    attack which leaves its factual and statistical basis severely impaired.
    See eg D Edgerton, 'The Prophet Militant and Industrial: The pecu-
    liarities of Coreli Barnett', *20th Century British History*, vol. 2, no.
    3, 1991.

Chapter 1

1 According to Roy Jenkins, Attlee was 'A very firmly established
   member of the English upper middle class' with 'a natural respect
   for conventional values and institutions' *Contemporary Review*,
   Summer 1988. 'He rarely attempted to raise the spirits of the PLP,
   and when he did, his attempts involved metaphors straight from
   his upper middle class background' David Howell *British Social
   Democracy*, Croom Helm, 1980, p 143.

2 K Middlemas, *Power, Competition and the State* vol I: *Britain in
   Search of Balance 1940–61*, Macmillan, 1986, p 115.

3 Bevin's admirers maintain that a man of such fiercely independent
   mind and temper as he was could not be subject to manipulation,
   and that he himself was the originator of and inspiration for
   postwar British foreign policy. If his positions *were* independently
   arrived at, one can only express astonishment at the perfection with
   which they mirrored the FO view of world reality. They can
   then only be regarded as a tribute to the effectiveness with which
   the ideas of the rulers had been converted into the ruling ideas of
   Labour leaders. The most comprehensive presentation of the case
   for Bevin as the guiding spirit is found in the third volume of Alan
   Bullock's biography: *Ernest Bevin, Foreign Secretary*, Heinemann,
   1983. Bullock specifically claims that 'Bevin did not succumb to

the aristocratic embrace', (p 77) but the weight of his discussion makes it clear that Bevin did, '... in every case where he might have justified a political appointment he chose a career diplomat instead' (p 73). Alexander Cadogan had been head of the Foreign Office since 1938 and fully expected to be retired, but Bevin specifically asked him to continue.

According to Lord Greenhill, the Permanent Secretary under George Brown, Bevin was 'a giant with an *instinctive* understanding of British interests.' Sir Frank Roberts, his Private Secretary insisted that Bevin did not always take Foreign Office advice, for, '*he would have been no use to us if he had*' (italics W T). Both remarks were made at conferences of the Institute of Contemporary British History, in 1988 and 1989 respectively.

4   The importance of Keynesian prescriptions for the maintenance of full employment and capacity working was taken for granted in the postwar years. The existence of this relationship has, of course, been a matter of loud dispute since the 1970s among both economists and politicians. Alan Booth has suggested, first, that Keynes importance may have been less in the sphere of demand management, as previously assumed, and more in the encouragement given to investment – and hence employment – by the low interest rates which he favoured and, secondly, that in promoting the IMF he made a significant contribution to the perpetuation of the eventual long boom conditions, the framework in which the corporate institutions of capital, labour and government could co-operate without the economic controls deemed unacceptable by the USA and the Treasury. ICBH Conference, 1988.

5   Keith Middlemas *Politics in Industrial Society*, Andre Deutsch, 1979 p. 323.

6   Middlemas actually prefers the concept of 'corporate bias', on the analogy of bowls – an inbuilt tendency, other things being equal, on the part of the institutions of labour, capital and state to seek co-operation with each other.

7   K O Morgan *Labour In Power 1945–51*, OUP, 1984, pp 28–31. Referring to the alignment of political forces as the end of the war approached, Middlemas writes:

What in modern terms ought to be called the struggle to establish future hegemony, by outlining the values and programme of peacetime before the postwar Election decided party balances replaced the banned struggle between the parties in Coalition.

Instead they sought to use the 'neutral' state apparatus to instil their own ideological preconceptions into the public mind. *Politics* ... p 359.

8   S L Carruthers, 'Manning the Factories': Propaganda and Policy on the Employment of Women 1939–47' *History*, June 1990, from which the above information and quotations are drawn.

9   Ibid p 254.

10 'Awareness of the need to take public opinion into consideration did not lead politicians and civil servants on to an acceptance of parliamentary democracy, *but rather the reverse*' (italics added) Middlemas, op cit, p 369.

[Historians] may perhaps be able to discern, behind the whitewash, outlines of monstrous things done by men and corporations shielded by official secrecy and the law of libel. Ibid p 389.

11 V L Allen *Trade Union Leadership*, Longman, 1957, p 22.

12 Initially the Labour leaders hoped that a united, independent India, disposing of a numerous and powerful army, could be recruited as a junior partner in upholding British imperial positions elsewhere in Asia. J G Darwin, *Contemporary Record*, Autumn 1987.

13 The prospect of being compelled to adopt a Swedish, let alone a Finnish, posture on the international scene appears to have terrified the FO mandarins no less than the possibility of foreign invasion or occupation. See J Saville, 'Labour and Foreign Policy 1945–1947: a Condemnation', *Our History Journal*, no 17, 1991.

14 In 1949 Bevin asserted that, 'In peace and war, the Middle East is an area of cardinal importance to the UK, second only to the UK itself.' Bullock, *Ernest Bevin* ..., p 113.

15 M Gowing, 'Britain and the Bomb', *Contemporary Record*, Summer 1988, notes that, 'It was not a response to an immediate military threat but arose, rather, from a fundamentalist and instinctive feeling that Britain must posess such a climacteric weapon,' and quotes Lord Cherwell, Churchill's scientific advisor, as claiming that unless Britain had an atomic bomb it would 'rank with other European nations who have to make do with conventional weapons'. In fact, intelligence reports in the spring of 1946 had indicated that the Soviet Union would not be ready to go to war before 1950 (Ray Smith, ICBH Conference, 1989), and the main threat to the British (and western) positions in Europe was perceived

as coming not from the USSR but from the Communist Parties of France and Italy. See M Gowing, *Independence and Deterrence: Britain and Atomic Energy 1945–1952*, Macmillan, 1972, for an exhaustive account.

16 K O Morgan, *Labour in Power*, p 282.

17 Ibid p 55. That impeccably Establishment figure, Sir Alec Cairncross, has described the burden of arms expenditure on the postwar economy as an 'incubus'. ICBH Conference, 1988.

18 M Gowing, 'Britain and the Bomb'. Tizard also remarked prophetically that, 'We are a great nation but if we continue to behave like a Great Power we shall soon cease to be a great nation,' and went on to quote Aesop's fable of the puffed-up frog.

19 Although the idea that Bevin persuaded a reluctant US government to re-assume a European role is a myth – the US troops had never withdrawn and had no intention of doing so, as early as 1949 they had no less than six contingency plans for armed intervention in the Mediterranean – the FO certainly did everything in its power to stiffen US antagonism to the Soviet Union. In 1945 Lord Halifax, arch-appeaser and Foreign Secretary until 1940, who had been pensioned off with the Washington Embassy and was still there at the end of the war, was complaining that the USA was far too friendly towards the Russians and lamenting the degree of popular sympathy then held about the USSR. P Boyle, 'British perspective on US/Soviet Relations 1945–55' ICBH Conference, 1990.

20 The degree of tenderness shown towards these sectional interests is nevertheless a bit surprising and again illustrates the disposition of Attlee's government to adjust itself to accepted establishment norms. Civil servants twice prevented Labour ministers from prohibiting restrictive practices by cartels (H Mercer, 'The Labour Government and Private Industry: The Control of Restrictive Practices – an Outline', paper to ICBH Conference, 1988). In 1947 a proposed tax on advertisments was withdrawn after lobbying from the FBI. N Rollings, 'Fiscal Policy and Private Industry 1945–1951: The Case of Incentives' Ibid.

21 D Howell, *British Social Democracy*, p 159.

22 Ibid p 157.

23 K Middlemas, *Power, Competition* ... p 167.

24 Ibid p 146.

25 'But the obligations set in 1944 also included others whose strict observance ran counter to the high level of domestic consumption ... These were the stability of sterling and the survival of the

sterling area ... It looked as though City values had triumphed over those of industry or labour ... The financial sector failed to develop a direct commitment to the performance of industry, as it did in Germany or France.' K Middlemas, 'Corporatism: its rise and fall', *Contemporary Record*, Spring 1988.

26   That the financial sector had its own conscious agenda, inherited from the prewar era and wholly contrary to the general thrust of official policy and public feeling, cannot be doubted. 'The financial sector tried to influence government first to defer Beveridge's initial report in 1942 and then to cripple the full employment package in autumn 1943 on the grounds that Britain's external situation after the war would be so critical that the nation simply could not afford this proposed generosity.' K Middlemas, *Power, Competition* ... p 93.

27   Ibid pp 99, 145, 183.

28   '... the Coalition did to a very large extent bind its successors, simply because in 1945 there was neither time nor willpower to think up an alternative *and because Labour's own leaders lacked faith in a "socialist alternative"'* Ibid p 109, (italics added).

29   P Anderson 'The Figures of Descent' *New Left Review* 161, (1987). See also Martin Weiner and his contentious *English Culture and the Decline of the Industrial Spirit 1850–1980*, Penguin, 1985.

30   See D Nicholls, 'Fractions of capital: the aristocracy, the City, and industry in the development of modern British capitalism,' *Social History*, January 1988.

31   In 1949 the TUC expressed opposition to the nationalisation of the chemical industry.

32   Proposals from the Labour Party's Home Policy Committee for very far-reaching planning measures, including a 40 hour week, price control and worker participation, alienated Attlee and Morrison. K Middlemas, *Power, Competition* ... p 73.

33   During the war the FBI had indicated that the price of its acceptance of future nationalisation measures would depend on the controllers of nationalised industry being drawn from existing management. Ibid p 61.

34   In 1950 Morrison listed the central problems of the nationalised industries. They were defined as: relations between the Ministries, the nationalised industries' Boards and Parliament; the control of efficiency; consumer satisfaction; worker/management relations (Ibid p 185) – in other words, much the same agenda as in 1945!

35   J Harris, ICBH Conference, 1988.

36 According to one analysis, the incoming Labour government had no strategic thinking on a national health service and deeply distrusted the Socialist Medical Association. The NHS concept did not form a central plank in the 1945 election manifesto. Bevan's colleagues would have preferred something more modest and Morrison thought that his scheme would place unacceptable demands upon the Exchequer. The Cabinet was persuaded by the argument that the cost would not be much more than what local authority funding would have required (£175 million) and were horrified by the actuality. Nor did the NHS achievement feature largely in the 1950 and 1951 election campaigns. Charles Webster, ICBH Conference, 1988.

37 Interlocking networks of control involving Labour Party branch and constituency organisations, local trade union bodies and council committees characterised these regions. The most notorious cases were probably the North East and Merseyside in England, West Fife in Scotland and South Wales. The most regular sources of corruption were building and development contracts, but positions in the local Co-op machinery featured as well. The Poulson and other spectacular scandals of the 1970s marked the culmination of lengthy developments in a culture of petty corruption.

38 K Middlemas, *Power, Competition* ... p 152.

39 While this was happening, the Board of Trade was arguing for the maintainance of retailers' margins and business profits in order to sustain private investment. Complaints from the shop floor and lower level trade union offficials were stifled by the TUC. Ibid p 161.

40 'If the two sides' willingness to make sacrifices in 1947–49 is compared on the basis of what they *said* they wished to do, the unions come out best.' Ibid p 162.

41 In view of the acute labour shortage of the time its acceptance was an extraordinary tribute to the level of discipline then prevailing in the labour movement.

42 V L Allen, *Trade Union Leadership*, p 112.

43 K Middlemas, *Politics in Industrial Society*, p 403.

44 K Middlemas, *Power, Competition* ... p 189.

45 Ibid p 167.

46 The experience of administering Marshall Aid in Britain highlighted the inadequacies of management, not of the workforce. This fact, however, was overshadowed by the exploitation of a red scare on the part of both government and press, directing attention instead

to unofficial strikes, communists in the London docks and Smithfield and the alleged lack of TUC leadership. See K Middlemas, ibid p 163. The BBC, to its credit, resisted pressure from Attlee personally to give air time to T&GWU leaders to condemn the dock strikes while denying it to the strikers.

47   'In the 1940s these two unions (the T&GWU and the NUM) together with the General and Municipal Workers formed the solid base on which the Attlee government was able to pursue its politics without much fear that it might have to face effective opposition from within its own party.' A Bullock, *Ernest Bevin*, p 58. He notes that the relationship formed between Bevin and the union leaders Arthur Deakin, Will Lawther and Tom Williamson was 'one of the keys to understanding the history of the 1940s' ibid p 59.

48   D Howell, *British Social Democracy*, p 138. Although no substantial criticism of the principle of British involvement in the Korean War emerged to trouble the government, US and South Korean military atrocities in December 1950 caused trouble among Labour Party branches. On the other hand, early in 1951 Hugh Gaitskell threatened to resign from the government unless the UK agreed to back a UN resolution condemning China as an aggressor. P Addison, ICBH Conference, 1989.

49   D Howell, *British Social Democracy*, p 146.

50   For Raph Samuel's nostalgic tribute to the political culture of the Communist Party in the 1940s, see *New Left Review* 154, 156 (1985–86). Middlemas notes that, in spite of the fact that from 1947 the TUC's most energetic political activity was anti-communism and opposition to the World Federation of Trade Unions, there remained a surprising amount of residual sympathy for the USSR among large numbers of workers. *Power, Competition* ... p 147. For the TUC and the WFTU see R Saville, 'Politics and the Labour Movement in the early Cold War,' *Our History Journal*, no 15, April 1990.

51   'The Labour Party of 1945 was led by an alliance of Oxbridge intellectuals and TUC oligarchs. Committed as they were to working class welfare, they had no interest in redistributing authority ... the ethos of the time was managerial, with orders and injunctions flowing down from on high; and Labour leaders expected the people to respond.' P Addison, 'Attlee', *New Statesman*, 17 December 1982.

52   D Howell, *British Social Democracy*, p 143.

53   V L Allen, *Trade Union Leadership*, p 35.

54   P Addison, ICBH Conference, 1989.

55 The armaments burden accepted by the 1950–51 Attlee government amounted to £4.7 billion, 14 per cent of the national income. By diverting resources from investment in the transport infrastructure, industrial construction, civil technology, housing and health, it derailed the industrial recovery which had been in process until that point and it was immediately cut back by the incoming Conservatives in October 1951. In the international economy, however, war demand stimulated the long boom which floated the British economy upwards in the 1950s and in Britain proved an asset to the engineering unions, particularly in relation to shopfloor activity.

56 Attlee proposed ferocious restrictive legislation against industrial unrest in the summer of 1950. He was dissuaded by Morrison, the Cabinet Office and the TUC leaders. K Middlemas, *Power, Competition* ... p 176.

57 V L Allen, *Trade Union Leadership*, p 180.

Chapter 2

1 The Liberal vote was 730,000 in 1951 as compared with 2,600,000 in 1950 (though votes per candidate increased slightly) and the percentage 2.6 against 9.1. Three of the nine seats won in 1950 were lost. The Liberal leader, Clement Davies, was offered a coalition and a Cabinet post by Churchill and the offer was seriously considered.

2 On the question of the postwar consensus see M Holmes and N J Horsewood, 'The Postwar Consensus', *Contemporary Record*, Summer 1988; B Pimlott, *et al* 'Is the 'Postwar Consensus' a Myth?' *Contemporary Record*, Summer 1989; R Lowe, 'The Second World War, Consensus and the Foundation of the Welfare State' *20th Century British History*, vol 1, no 2, 1990.

3 R Martin and B Rowthorn (eds) *The Geography of De-industrialisation*, Macmillan, 1986, p 5.

4 T O Lloyd, *Empire to Welfare State: English History 1906–1976*, OUP, 1979, Table 8. Between 1951 and 1954 the average wealthy person more than doubled their capital without effort, but a shrewd investor could have tripled it. John Saville, 'Labourism and The Labour Government', *Socialist Register*, 1967.

5 M Dobb, *Studies in the Development of Capitalism*, Routledge & Kegan Paul, 1946, Chapter 8.

6 See A Gamble, *Britain in Decline*, Macmillan, 1981; Sydney Pollard, *The Wasting of the British Economy*, Croom Helm, 1982.

7 For an informative account see V Allen, *Trade Union Leadership*, Longman, 1957.

8 In 1954 110 unofficial stoppages occurred in the engineering trades. In 1960 the comparable figure was 400. Forty-nine days per 1,000 employees were lost in the former year, 291 in the latter. K Middlemas, *Politics in Industrial Society*, Deutsch, 1979, p 401.

9 Or perhaps better. In 1951 Churchill informed Walter Monckton, his new Minister of Labour to conciliate and keep the peace or his 'head would fall'. See Middlemas, ibid; K O Morgan, *The People's Peace*, OUP, 1990; Justin Davis Smith, *The Attlee and Churchill Administrations and Industrial Unrest 1945–55: a study in consensus*, Pinter, 1990.

10 Revelations in 1991 confirmed what had long been suspected, that in the drafting of the programme Stalin had exercised major influence. See G Matthews, 'Stalin's British Road?', *Changes* no 23, 14–27 September 1991.

11 See R Gray, *The Aristocracy of Labour in Nineteenth-century Britain c. 1850–1914*, Macmillan, 1981.

12 W Osgerby, '"Well, it's Saturday night an' I just got paid": Youth, Consumerism and Hegemony in Britain 1945–1990', Institute of Contemporary British History conference, 1990.

13 Collectively termed the 'Angry Young Men', most likely from the title of John Osborne's *Look Back in Anger*. For a perceptive, though sometimes contentious, examination of British cultural development during this period see A Sinfield, *Literature, Politics and Culture in Postwar Britain*, Blackwell, 1989.

14 J Callaghan, *The Far Left in British Politics*, Blackwell, 1987, p 71.

15 For Gaitskell see the biography by Philip Williams, *Hugh Gaitskell, a Political Biography*, Cape, 1979.

16 Middlemas, *Politics* ..., K O Morgan, *People's Peace* ...

17 Macmillan reneged on Eden's commitment of 1956 to support the Engineering Employers' Federation in taking on the unions. In refusing government backing he told the EEF to settle on whatever terms it could obtain. K Middlemas, *Politics* ... p 400. For Macmillan, see the biography by Alastair Horne.

18 In 'The Sickness of Labourism', *New Left Review* No 1, 1960, Ralph Miliband made the first full exposition of the indictment and also popularised, if he did not invent, the term 'labourism'.

19 K Middlemas, *Power, Competition and the State*, vol II, *Threats to the Postwar Settlement: Britain 1961–74*, Chapter 1.

20 K Middlemas, *Power* ..., vol I, *Britain in Search of Balance, 1940–61*, Macmillan, 1988, pp 292, 297, 343–44.

21 The collection of essays published in 1960 as *Out of Apathy* and containing chapters by, among others, Stuart Hall, E P Thompson and Raphael Samuel, made a considerable impression at the time.

Chapter 3

1 Recently some attempt has been made to rehabilitate the record of the Wilson and Callaghan administrations. See, for example, R McKibben, 'Homage to Wilson and Callaghan' *London Review of Books*, 24 October 1991. The argument however is scarcely convincing. (Even Tony Benn has recently expressed surprising indulgence; 'The Case for Dismantling the Secret State', *New Left Review* 190, [1991].)

2 D Coates *The Labour Party and the Struggle for Socialism*, CUP, 1975, p 101.

3 See A Glynn and D Sutcliffe 'The Critical Condition of British Capital', *NLR* 66, (1971), expanded in *British Capitalism, Workers and the Profit Squeeze*, Penguin, 1972; D Yaffe, 'The Crisis of Profitability: a Critique of the GLYN–Sutcliffe Thesis', *NLR* 80, (1973).

4 D Coates *Labour Party* ... p 113.

5 Ibid p 106.

6 Ibid p 99.

7 Though the US demand to contribute troops was refused: it is unlikely that public feeling would have tolerated the prospect of British casualties in this war.

8 See for example P Foot, *The Politics of Harold Wilson*, Penguin, 1968; D Howell, *British Social Democracy*, Croom Helm, 1980; D Coates, *Labour Party* ...; C Ponting, *Breach of Promise: Labour in Power*, Penguin 1990.

9 See for example K Middlemas, *Power, Competition and the State* vol II, *Threats to the Postwar Settlement: Britain 1961–1974*, Macmillan 1990.

10 D Howell, *British Social Democracy*, p 267.

11 Ibid p 250.

12 See J Callaghan, *The Far Left in British Politics*, Blackwell, 1987.

13 See J Callaghan, ibid, and *British Trotskyism*, Blackwell, 1984.

14   See M Shaw, 'The Making of a Party', Socialist Register 1978 and
     I Birchall, 'The Premature Burial: a Reply to Martin Shaw',
     Socialist Register 1979.
15   See J Callaghan, *Far Left* and *British Trotskyism*; M Crick, *The
     March of Militant*, Faber 1986.
16   R Blake, *The Conservative Party from Peel to Thatcher*, Fontana,
     1979, p 309.
17   K Middlemas in *Threats* ... is at pains to stress the degree of
     continuity in industrial and labour policies between the two
     administrations.
18   See J Foster and C Woolfson, *The Politics of the UCS Work-in*,
     Lawrence & Wishart, 1986. K Middlemas in *Threats* ... underplays
     the significance of the episode.

Chapter 4

1   D Coates, *Labour in Power?*, Longman, 1980, p 183.
2   Ibid p .162.
3   Although Keith Middlemas, without access to any such sources,
     succeeds in *Power, Competition and the State* vol III, *The End of the
     Postwar Era: Britain since 1974*, Macmillan, 1991, in presenting a
     detailed and comprehensive account of the official mind over this
     period.
4   See for example David Leigh, *The Wilson Plot*, Heinemann, 1988;
     S Dorril and R Ramsay, *SMEAR – Wilson and the Secret State*,
     Fourth Estate, 1991.
5   See, for example, the discussions published in the *Socialist Register*
     of the period: R Miliband, 'Moving on', 1976; D Hallas, 'How Can
     we Move on?', 1977; P Jenkins, 'The Labour Party and the Politics
     of Transition', 1977; R Miliband, 'The Future of Socialism in
     England' (sic), 1977; L Panitch 'Socialists and the Labour Party: a
     Reappraisal', 1979.
6   J Callaghan, *The Far Left in British Politics*, Blackwell. 1987, Chapter
     4; M Shaw, 'The Making of a Party', *Socialist Register,* 1978.
7   D Coates, *Labour in Power?*, p 5.
8   The fullest account of internal developments within the Labour
     Party following the loss of the 1970 election is given in P Seyd, *The
     Rise and Fall of the Labour Left*, Macmillan, 1987.
9   For example, R Miliband, *Parliamentary Socialism*, Merlin Press,
     Postscript, 1973 edition, and the response by K Coates, 'Socialists
     and the Labour Party', *Socialist Register*, 1973.
10   P Anderson, 'The Figures of Descent', *New Left Review* 161, (1987).

11 K Middlemas *End of the Postwar Era* ... argues that Heath would almost certainly have won had his timing been slightly better.

12 G Taylor, 'The Marxist Inertia and the Labour Movement' *Politics and Power* no. 1.

13 D Coates, *Labour in Power?*... p 203.

14 Ibid, p.34, 84; K Middlemas, *End of the Postwar Era*, Chapters 5 and 6, esp. pp 149–56; Symposium, '1976 IMF Crisis' in *Contemporary Record*, vol 3, no 2, November 1989.

15 K O Morgan, *The People's Peace*, OUP, 1990, p 398. For the comment of a repentant Denis Healey, see *The Time of my Life*, Penguin, 1990, pp 455–56, where he concedes the error of the Chevaline project.

16 D Coates, *Labour in Power* ... p 57.

17 Ibid p 58.

18 B Campbell and M Jacques, 'Goodbye to the GLC', *Marxism Today* April 1986.

19 E J Hobsbawm, 'The Forward March of Labour Halted?' *Marxism Today* September 1978.

20 F Wood, 'Scottish Labour in Government and Opposition 1964–1969' in Ian Donnachie ed, *Forward! Labour Politics in Scotland 1888–1988*, Polygon, 1989.

21 Ibid.

22 For an account of the Scottish Labour Party see H M Drucker, *Breakaway!*, EUSPB, 1978.

23 Seyd, *Rise and Fall*... p 124.

24 Ibid p 102.

25 N Geras, 'Post-Marxism?', *NLR* 163, (1987).

26 Seyd, *Rise and Fall*... p 128.

27 G L Williams and A L Williams, *Labour's Decline and the Social Democrats' Fall*, Macmillan, 1989, p 112.

28 Seyd, *Rise and Fall*... p 102.

29 Healey's autobiography, *The Time of My Life*, Penguin, 1990, is a good deal more readable than most politicians', but no less tendentious.

30 Seyd, *Rise and Fall*... p 178.

Chapter 5

1 For a perceptive comment on the erosion of civic culture see R McKibben, 'With or without the workers', *London Review of Books*, 25 April 1991, reviewing D Marquand's *The Progressive Dilemma*.

2 See S Hall and M Jacques, eds. *The Politics of Thatcherism*, Lawrence & Wishart, 1983. Labour's paralysis was manifest in spite of the fact

that, 'Under Mrs Thatcher as Prime Minister and Sir Geoffrey Howe at the Exchequer, the present government has done more damage more rapidly than any previous administration, or indeed than could have been conceivable even two years ago.' S Pollard, *The Wasting of the British Economy*, Croom Helm, 1982.

3   A Barnett, 'Iron Britannia', *New Left Review* 134, (1982) special issue on the Falklands War, pp 10–29.

4   For a succinct analysis of the significance of the strike see J Saville, 'An Open Conspiracy: Conservative Politics and the Miners' Strike 1984–5', *Socialist Register*, 1985–86. Also R Hyman, Reflections on the Mining Strike', ibid.

5   See V Seddon, ed, *The Cutting Edge: Women and the Pit Strike*, Lawrence and Wishart, 1986.

6   E P Thompson *The Making of the English Working Class*, Penguin, 1968, p 690.

7   C Coles, 'A Miner in the House', in Seddon, *Cutting Edge ...*

8   For an account see M Crick, *The March of Militant*, Faber, 1986, Chapters 12–13.

9   Following the Liverpool Militant episode, Hatton became a businessman and public relations consultant, later tried and acquitted on corruption charges.

10 M Crick, *March ...* pp 276–78.

11 J Callaghan, *The Far Left in British Politics*, Blackwell, 1987, pp 213–14.

12 K Livingstone, *If Voting Changed Anything, They'd Abolish It*, Fontana, 1988, Chapter 8.

13 See especially S Hall and M Jacques, *The Politics of Thatcherism*.

14 Nevertheless, the attempt is now beginning to be made. See Chapter 3, note 1, above.

15 See D Edgerton, 'Liberal Militarism and the British State', *NLR* 185, (1991) for an analysis of the importance of military science for technological development in Britain.

16 The same strategem was even used against Michael Heseltine when he challenged Thatcher for the Conservative Party leadership in 1990. He was accused of being a crypto-socialist – and a crypto-communist by implication.

Conclusion

1   In Scotland, however, the Scottish TUC, though not advocating refusal to pay, was involved in active campaigning against the Poll Tax.

2 Somebody commented that the main barrier to Robin Cook, the able Shadow Health Secretary, becoming Labour Party leader was the fact that he had a beard.

3 The leaders of Sheffield City Council admitted openly that they had based their 1991–92 expenditure plans on the presumption of a Labour government and the opening of the Westminster purse strings. With these expectations confounded, they were faced with a ruinous deficit.

4 See G Therborn, 'The Life and Times of Socialism', *New Left Review* 194, (1992).

5 John Smith must have been privately very relieved he wasn't Chancellor in September 1992.

6 'As the treaty proposes no new institutions other than a European bank, its sponsors must suppose that nothing more is needed ... It is a crude and extreme version of the view which has for some time now constituted Europe's conventional wisdom ... that governments are unable, and therefore should not try, to achieve any of the traditional goals of economic policy, such as growth and full employment.' W Godley, 'Maastricht and All That', *London Review of Books*, 8 October 1992.

Bibliography

Books

(Place of publication London unless otherwise indicated.)

Aaronovitch, S, *The Road from Thatcherism: The Alternative Economic Strategy* (Lawrence & Wishart, 1981).

Addison, P, *The Road to 1945* (Cape, 1975).

Allen, V L, *Trade Union Leadership* (Longman, 1987).

Anderson, P et al *Towards Socialism* (New Left Review/Fontana, 1965).

Archer, R et al (eds), *Out of Apathy: Voices of the New Left Thirty Years On* (Verso, 1989).

Artis, M and Cobham, D (eds), *Labour's Economic Policies, 1974–1979* (Manchester, Manchester University Press, 1991).

Blackburn, R and Cockburn, A, *The Incompatibles: Trade Union Militancy and the Consensus* (Harmondsworth, Penguin, 1967).

Blake, R, *The Conservative Party from Peel to Thatcher* (Fontana, 1979).

Bullock, A, *Ernest Bevin, Foreign Secretary* (Heinemann, 1983).

Cairncross, A, *Years of Recovery: British Economic Policy 1945–51* (Methuen, 1985).

Callaghan, J, *British Trotskyism* (Oxford, Blackwell, 1984).

——, *The Far Left in British Politics* (Oxford, Blackwell, 1987).

Campbell, J, *Roy Jenkins: a Biography* (Weidenfeld and Nicolson, 1983).

Coates, D, *The Labour Party and the Struggle for Socialism* (Cambridge, CUP, 1975).

——, *Labour in Power?* (Longman, 1980).

Coates, K, *Democracy in the Labour Party* (Nottingham, Spokesman, 1977).

——, (ed) *What Went Wrong?* (Nottingham, Spokesman, 1979).

Cook, C and Taylor, I, *The Labour Party: An Introduction to its History, Structure and Politics* (Longman 1980).

Crick, M, *The March of Militant* (Faber, 1986).

——, *Scargill and the Miners* (Harmondsworth, Penguin, 1985).

Crosland, C A R, *The Future of Socialism* (Cape, 1956).

Crosland, S, *Tony Crosland* (Cape, 1982).

Curran, J ed, *The Future of the Left* (Cambridge, Polity Press, 1984.)

Dobb, M, *Studies in the Development of Capitalism* (RKP, 1946).

Dockrill, M, *British Defence since 1945* (Oxford, Blackwell, 1988).

Donnachie, I (ed), *Forward! Labour Politics in Scotland 1888–1988* (Edinburgh, Polygon, 1989).

Donoughue, B and Jones, G W, *Herbert Morrison: Portrait of a Politician* (Weidenfeld & Nicolson, 1973).

Doril, S and Ramsay, R, *SMEAR - Wilson and the Secret State* (Fourth estate, 1991).

Drucker, H M, *Breakaway! The Scottish Labour Party* (Edinburgh, EUSPB, 1979).

Foot, P, *The Politics of Harold Wilson* (Harmondsworth, Penguin, 1968).

Foote, G, *The Labour Party's Political Thought: a History* (Croom Helm, 1985).

Foster, J, *Class Struggle and the Industrial Revolution* (Gollancz, 1963).

——, and Woolfson, C, *The Politics of the UCS Work-in* (Lawrence & Wishart, 1986).

Gamble, A, *Britain in Decline* (Macmillan, 1981).

Glynn, A and Sutcliffe, D, *British Capitalism, Workers and the Profit Squeeze* (Harmondsworth, Penguin, 1972).

Gowing, M, (assisted by Arnold, L) *Independence and Deterrence: Britain and Atomic Energy 1945–1952* (Macmillan, 1974) vol. I *Policy Making*: vol. II *Policy Execution*.

Gray, R, *The Aristocracy of Labour in Nineteenth-century Britain c. 1850–1914* (Macmillan, 1981).

Hall, S, *The Hard Road to Renewal: Thatcherism and the Crisis of the Left* (Verso, 1988).

Hall, S and Jacques, M eds. *The Politics of Thatcherism* (Lawrence & Wishart, 1983).

Hall, S et al *Policing the Crisis; Mugging, the State and Law and Order* (Macmillan, 1978).

Harris, K, *Attlee* (Weidenfeld & Nicolson, 1982).

Healey, D, *The Time of my Life* (Harmondsworth, Penguin, 1990).

Hobsbawm, E J, *Industry and Empire* (Weidenfeld & Nicolson, 1968).

Holland, S, *The Socialist Challenge* (Quartet, 1975).

Howell, D, *British Social Democracy* (Croom Helm, 1980).

Hunter, L, *The Road to Brighton Pier* (Arthur Barker, 1959).

Keegan, W, *Mrs Thatcher's Economic Experiment* (Harmondsworth, Penguin, 1984).

Kennett, W (ed), *The Rebirth of Britain* (Weidenfeld & Nicolson, 1982).

Leigh, D, *The Wilson Plot* (Heinemann, 1988).

Marquand, D, *The Unprincipled Society: new demands and old politics* (Fontana, 1988).

Martin, R and Rowthorn, B (eds), *The Geography of Deindustrialisation* (Macmillan, 1986).

Livingstone, K, *If Voting Changed Anything, They'd Abolish It* (Fontana, 1988).

Middlemas, K, *Power, Competition and the State*: vol. I *Britain in Search of Balance 1940–61* (Macmillan, 1985); vol. II *Threats to the Postwar Settlement* (Macmillan, 1990); vol. III *The End of the Postwar Era: Britain since 1974* (Macmillan, 1991).

——, *Politics in Industrial Society* (Andre Deutsch, 1979).

Miliband, R, *Parliamentary Socialism* (Allen & Unwin, 1961).

Morgan, K O, *Labour in Power* (Oxford, OUP, 1984).

——, *The People's Peace* (Oxford, OUP, 1990).

Morris, R J, *Class Consciousness in the Industrial Revolution* (Macmillan, 1979).

Nairn, T, *The Break-up of Britain: Crisis and Neo-nationalism* (New Left Books, 1977).

——, *The Enchanted Glass: Britain and its Monarchy* (Radius, 1988).

Panitch, L, *Working Class Politics in Crisis: Essays on Labour and the State* (Verso, 1986).

Parkin, F, *Middle Class Radicalism: The Social Basis of the British Campaign for Nuclear Disarmament* (Manchester, Manchester University Press, 1968).

Pimlott, B, *Hugh Dalton* (Cape, 1985).

Pollard, S, *The Wasting of the British Economy* (Croom Helm, 1982).

Ponting, C, *Breach of Promise: Labour in Power* (Harmondsworth, Penguin, 1990).

Seddon, V, *The Cutting Edge: Women and the Pit Strike* (Lawrence & Wishart, 1986).

Seyd, P, *The Rise and Fall of the Labour Left* (Macmillan, 1987).

Sinfield, A, *Literature, Politics and Culture in Postwar Britain* (Oxford, Blackwell, 1989).

Sked, A, *Britain's Decline* (Blackwell, 1987).

Smith, J D, *The Attlee and Churchill Administrations and Industrial Unrest 1945–55: a study in consensus* (Leicester, Pinter, 1990).

Stedman Jones, G, *Outcast London* (Oxford, OUP, 1971).

Thompson, E P, *The Making of the English Working Class* (Harmondsworth, Penguin, 1968).

——, (ed), *Out of Apathy* (Stevens, 1960).

Wainwright, H, *Labour: a Tale of Two Parties* (Hogarth Press, 1987).

Whiteley, P, *The Labour Party in Crisis* (Methuen, 1983).

Wiener, M J, *English Culture and the Decline of the Industrial Spirit 1850–1980* (Harmondsworth, Penguin, 1985).

Williams, G L and Williams, A L, *Labour's Decline and the Social Democrats' Fall* (Macmillan, 1989).

Williams, P M, *Hugh Gaitskell: a Political Biography* (Cape, 1979).

Articles

Aaronovitch, S, 'The Alternative Economic Strategy: Goodbye to All That?', *Marxism Today*, February 1986.

Addison, P, 'Attlee', *New Statesman*, 17 December 1982.

Anderson, P, 'The Left on the Fifties', *New Left Review*, no. 29 (Jan–Feb 1965).

——, 'The Figures of Descent', *New Left Review*, no. 161 (Jan–Feb 1987).

Arblaster, A, 'Labour's Future and the Coalition Debate', *New Left Review*, no. 157 (May–June 1986).

Barnett, A, 'Iron Britannia', *New Left Review*, no. 134, (Jul–Aug 1982).

——, 'Whistling in the Wind?, *New Socialist*, January 1986.

——, 'National Boundaries: the Uses of National Security', *New Socialist*, March 1987.

Bassett, P, 'All Together Now?', *Marxism Today*, January 1989.

Beechey, V, 'The Shape of the Workforce to Come', *Marxism Today*, August 1985.

Benn, T, Interview, *Marxism Today*, October 1980.

Benton, S, 'Reaching New Parts', *Marxism Today*, April 1988.

Birchall, I, 'The Premature Burial: a Reply to Martin Shaw', *Socialist Register*, 1979.

Bloomfield, J, 'Labour's Long Haul', *Marxism Today*, December 1980.

Campbell, B and Jacques, M, 'Goodbye to the GLC', *Marxism Today*, April 1986.

Carruthers, S L, '"Manning the Factories": Propaganda and Policy on the Employment of Women 1939–47', *History*, vol. 75, no. 244 (June 1990).

Coates, D, 'Labourism and the Transition to Socialism', *New Left Review*, no. 129 (Sept–Oct) 1981.

——, 'The Labour Party and the Future of the Left', *Socialist Register* 1983.

Coates, K, 'Socialists and the Labour Party', *Socialist Register* 1973.

——, 'The Choices Before Labour', *New Left Review*, no. 131 (Jan–Feb 1982).

——, 'The New Age of Trade Unionism', New Socialist, October 1985.

Coates, K, and Bell, G, 'Labour and Imperialism', *New Socialist*, Jul–Aug 1982.

Cook, R, 'A Hole in Labour's Heart', *Marxism Today*, August 1987.

Coote, A, 'The AES: a new starting point', *New Socialist*, Nov–Dec 1981.

Corrigan, P, 'The Local State: the Struggle for Democracy', *Marxism Today*, July 1979.

Crewe, I, 'Centre of Attraction', *Marxism Today*, May 1980.

Davies, I, 'The Labour Commonwealth', *New Left Review*, no. 22 (Nov–Dec 1963).

Darwin, J G, 'The End of Empire', *Contemporary Record*, vol. 1, no. 3 (Autumn 1987).

Edgar, D, 'Bitter Harvest', *New Socialist*, Sep–Oct 1983.

Edgerton, D, 'Liberal Militarism and the British State', *New Left Review*, no. 185 (Jan–Feb 1991).

Edmonds, J, 'Thoroughly Modern Movement', *Marxism Today*, September 1988.

Freeman, M, 'The decline and fall of British Labourism', *Confrontation*, no. 4 (Summer 1988).

Gamble, A, 'The Free Economy and the Strong State', *Socialist Register*, 1979.

——, 'Crawling from the Wreckage', *Marxism Today*, July 1987.

Griffiths, D and Holmes, C, 'To Buy or not to Buy?', *Marxism Today*, May 1984.

Glynn, A and Sutcliffe, D, 'The Critical Condition of British Capital', *New Left Review*, no. 66, (March–April 1971).

Gowing, M, 'Britain and the Bomb', *Contemporary Record*, vol. 2, no. 2 (Summer 1988).

Hall, S, 'The Battle for Socialist Ideas in the 1980s', *Socialist Register*, 1982.

——, 'The Culture Gap', *Marxism Today*, January 1984.

——, 'Blue Election, Election Blues', *Marxism Today*, July 1987.

——, 'Thatcher's Lessons', *Marxism Today*, March 1988.

Hall, S and Jacques, M, 'March Without Vision', *Marxism Today*, December 1990.

Hallas, D, 'How Can We Move On?', *Socialist Register*, 1977.

Hart, N, 'Gender and the Rise and Fall of Class Politics', *New Left Review*, no. 175 (May–June 1989).

Hobsbawm, E J, 'Some Reflections on "The Break-up of Britain"', *New Left Review*, no. 105 (Sept–Oct 1977).

——, 'The Forward March of Labour Halted?', *Marxism Today*, September 1978.

——, 'Labour's Lost Millions', *Marxism Today*, October 1983.

——, 'Out of the Wilderness', *Marxism Today*, October 1987.

——, 'No Sense of Mission', *Marxism Today*, April 1988.

Holmes, M and Horsewood, N J, 'The Postwar Consensus', *Contemporary Record*, vol. 2, no. 2 (Summer 1988).

Hughes, J, 'British Trade Unionism in the Sixties', *Socialist Register*, 1966.

Hyman, R, 'Reflections on the Mining Strike', *Socialist Register*, 1985–86.

Jenkins, P, 'The Labour Party and the Politics of Transition', *Socialist Register*, 1977.

Jenkins, R, 'Changing Patterns of Leadership', *Contemporary Record*, vol. 2, no. 2 (Summer 1988).

Jessup, B et al 'Authoritarian Populism, Two Nations and Thatcherism', *New Left Review*, no. 147 (Sept–Oct 1984).

——, 'Thatcherism and the Politics of Hegemony: a Reply to Stuart Hall', *New Left Review*, no. 153 (Sept–Oct 1985).

Kiernan, V G, 'India and the Labour Party', *New Left Review*, no. 42 (March–Apr 1967).

Leadbeater, C, 'The Sid in Us All', *Marxism Today*, January 1987.

——, 'In the Land of the Dispossessed', *Marxism Today*, April 1987.

——, 'A Head Without a Heart', *Marxism Today*, July 1990.

Livingstone, K, 'Rate-capping and Realignment', *Marxism Today*, May 1985.

Livingstone, K and Campbell, B, 'Labour and the People', *Marxism Today*, December 1984.

Lowe, R, 'The Second World War, Consensus and the Foundation of the Welfare State', *20th Century British History*, vol. 1, no. 2, (1990).

McKibben, R, 'Homage to Wilson and Callaghan', *London Review of Books*, 24 October 1991.

——, 'With or Without the Workers', *London Review of Books*, 25 April 1991.

McLennan, G, 'Class Conundrum', *Marxism Today*, May 1984.

Marxism Today Roundtable, 'The Miners' Strike: a Balance Sheet', *Marxism Today*, April 1985.

Massey, D et al 'Stop the Great Male Moving Right Show!', *New Socialist*, Jan–Feb 1984.

Middlemas, K, 'Corporatism: Its Rise and Fall', *Contemporary Record*, vol. 2, no. 1 (Spring 1988).

Miliband, R, 'The Sickness of Labourism', *New Left Review*, no. 1, (Jan–Feb 1960).

——, 'Labour Policy and the Labour Left', *Socialist Register* 1964.

——, 'Moving On', *Socialist Register*, 1976.

——, 'The Future of Socialism in England', *Socialist Register*, 1977.

——, 'Socialist Advance in Britain', *Socialist Register*, 1983.

Minkin, L, 'Polls apart: the Union battle to stay in politics', *New Socialist*, December 1984.

Mulgan, G, 'The Vision Thing', *Marxism Today*, August 1989.

Nairn, T, 'The English Working Class', *New Left Review*, no. 24 (March–Apr 1964).

——, 'The Nature of the Labour Party', *New Left Review*, nos. 27–28 (Sept–Oct/Nov–Dec 1964).

——, 'British Nationalism and the EEC', *New Left Review*, no. 69 (Sept–Oct 1971).

——, 'The Left Against Europe', *New Left Review*, no. 75 (Sept–Oct 1975).

——, 'Great Britain: A Legitimation Crisis?', *New Left Review*, no. 129 (Sept–Oct 1981).

Nicholls, D, 'Fractions of Capital: the Aristocracy, the City and industry in the development of Modern British capitalism', *Social History*, vol. 13, no. 1 (January 1988).

Panitch, L, 'Socialists and the Labour Party: a Reappraisal', *Socialist Register*, 1979.

——, 'Trade Unions and the State', *New Left Review*, no. 125 (Jan–Feb 1981).

——, 'Socialist Renewal and the Labour Party', *Socialist Register* 1988.

Pimlott, B, 'Labour's Shadow Boxing', *New Socialist*, February 1987.

Pimlott, B et al 'Is the "Postwar Consensus" a Myth?', *Contemporary Record*, vol. 2, no. 6 (Summer 1989).

Rodrigues, J, 'The Riots of '81', *Marxism Today*, October 1981.

Ross, G and Jenson, J, "Post-war Class Struggle and the Crisis of Left Politics', *Socialist Register*, 1985–86.

Rowthorn, B, 'The Politics of the Alternative Economic Strategy', *Marxism Today*, January 1981.

Rustin, M, 'The New Left and the Crisis', *New Left Review*, no. 121 (May–June 1980).

——, 'Labour's Strategy', *New Socialist*, March–Apr 1982.

——, 'Different Conceptions of Party: Labour's Constitutional Debates', *New Left Review*, no. 126 (March–Apr 1981).

Samuel, R, 'The Lost World of British Communism', *New Left Review*, no. 154 (Nov–Dec 1985).

——, 'Staying Power: The Lost World of British Commmunism, Part Two', *New Left Review*, no. 156 (March–Apr 1986).

Saville, J, 'Labourism and the Labour Government', *Socialist Register*, 1967.

———, 'C R Attlee: An Assessment', *Socialist Register*, 1983.

———, 'Ernest Bevin and the Cold War', *Socialist Register*, 1984.

———, 'An Open Conspiracy: Conservative Politics and the Miners' Strike 1984–5', *Socialist Register*, 1985–86.

———, 'Labour and Foreign Policy 1945–1947: a Condemnation', *Our History Journal*, no. 17 (May 1991).

Saville, R, 'Politics and the Labour Movement in the Early Cold War', *Our History Journal*, no. 15 (April 1990).

Scargill, A, 'The New Unionism', *New Left Review*, no. 92 (Jul–Aug 1975).

———, Interview, *Marxism Today*, April 1981.

Schwartz, B, 'The Thatcher Years', *Socialist Register*, 1987.

Seyd, P, 'Labour's Left in Crisis', *New Socialist*, March–Apr 1983.

———, 'Labour Members', *New Socialist*, December 1987.

Shaw, M, 'The Making of a Party', *Socialist Register*, 1978.

Stewart, J, 'Storming the Town Halls: a Rate-Cap Revolution', *Marxism Today*, April 1984.

Taylor, G, 'The Marxist Inertia and the Labour Movement', *Politics and Power*, no. 1, (1980).

Taylor, I, 'Law and Order, Moral Order: the Changing Rhetorics of the Thatcher Government', *Socialist Register*, 1987.

Wainwright, H, 'The Limits of Labourism: 1987 and Beyond', *New Left Review*, no. 164 (Jul–Aug 1987).

Wallace, W, 'Pride and Prejudice', *Marxism Today*, October 1991.

Ward, M, 'Labour's Capital Gains: the GLC Experience', *Marxism Today*, December 1983.

Williams, G A, 'Land of our Fathers', *Marxism Today*, August 1982.

Wilson, E, 'Thatcherism and Women: After Seven Years', *Socialist Register*, 1987.

Wolmar, C, 'Divided We Stand', *New Socialist*, December 1984.

Yaffe, D, 'The Crisis of Profitability: a Critique of the Glynn-Sutcliffe Thesis', *New Left Review*, no. 80 (Jul–Aug 1973).

Index

TRESSOLL
MEEK
SHINWELL
BRADDOCK
BEVIN
BEVAN